The Therapeutic Potential of Creative Writing

Writing Myself

Gillie Bolton

Foreword by Sir Kenneth Calman

Jessica Kingsley Publishers
London and Philadelphia

Acknowledgements

Every reasonable effort has been made to contact the copyright holders of material reproduced in this book, and the author and publisher would like to thank the following: Anne Frank – Fonds for permission to reproduce the passage from *The Diary of Anne Frank* on page 31; Random House for the use of material from *The Diary of Virginia Woolf* on page 31; Shambhala Publications for the quotation from *Writing Down the Bones* by Natalie Goldberg on page 49; Faber and Faber Ltd, Harcourt, Brace and Company and the Eliot Estate for permission to reproduce the lines by T.S. Eliot from 'Burnt Norton' on page 61, from 'East Coker' on pages 67 and 212, and from *Selected Essays* on page 98; Bloodaxe Books for the quotation from 'Poetry for Supper' in *Selected Poems 1946–68* by R.S. Thomas on page 61; the National Committee of Gibran for permission to use the passage from *The Prophet* by Khalil Gibran on page 69; James MacGibbon for 'Thoughts About the Person From Porlock' from *The Collected Poems of Stevie Smith* (Penguin Twentieth Century Classics) reproduced on pages 94–5; Spike Milligan Productions for permission to reproduce 'String' by Spike Milligan on page 98; Peter Reading for the quote on page 169 from his poem in *C*, published by Secker and Warburg; Faber and Faber for the line from *The Bell Jar* by Sylvia Plath quoted on page 183; HarperCollins Publishers for permission to use the passage from *Little House in the Big Woods* by Laura Ingalls Wilder on page 183; Ted Hughes for allowing the reproduction of the passage from his foreword to *What Rhymes with Secret?* by S. Brownjohn, published by Hodder and Stoughton, on pages 195–6; and Faber and Faber for the passage from *Poetry in the Making* by Ted Hughes quoted on page 211. All rights reserved.

First published in the United Kingdom in 1999 by
Jessica Kingsley Publishers Ltd
116 Pentonville Road
London N1 9JB, England
and
325 Chestnut Street
Philadelphia PA 19106, USA.
www.jkp.com

Second impression 2000

Library of Congress Cataloging in Publication Data
A CIP catalog record for this book is available from the Library of Congress

British Library Cataloguing in Publication Data
The therapeutic potential of writing : writing myself
1. Creative writing – Therapeutic use
I. Title
616.8'916.5

ISBN 1 85302 599 2

Printed and Bound in Great Britain by
Athenaeum Press, Gateshead, Tyne and Wear

The Therapeutic Potential of Creative Writing

of related interest

The Self on the Page
Theory and Practice of Creative Writing in Personal Development
Edited by Celia Hunt and Fiona Sampson
ISBN 1 85302 470 8

Writing Well
Creative Writing and Mental Health
Deborah Philips, Debra Penman and Liz Linington
ISBN 1 85302 650 6

Contents

This book is dedicated to the angel who said:

on my lectern wings
open your unwritten book
and write what you read

Acknowledgements

This book would not have been possible without the generous support of rather a lot of people. The text owes much of its vitality, and range of experience and knowledge, to the many voices other than my own within it. I would like to thank all these, whether their name appears or not, as well as everyone with whom I have worked over the last fifteen years. Each of these many people – patients, clients, colleagues, students, friends, family – has played a significant role in the development of my theories, ideas and practice.

Particular thanks go to Rosie Field, Amanda Howe, Kate Billingham and the members of the 'Reflections in Writing for GPs' group for inspiration and ideas; David Hannay, Nigel Mathers, Sam Ahmedzai, Tony Bethell, Pat Lane and Len Barton for research support; David Hart, Jackie Brown, Catherine Byron, Rob Hamberger and the members of Off the Page for believing in me and offering help – from the placing of a comma to the fine-tuning of a theory; Marilyn Lidster for smoothing my blunders with such humour and for locating scattered papers (as well as confidence).

Finally, I would like to celebrate the contribution of Stephen Rowland, who has always been here throughout the work and the writing – restructuring infelicitous sentences, helping to open windows in my mind onto wider human and intellectual vistas, and always ready with tea, water or champagne.

Foreword

Quality of life for patients and professionals is clearly important. We need to change our understanding as to how it might be improved. Physical problems, pain and disability, have always received a great deal of attention, and psychological problems, such as anxiety and depression, are being increasingly investigated. Writing therapy is a relatively new development. It provides opportunities for self-reflection for both patients and practitioners. Putting down on paper what you feel and how you are responding to a personal or professional issue can be therapeutic. Gillie Bolton's book emphasises the role of creative writing and begins an evaluation of its potential.

It is part of a broader movement of linking the arts (visual, dramatic, literature, etc.) to the physical, psychological and social problems of patients in communities. Such initiatives are to be welcomed as they open up new possibilities for improving well-being in the broadest sense. An assessment of its value is also important to ensure that time and effort are appropriately directed.

I therefore welcome this volume as a contribution to improving both patient care and the understanding of professional staff in dealing with complex patient problems.

Sir Kenneth Calman, Chief Medical Officer
March 1998

CHAPTER ONE

Introduction

Trust yourself
You can't write the wrong thing
Give yourself the gift of this writing

These are the three basic tenets of the therapeutic writing method outlined in this book. If you trust yourself you cannot write the wrong thing. That trustworthy self will help you to write material which you will learn from but not allow you to write things which you would find unbearable to read and relate to. Most of the writing suggested in this book will be completely enjoyable. In fact, the book should come with a warning to colleagues, family, lovers and friends. Writing in this way can become compulsive; it is a way of life, not just something to try. Hence the third cornerstone: the kind of writing suggested in this book feels like a gift to oneself, a luxury. You deserve the gift of some prime time on your own for yourself.

You can trust yourself to know: when would be a good time to write; when to stop; when and whom to ask for support; where and how you should write; what are the appropriate subjects for you to write about intensely and which to skim; and why you should be writing. *The Therapeutic Potential of Creative Writing* offers routes towards gaining that essential trust and faith in yourself.

Writing the right thing will not mean that there will never be painful or even intensely distressing parts of your writing. There will be. There should be. Unfortunately, these will be the right things at that time. All of us have memories, fears and horrors buried inside which cause problems either some of or much of the time. We can choose to live with these issues, and the problems they create, for the rest of our lives and not face the pain of examining them. Or we can choose to undertake an exercise like therapeutic writing.

Writing is a kind and comparatively gentle way of facing whatever is there to be faced. You can trust it to pace itself to your needs and wants rather than to anyone else, such as a therapist. It can be private until you decide to share it.

Who are you, my reader?

I think you would like to understand yourself better by writing. You might work with patients, clients or students who would benefit from therapeutic or reflective writing. You may be a healthcare worker or a group leader or an established writer seeking to extend the depth of your writing. This book is primarily addressed to a *you* who is a writer or potential writer. Trying out the methods and processes before you suggest them to others is an essential part of the process. The suggestions in this book, when undertaken sincerely, are powerful. This needs to be fully understood.

The format and contents of this book

This book is a straightforward how-to guide to therapeutic writing, from starting off to further development possibilities; some background and history of this area in Britain, and, to some extent, from the USA, relating it to other therapies; in-depth advice on how to get the most out of a writing group; suggestions on working with patients/clients/students and within institutions; and the relationship of writing with mental distress or illness.

The book is arranged in a logical progression and will benefit from being read from beginning to end. Some parts, however, will be of more value to some readers than others. The text will be perfectly useful read in any order, though I recommend all readers to begin with the first two chapters and finish with the final one.

There are a variety of authorial voices within this book: poets, novelists and playwrights who have either worked with others or felt the therapeutic benefit of writing themselves; patients, clients and students; and nurses, doctors and therapists. This gives a wide range of experience, knowledge and examples of writing. All the suggestions in this book have been used by their writers. My own vital therapeutic journey has been through writing.

Therapeutic writing vs creative writing

There is no real distinction. Both creative writing and therapeutic writing would lose much of their power if there was. Literature relies for its impact on highly charged material. That charge comes from the emotional relationship of the writer with their writing: their desire or need to write the novel, the poem, the play, the autobiography. And this is why we read literature. It not only contains insights, acute observations, gripping plots and style, but carries an urgency, a deep need to express and communicate something about the human condition. We cry when we read, we laugh, we grip the book with tense fingers. Can the writer have been passionless when they put these emotions on the pages? Why does a poet choose to devote a whole book to the pain of infertility and childlessness, or to the experience of being adopted? Why does a novelist tell the searing story of an unloved outcast wretch? Budding writers have often said to me: 'I am going to get rich quick and write a romance/bodice ripper/thriller.' I shake my head. Even the writers of these genres have their hearts in what they write.

Most writers will tell you that they need to write. Writing is not just a job like so many others (though there are many utterly job-like aspects – editing, sorting out references, redrafting according to the wants of the producer/publisher, filling in tax returns). I cannot, however, maintain that all creative writing has a therapeutic element or stage, even if that is what I believe, since there are writers who deny it of their own work.

Much creative writing is deeply therapeutic, whether undertaken for writing groups and classes, by novelists, poets and playwrights; or by people writing on their own – in the hope of publication or not. Poetry seems to be a particularly therapeutic medium; so many poems in collections, anthologies and journals have such a clear therapeutic base. And people who don't habitually write often turn to the poetic form when in trauma or emotional disturbance.

And, of course, therapeutic writing is creative. Its very creativity is one of the therapeutic benefits (see later chapters). And, conversely, its power to help its writer is the force which makes much of this writing an extremely good read. My many volumes of diary have all been deeply mined for material for poetry. Many of the people I, and other writers in healthcare, have worked with have crafted and redrafted their writing for publication – often as a way of sharing a journey of pain with other sufferers or their relatives. Occasionally, a therapeutic piece is publishable with no working.

But is therapeutic writing Art? It might be or it might, on redrafting and crafting, become art, but no beginning or therapeutic writer will benefit from thinking their writing may be shareable with a wide audience as an art (see Chapter Fourteen). This issue is debated by writers, many of whom make a complete distinction between their writing and therapeutic splurges. Writing novels, stories, poetry or plays is a skill and an art. Therapeutic writing is deeply supportive, self-illuminating and personal.

So do it. Don't think about whether the writing is an art, or even whether it is being therapeutic. Write for yourself. That way you will write the most vivid material which will offer you the most personal benefit and may well communicate best to a reader, if you decide later that that is what you want. Pick up a pen and begin.

CHAPTER TWO

Therapeutic Writing: How and Why

The Healing Pen

I even enjoy the physical holding of the pen, the shaping of the words, and I like the way it unfolds before me, like thought unravelling. The rest of the book is blank; I wonder what the next chapter will be?

(Jenny)

A wise man ought to realise that health is his most valuable possession and learn how to treat his illnesses by his own judgement.

(Hippocrates 1983, p.276)

The healing pen

Writing can be powerful therapy.
It raises curtains, brings the past to light.
Often what I write surprises me.

Dreams and fears that linger threateningly
Appear in a new light in black and white.
Writing can be powerful therapy.

Confidences in my diary
Reveal my longings, prejudices, spite.
Often what I write surprises me.

Spirits from my past have haunted me
Until I wrote their names. Then they took flight.
Writing can be powerful therapy.

A pen gives sorrow words, dumb guilt a plea.
Then love can offer comfort, mercy's might.
Often what I write surprises me.

Our souls are full of stars. We only see
How bright some are if healing primes their light.
Writing can be powerful therapy.
Often what I write surprises me.

(Averil Stedeford)

There is writing and writing. There is writing which expresses things from deep within us, explores things we didn't know we knew, felt or remembered. It offers endlessly creative questions and tantalising paths to follow, rather than answers. This book concerns such writing. It is not about the kind we were taught at school: essays with introductions, logical texts and analytical conclusions or poems with set forms. This expressive and explorative writing can be deeply healing and therapeutic. A pen/pencil and paper are almost free and can easily be carried and stored. The way of writing described in this book is so simple too. Those beginning will need to unremember all those rules they learned about writing. The most important rule for this kind of writing is that *there are no rules.*

How to write therapeutically

Making contact with the trustworthy, strong, wise, healing self (see Introduction) within is a great deal easier than people might think. No expensive professional help or equipment is necessarily required, merely your favourite writing tool, some blank paper and a willingness to trust your hand to write whatever comes, in whatever order, in whatever way, without worrying about spelling, punctuation or even sentencing and paragraphing. Here is a summary of the guidelines I have given to those who would like to start writing:

Writing for healing

Why?

Writing is

- fun, stimulating, exciting
- helps you explore and express important things
- helps you remember memories allows you to sort out your thoughts/feelings

- enables you to create something beautiful, like a poem
- can speak to other people
- leaves a record for children/grandchildren/friends.

In what way?

- Whatever you write is right. You can't write the wrong thing!
- This writing is only for you to read, at first. You might even want to tear it up. You might keep it to read again later. You might share it with
    - a relative
    - a friend
    - or some with your nurse/doctor.
- Because this writing is for you, it doesn't have to be in proper English: write it like poetry is written – if you like – not in sentences, and with your own spelling.
- You may think you have nothing to write. When you start, you will find your pen has a great deal to say. It may seem odd at first, sitting on your own, scribbling something that isn't a letter, list or report.
- You do deserve the gift of some time – just for you.
- Be relaxed about it. Enjoy it. Watch it grow.

How? When? Where?
Write when and where you feel like it

- day or night
- in bed, in a cafe
- (difficult on a bike).

Write only two lines, or lots

- in a notebook
- on scraps of paper
- perhaps in a folder.

Write when and where you can be on your own, if that feels right for you. It doesn't matter if someone is in another room. Sit somewhere comfortable, warm, yet airy. Make sure you have a cup of tea if you want one.

What to write

You may feel you know. If you don't:

1. Scribble whatever comes into your head for 6 minutes
   - don't stop to think
   - it might be a list, or some odd words and phrases
   - spelling and proper sentences don't matter.

2. Now:

You may want to carry on with some ideas that have started in this writing.

If not,

write about:

- a dream
- a memory from a long time ago
- a memory of a Christmas or birthday
- something that happened last week/year
- a time you were told off
- a time of great happiness
- a time of loss
- a poem
- anything else that occurs to you;

or: Make a list of all the important people in your life, or draw a family tree (including friends). It doesn't matter if they are alive or dead now. Choose one. Describe them. What kinds of things did they say?

If you wrote a letter or talked to them, what might you say to them now? How might they reply? Write as if you are writing those letters.

The best things in life are free! But – the more you put into this – the more you get out.

Good luck – learn a lot – enjoy it.

A reader

A good friend/nurse/sister/GP/priest/therapist/counsellor with whom to share this writing at the right stage (whenever that is for each writer) can be invaluable. Encouragement and support is very heartening. This work can occasionally be difficult and lonely. Any process bringing dynamic change to a person in need of therapeutic help is going to be uncomfortable at times.

The right reader can offer support and encouragement at the right time. This person may not be the obvious one, such as partner or best friend. The best way to find the appropriate reader for you (if you need one at all) is to ask the writing. Thus the choosing of the reader will come from the same place as the writing. Write the simple question 'WHO?' on your next page and then write whatever comes into your head (free-intuitive writing, see Chapter Three). You may not get the answer straight away but you will certainly get the right one in time – and it may surprise you.

Make a gift of writing for yourself

This writing is, and should be, mostly enjoyable. Look after yourself and only write if you are respecting it, and either enjoying it or feel it is the right thing to be doing at that time:

1. Give yourself the luxury of nice paper (notebook/file), coloured pens, a good pen/pencil (I like 2B, with a rubber on the end), a lamp in the right place...
2. Allow yourself plenty of breaks, exercise, fun.
3. Choose your right writing place (airy but warm enough): the bustle of the kitchen/an impersonal library/a secluded study or bedroom.
4. Discover your writing pattern, the right time/space for you: 6 am or midnight; in frequent half-hour snatches, or five days living, eating and sleeping it.
5. If you are writing something lengthy, leave your work each session at an interesting beginning of something. Do not stop at an end of a section. Push yourself to begin the next bit or allow yourself to stop before the end. You'll feel much keener to start again.
6. You *can* tell children/co-committee members/mother you are unavailable for half-an-hour/six months. Telephone bells can be switched off for a while too.

7. Every writer has delaying strategies; what are yours? One successful novelist friend says she knows when it's a writing day, all her boring household tasks are done first. I have to prevent myself working through everything in my in-tray before I can start.
8. Pile everything else away from your desk/table. List and file your mind's clutter (dripping tap to fix/what to buy for that birthday). They'll all keep till later when you can give them proper time.

Why and how writing works

One of the reasons we need the help of such lifelines as therapeutic writing is that our modern culture tries to force our understanding of our lives into the school essay form. Life, on the contrary, is extraordinarily muddled and chaotic, certainly not made up of clear beginnings, middles and ends, so the writing we are concerned with here is just as formless. The *content*, and the *process* of creating the writing are the vital elements. 'It is a truth which flows through my arm. There is no *should*... it can't be put aside. Writing puts me in touch with my purpose, my Self, and therefore my direction' (Massereene-James, personal communication). The focus is not on the perfecting of creative writing forms such as poetry, short stories, autobiography and so on, though such very effective products may be unlooked-for rewards.

When an explorative, expressive attitude to writing is accepted – when the writer allows their hand to put on the paper whatever arrives at the end of the pencil – they *can't write the wrong thing*. It might be distressing or even shocking but it is likely to be the right thing for them at that time.

One of the vital starting points for this kind of writing seems to be the attitude of mind when writing. I always tell people when they start: 'do not think! Believe it or not, thinking inhibits creativity. Write without stopping to think.' You could call this not thinking 'absent minded' (Freud 1950) or, in Coleridge's words: 'That willing suspension of disbelief for the moment, which constitutes poetic faith' (in the *Biographia Literaria*); or as Hughes (1982) put it: 'The progress of any writer is marked by those moments when he manages to outwit his own inner police system'.

Hughes is referring to a 'police system' which keeps all sorts of elements of our experience down and out of consciousness, down in the deep well of ourselves (to mix my metaphors!). This can be an uncomfortable restriction for a writer, or someone suffering from depression or anxiety, as it can prevent them from expressing and exploring deep fears, anxieties, emotions, experiences, memories. It would certainly be inappropriate to deal with these in public. But, within the privacy of solitude, with a pencil and sheet of paper, it can be safe and healing (if, at times, uncomfortable or even painful) to give them conscious space. Writing does not seem to allow onto the page more than the writer can bear at that time.

Fear of what is sometimes seen as lurking depths within the mind can be a block to trying this kind of activity. Since Freud and Jung, there has come to be an anxiety over the contents of what is seen as the subterranean mind – a fear there may be monsters within. Yet what is down there is no more than ourselves, our own memories, thoughts, fears, experiences. Wordsworth (1798, p.360, lines 105–107) explored a similar problem, saying we 'half create' what we perceive: blow it up to be much bigger and perhaps more fearsome than it really is. Wordsworth borrowed this idea from the eighteenth century poet, Edward Young, who wrote in *Night Thoughts,* 'and half create the wondrous world they see' (1975, p.103, line 426).

Writing offers access to our inner words in a process within which the writer can feel confident. The self the writing hand makes contact with seems to be trustworthy. The process of writing in this way is gentle. Above all, it is paced. That strong inner, healing self who guides the writing hand once the policeman of the brain has been caught napping knows how much we can bear at any one time. I must have worked with hundreds of people. The writing has never brought up the wrong thing – uncomfortable, painful even, but never wrong. There is no one to ask probing questions, pushing us further than we want to go; no one to hear and take in our secrets. The writer is in the safety of aloneness, until they themselves decide to share the writing or its contents.

Why writing?

Gordon Wilson, who has now written about the death of his daughter, Marie, at Enniskillen, says: 'I have felt lighter of heart since I did the book. It's been a sort of therapy.'

> And if only GPs who are so quick to prescribe instant tranquillisers to silence distress would suggest the cleansing therapy of putting pen to paper instead. It's healing in rejection, grief, heartache or despair. It can clear our heads when we're faced with choice and indecision. It doesn't make you fat, sick or wreck your liver. And since nobody can possibly

> know more about us than we know about ourselves, infinitely superior to any psychiatrist. (Potter 1990)

Why write, when most of us tell our narratives over coffee, beer, cocoa? Writing is essentially different from talking because:

- Writing seems to create a pathway to memories, feelings and thoughts you did not know you had. You can discover, explore, clarify and make connections with the present. It is a way of grasping experiences which seem otherwise lost in the depths of the mind.
- Issues, ideas, inspirations you are aware of, but are almost impossible to *say*, can often be expressed in writing.
- Writing helps you work on things. It stays there on the page in the same form. It doesn't go away and so can be worked on. Thoughts, ideas, inspirations can be organised and clarified later (next day/year). Logical thought may be useful at this later stage, but not at the initial one. Thinking or talking can go round in circles like Chinese Whispers then evaporate: 'what was it I said or thought that seemed so vital yesterday???'
- Writing is private, a communication with the self, until you decide to share it – usually after solitary reflective rereading. Or it can be destroyed unshared, if necessary, even with yourself. Once something has been said and heard, it can never be unsaid. Things can be blurted out so fast, then regretted for a lifetime – as we all know from things we've devastatingly yelled in a row with a loved one. Writing is a staged process of rereading and redrafting and sharing when ready. Unshareable things can, therefore, be expressed relatively safely in writing.
- Writing offers a lasting record for the self, family, friends.
- The creative process of writing is rewarding (often exciting and fun), increasing self-confidence and self-esteem.
- Discussions around pieces of writing tend to have a depth and significance. A writing group can be a relatively safe, supportive, yet challenging environment to explore and share vital elements within a changing, sometimes joyful, but often depressing or even scary world (see Chapter Nine). A discussion with one significant

reader, such as a nurse, friend, doctor or therapist can be illuminating.

A new writer commented: 'In writing I can express that inner person I can't express to anyone else.' And another:

> Writing about yourself may inform *you*... almost like a map with landmarks which show you how you feel and what you need to do about it. It can be cathartic – releasing all the pain you held within, that swirled around inside your head and from which there seemed to be no escape. On paper it is captured – you don't have to think about it any more. A verbal cremation.
>
> In writing there's a power that is all yours. You can create whatever you wish; achieve your heart's desire; fulfil every ambition through your characters; use your imagination; flex and stretch it; give it exercise. It is boundless. Nothing is impossible with your pen.

A piece of paper and pencil is nearly always available, unlike the doctor or counsellor, like having a private therapist day and night. This is wonderful if you are writing on your own. If you are in therapy or counselling, it extends the possibilities: a twenty-minute or one-hour consultation may not only be too desperately short but might also come at just the wrong time for the patient. You can write in between sessions and take it in for the practitioner to see, or use it to inform what you do.

The physical business of writing, the co-ordination of hand and eye and mind seems to hold the writer to the explorative process. The act of moving the pen/pencil over the page can be soothing and creative, enjoyable in itself, as Jenny has pointed out at the beginning of the chapter. It can become addictive – but, perhaps, a fairly harmless addiction compared to others. Here is the testimony of a brand new writer in a group, translated by her from French, her first language:

> It is something that I've got deep down in my stomach, and I cannot describe it. How do they say in English? Guts feeling ... It is said it helps to talk but I find that writing is much better, it's between me and the paper. If I talk, how can I trust the others, and also it is said 'walls got ears'. Writing is ideal, frustration goes on the paper. I don't want to hassle anyone, if the tension goes up I can press harder with my pencil... Oh how much I like writing, I feel much better, it is like getting rid of a big load. Also on paper you can reread it, correct it, cross it, rub it off, tear it off, burn it, throw it in a bin. But why get rid of it? I want to read it again. But if I share it with the group, I won't be able to take my words back.

> They might interrupt me, ask questions, make some comments or they might say what I want to hear. The paper won't answer back – it won't say a thing – I like that. I want to do it again. Maybe at home? In a private corner, isolated in my solitude? (Marie Claude Maisey)

She did share her writing with the group, translating as she read. Some, however, need discipline when they first begin to help overcome their anxiety that they won't be able to write. I have often suggested an alarm clock set for twenty minutes – a comfortingly short period. I have, on occasion, told myself I must complete a piece during a train journey.

'Writing can be ... the place where the tough, the raw, the uncomfortable and the unresolved can first see the light of day and be given form' (Miles 1996). The writer puts his or her hand to the page without really knowing what is going to appear there, a process which has been likened to dropping a bucket into the well of the mind – the writer often does not know what will be dragged up (Byron 1995; Sansom 1994). I have known therapists or counsellors in workshops amazed, or crying, at reading what they have just written (Bolton 1995) This sounds possibly risky yet, perhaps because writing is so much slower than talking and thinking, it never seems to exceed what the writer can cope with.

Writing is a comparatively slow staged process. It is gentle and trustworthy. Material is often drawn up in the bucket in image form (metaphors for example). These images will only fully be understood when the writer is ready. The process of understanding might be straightforward, though, often stunningly simple – 'oh I see!' kind of stuff – bearable if painful. Here is Paul Pritchard being interviewed about his book (Pritchard 1997) about climbing:

> My stories of friends who have died and of my big accident are written to myself. The process helped me cope with the grief I was feeling and reasserted what they meant to me. Writing about my accident in Wen Zawn was pure therapy. I was so confused and lost after that, yet when I had finished ordering all the chaos I felt inside, I was able to see clearly how a painful experience could help me see my world in a more positive way than ever before. I will always be a climber first, but writing it all down has opened up new avenues of thought for me and it has been, almost, as rewarding as the travels and the climbs themselves.

Rewriting

Just as often, however, the written image is as clear as mud, in terms of personal meaning, until redrafting is undertaken. Redrafting is writing and rewriting to clarify and understand, to bring the writing closer and closer to what is in their mind, an artistic, crafting process, useful to borrow here. The writer will know if the image is worth exploring in this time-consuming way by the amount of energy (anger, fear, pain, joy, etc.) generated by rereading the initial writing.

The reworking of therapeutic writing creates communication back with the writer again. This is slightly different from the crafting of a poem intended for publication (for example), which is done in order to achieve a product which will communicate effectively with the reader/listener. On rewriting, sharper details of a memory come to mind (such as specific smells), errors are noted (no, the dress was not bottle green but navy blue; I wore that when I was very much younger). These details can make astonishing differences in comprehension of what the writing is telling the writer.

Redrafting is a process of re-experiencing, or creeping back into, the experience that led to the writing in order to find the words that most closely evoke it. This pushes out the boundaries of the memory, extending and clarifying it to encompass colour, shape, texture, quality of light, sound, smell, heat, cold, taste, exactly what words and tone of voice, and so on.

> Take that old, material utensil, language, found all about you, blank with familiarity, smeared with daily use, and make it into something that means more than it says. What poetry is made of is so old, so familiar, that it's easy to forget that it's not just the words, but polyrhythmic sounds, speech in its first endeavours (every poem breaks a silence that had to be overcome), prismatic meanings lit by each other's light, stained by each other's shadows. (Rich 1995, p.84)

Our memories are created by language. The finding of just the right words sharpens and enhances our understanding of ourselves. This is healing and self-affirming, whether the experience (and resulting writing) is comedy or tragedy. If it is the latter, 'opening the pus-filled wound and allowing it to drain through the writing' (Peter Connolly, see autobiography in Chapter Seven) can bring relief as well as great creative products. A hospice patient said: 'I had that poem inside me for ages. I couldn't get it out until I got my electric typewriter. I couldn't have dictated to anyone, it was too personal... I actually felt a burden roll off me. There was still the pain, but the burden had gone' (Frampton 1986).

Communication

Writing can be an extra form of communication with another – invaluable to a practitioner, if it is being pursued as part of therapy/counselling or other caring relationship (such as patient and doctor). Patients are usually in a position of dependency or vulnerability, from which saying what they think and feel is often hard. Writing a letter or list, or diary entry in the security of their own home, and taking it to the appointment, may enable them to communicate with the practitioner in their own way.

GPs have found it has offered diagnostically useful insight into the patients and not overwhelming in quantity (see Chapter Eleven). As Robin Philipp has said: 'Poetry extends ways of communicating in medicine. It can help both patient and physician express themselves' (Philipp 1994; see Chapter Thirteen). As a GP commented: 'you can't mishear what is written.'

Creativity in itself has a beneficial effect. 'There is a happiness in creation that is not without its own pain and struggle, a sensation that feels sometimes ... like lighting fires in snow, sometimes like untying knots in which you have been bound' (Rich 1995). It not only makes valuable use of otherwise unfulfilling leisure time (particularly useful for the depressed and anxious) but it also ensures a product of some sort. And, often, this product is from someone who would never see themselves as a creative artist. 'By writing the patient is transformed into a writer – creating an art which others can read and share: instead of a victim, we have someone with status; the patient is a writer (Sampson 1995). Even more important than this creation of a product is the re-creation of life that often happens with this kind of writing. 'In telling/writing the story of your life you are creating/recreating yourself' (Kopp 1972).

Writing in the healing professions

There is art therapy, music therapy, drama therapy, dance therapy, even smelling therapy (aromatherapy), but where is writing therapy? The potential of writing within mainstream medical care has never been seriously trialled in Britain, or instituted like these other arts. A list of healing therapies in a magazine, subtitled *How Do the Arts Heal?* (Caduceus 1996), carries a two-page list of artistic opportunities to enhance our creative experience, none of them writing.

Caring institutions in Britain support a great deal of writing activity, as the chapters of this book testify, and even more in the USA. Many writers facilitating others to write would not use the word therapy, feeling it unnecessary since they know writing to be essentially therapeutic. These are practising writers themselves, bringing the art of writing into the lives of those who suffer. These practitioners do not question whether the new writer is getting better thereby because they are concentrating on the writing rather than the mental or emotional state of the writer.

Writers support sufferers who write because they know, as all of us know who write, that writing is good for you. This almost seems like a well-kept secret by writers over the centuries. But the illuminating and healing benefits of writing have been kept from people by their fear that only clever people, those born to be artists, can write. This has held people away for too long from an invaluable form of communication both with the self and others.

One day there *may* be specialists with the label 'Writing Therapist' (Fine 1995). I am not certain this is the very best thing. Psychoanalytic art therapy and counselling often have interpretative agendas (Sampson 1995). But writing does not necessarily need an outsider to enable the writer to make sense of their work. Writing, unlike visual or plastic art, uses our everyday communicating medium – words. Very often, the writer will not understand clearly what the writing is telling them. A specialist interpretation is not necessarily the best thing at this point. The stages of non-understanding are an essential part of the therapeutic process. Writing, rewriting and writing additional related material will often bring the writer naturally to understand their own images and expressions. The writer may need careful support in sticking with the images when they seem incomprehensibly emotive. This support, as well as advice on methods, can well be offered by a medical, nursing or therapeutic practitioner.

Poetry or storymaking is therapy for both the body and the soul. The Greek noun *therapon* meant 'Waiting man in freely given service; minstrel or poet serving the muses' (quoted by Rigler 1996). Hellenistic philosophy was therapy for the soul, just as medicine was therapy for the body (Nussbaum 1994). The Hippocratics believed in the healing power of nature and the necessity of very careful listening to the patient for diagnosis and treatment. They also believed that suffering was part of the healing process (this understanding is present also in Oriental philosophy and medicine – Zen and acupuncture for instance). 'Personal growth through suffering is something that can be encouraged and stimulated' (Frampton 1986).

The kind of writing discussed here is a healing journey which involves suffering. It is a personal philosophical journey (using the SOD definition of philosophy as 'the love, study or pursuit of things and their causes').

Scientific inquiry was classically considered to be a part of philosophy. Science has, in modern times, cut itself off from the other branches. Medicine is now beginning to reclaim the other areas, and the arts:

> There are other aspects of medicine other than the purely scientific, such as communication ethics and empathy, aspects of healing other than the purely drug induced or surgical (e.g. the placebo effect), and aspects of ill-health that do not conform to a predict able scientific model (e.g. psychosomatic illness). These may be impossible to subject to scientific measurement as they are concerned with emotional states, yet they need to be addressed within medical education... Serious study or creative involvement with the arts demands an approach that is at least as rigorous and critical as any scientific approach; conclusions drawn or works created need be no less valid or valued through absence of quantitative data. (Smith and Taylor 1996, p.250)

Helping myself

The doctor looks after my body, the psychiatrist treats my mind, the parson takes care of my soul, lawyers and accountants see to my affairs – but who can help me? Hippocrates (1950) says I am the best person to help me. Writing is one of the best, and most enjoyable, ways of doing this. People are looking for some way to express their pain, for ways to tell the stories of their own and others' lives which are important to them.

The death of Princess Diana has proved this. There was an orgy of grieving for a woman few of the mourners ever knew (one man who was interviewed confessed never to having grieved for his mother but was grieving for Diana). It provided an allowable focus for an emotional expression which was otherwise held back. This holding back tends to lead to stress, depression, anxiety and other physical symptoms. And writing poured out of these mourners – poetry mostly. They needed to express something vital and this was the way they chose to do it. David Hart (1998), who has worked in writing and health for many years has said of post-traumatic therapeutic writing: '*talk* in these situations was perceived as not enough, language had to be shaped, poetry was essential to what needed to be shared' (pp.12–15).

CHAPTER THREE

Keeping a Journal

'The Diamonds of the Dustheap'

I never travel without my diary. One should always have something sensational to read on the train.

(Oscar Wilde, *The Importance of Being Earnest,* p.32)

Only good girls keep diaries, bad girls don't have the time.

(Tallulah Bankhead)

'Great God! merciful God! Let me be calm, for out of that way lies madness indeed. I begin to get new lights on certain things which have puzzled me. Up to now I never quite knew what Shakespeare meant when he made Hamlet say:

My tablets! Quick my tablets!
'Tis meet that I put it down, etc..,

for now feeling as though my own brain were unhinged or as if the shock had come which must end in its undoing, I turn to my diary for repose. The habit of entering accurately must help to soothe me.'

(Bram Stoker, *Dracula,* p.50)

Not a filofax!

A diary is a friend, the best friend you will ever find yourself. It is always there, always receptive and it is the only time you can talk openly and be certain that you will not be questioned and that what you say will not be repeated to anyone else. And it's quiet, blessedly quiet 'Through diary writing we can create our own identities in this private space' (Simons 1990, p.36). This is the '*journal intime*', the private or secret diary in which the diarist can explore and examine whatever they want or need to about themselves and their environment. Within this particular kind of diary there are as many different approaches and as many different ways of writing as there are diarists, and their needs, wants and moods. This chapter offers an introduction to some of these. There is no right way to write but there are all kinds of things you can do to make your writing do more for you. There are other kinds of journal, daybook, engagement diary and so on for recording events or other data which are beyond the scope of this book. We are particularly not talking here about a filofax.

A diary is written for its own sake, for the joy, the painful release, the discovery, the ordering and making sense, the creation, the re-experiencing, the reaffirmation of the self. This kind of writing can be a comforting process, with pattern and repetition. Writing regularly or often, taking the object (the book/folder/pad) around with one, is rather like having a grown-up security blanket or teddy to talk to. This is completely different from any other kind of writing we are likely to do (from shopping lists to reports to novels) – all with a purpose, often for a specific audience.

A diary offers a haven, a sense of continuity, and a sense of wholeness. If I wrote on these pages yesterday/last week/twenty years ago, I must not only exist but I must be more or less the same person as I was then.

Rereading a diary gives a sense of continuity and selfhood. It can connect you up to the person you were then. Writing a diary can also connect you to your future self who will read your pages. Virginia Woolf (1979) thought of herself at 50 reading her 37-year-old writings: 'But how I envy her the task I am preparing for her!'

Reading published diaries is also useful. Quite apart from gratifying a nosiness, which we all share, 'Reading diaries, in the same way as reading biographies, can help us in the subconscious search for a pattern in life' (Cleveland Peck 1995).

The diary also offers a place for experimenting, for fantasising, for trying out being someone else. The persona who emerges from the pages of a diary will be just that – a constructed character. Some diarists have been aware of the persona they are creating in their diary. Anne Frank, for example, wished to record the angst-ridden young person her friends did not know. Truth and facts are slippery things. Even if you always tried to stick rigidly to them, you would be kidding yourself. What is the truth? You would find you didn't know. Even if you thought you did, you would inevitably become bogged down by boring detail and anxiety. The joy of a diary is that it can skip over the ordinary, embroider dull bits, experiment with opposites, express extremes, open doors to fantasies. Here are 13-year-old Anne Frank's reasons for beginning a journal:

> It's an odd idea for someone like me to keep a diary because it seems to me that neither I – nor for that matter anyone else – will be interested in the unbosoming of a thirteen-year-old schoolgirl. Still, what does that matter? I want to write, but more than that, I want to bring out all kinds of things that lie buried deep in my heart.
>
> There is a saying that 'paper is more patient than man'; it came back to me on one of my slightly melancholy days, while I sat chin in hand, feeling too bored and limp even to make up my mind whether to go out or to stay at home... And now I come to the root of the matter, the reason for my starting a diary: it is that I have no ... real friend ... Hence, this diary. In order to enhance in my mind's eye the picture of the friend for whom I have waited so long, I don't want to set down a series of bald facts in a diary like most people do, but I want this diary itself to be my friend, and I shall call my friend Kitty. (1997, p.6)

One diarist, writer and teacher of diarying, Christina Baldwin, was fired as a child to begin a journal by seeing a play of Anne Frank's diary. The next day she created a locked journal and a space in the basement for herself: 'Its entrance, camouflaged by piles of musty books, was hidden from the rest of the family. I had made myself a secret annex and a journal. I started to write'(1991). And here is another young diarist, Eleanor Field:

> I have written diaries on and off for as long as I can remember, but I suppose I started to write a diary regularly four years ago when I was twelve and went off travelling around the world. I managed to write something every day but it turned out that I only wrote about the places I went and the things we did. I wrote very little about my thoughts and feelings during this period, perhaps it was because I was too tired, but I think maybe I was too young to write down exactly what I was feeling.
>
> Now I don't feel I need to write every day. I just write when I feel like it as I've realised it's pointless to write if I haven't anything to say.
>
> Writing a diary enables me to let out my feelings in a form which has no rules about language, punctuation, grammar or spelling. You can express yourself in the way which suits you and the way you think is the best. Mostly what I write is just a muddle of feelings, which helps me work out what's happening in my life. It helps me decide what I think about things and it helps me to let out my feelings, which I would otherwise suppress, for example anger, and frustration.

> I think it's a valuable record of growing up and I often look back on things I have written and remember sad times, happy times, holidays, people and of how I coped and that the bad times always pass. Recently when I have been getting stressed out with exams, reading old bits of diary reminds me how I coped with it the last lot. It is also a way of storing memories as I forget a lot of my feelings after a while.
>
> I stick in photos of friends, holidays, parties and any other special occasions so that when I'm older I have a visual reminder of how everything looked. I write quotes from songs, poems, sayings and mottoes that mean something to me and that relate to the situation I am in. I put in things my friends have done, for example, letters they have written to me or pictures they have drawn. I stick in things like train tickets which remind me of trips I've been on. Sometimes I stick in letters I wrote but never sent, and some of the nice things people have said.
>
> I sometimes read some bits to my friends but mostly it's really private. I write it with the intention of no-one reading it, and I sometimes feel really uncomfortable when my friends read me bits from their diary because I think some bits should be kept private. (Eleanor Field)

Anyone who can write, can write a journal. Anyone can take a pencil and piece of paper and scrawl words on it. They might write about what they did yesterday, who they met and what was said. Or it might be an account of all the thoughts they had during the day. Or... read on for many, many more ideas.

Variety

There must be as many different kinds of journal/daybook/diary as there are diarists. Of course, what makes them so useful as a vehicle for personal exploration is that they are designed only to be read by the writer (unless you decide otherwise). So there will never be an imagined reader leaning over your shoulder criticising your style or grammar, or tut-tutting over the contents, or querying all the inconsistencies. You can't go wrong – write it your own way.

A diary can be many things. Virginia Woolf (1979) called hers a 'capacious holdall in which one flings a mass of odds and ends'. It can do many, many things for you. A diary can:

Inspire
express ideas
defuse dilemmas
sort out problems
extend awareness
rescue vivid memories
offer confidence in the future
integrate dreaming into waking life
provide a record for future generations
reconnect the adult with the child with the old person
help to heal relationships (even with the dead)
store a creative bank for poetry/prose
enable the facing of hurt/pain/trauma
help you work out who you are
validate uncertain memories
organise/clarify thinking
preserve experiences
discover thoughts
cry out opposites
create images

Marion Milner wrote a series of books about diarying, all drawn from her own diaries (Milner 1986a, 1986b, 1987). She was a psychoanalyst who decided to use free-intuitive writing or free association in writing to try to find certain things out about herself, such as 'what makes me happy?' She decided not to use any psychoanalytic techniques to help her understand her writings but to rely on her own intuitions. These were the books which started me writing, particularly *On Not Being Able to Paint* (which title I read as: *On Not Being Able to Write*) (Milner 1971).

Overcoming beginners' blocks

You may well feel embarrassed as you begin to write. You imagine someone at your elbow reading your intimate thoughts, feelings, ideas and ramblings. Because we are only privy to our own thought processes (except when reading literature), we tend to downgrade them: they are only my thoughts/ideas, so they must be rubbish. Only the big thinkers –

philosophers, mystics etc. – or those with literary genius have the right to express themselves in writing, we think.

You imagine that writing should have a proper form and contain only sensible, thought-out ideas in logical progression. This is what we were taught in school or college: an essay should have a beginning, a middle and an end. You should tell your reader in the introduction what you are going to say; say it logically in the main body of the work; then reiterate your main points incisively in the conclusion. Then the teacher (or lecturer) would go through it with a red pen and write a condescending comment at the bottom. 'I had come to believe that writing involved the inevitable haemorrhaging red pen, bleeding over my lines with all sorts of correct "teacher language"' (Luidens 1997).

This wasn't real writing. Real people were never expected to read your writing, only teachers who we thought knew a great deal better. The ghosts of those teachers are still at our elbows, criticising. These ghosts must be exterminated, just as Virginia Woolf killed the angel of the house (Woolf 1993).

Or, perhaps, you have had to write reports for work, or minutes or articles, or have tried writing stories for publication – stories which also have to have a particular form and be of interest to an audience.

Diary writing is qualitatively different – it is organic. The purposes are all intrinsic. You can't go wrong but you can dry up. You can begin to feel your writing is becoming repetitive. You stop because you are bored and beginning to make a chore of it. Never force it. Stop when you are bored or feel you should stop. Respect your own intuitions. If you need a change, be imaginative or try out lots of the following ideas.

Foundations

Tristine Rainer (1978) identifies four main 'diary devices', corresponding to Jung's basic modes of human perception:

- free-intuitive writing is the language of intuition
- catharsis releases and expresses the emotion
- description conveys the information perceived by the senses – sight, touch, small, taste and hearing
- reflection is the contemplation of the intellect.

Free-intuitive writing

The cornerstone of diary and therapeutic writing: this is a voyage of discovery. I think a session started with six minutes of this type of writing will inevitably be valuable. Six minutes seems to be a magic length of time for this. Not too long so the hand just gets exhausted but long enough for something to happen. Of course, if it is flowing well, longer time spent at this kind of writing can only be better. But don't push it beyond what seems right at the time – it will only be a waste of time.

Thinking gets in the way of creativity – at least of this stage of creativity in which the mind is bubbling all on its own, making the hand write all sorts of things the consciousness might not even know is there. An example:

> I got on the train/tram
> was welcomed by the conductor
> But I never got to the North Pole
> I had to be satisfied with a film.
> You saw me as a two faced woman
> a woman whose face was too soft to face
> the arctic wind. A woman who put a mask
> on the back of her head to fool you
> she was looking at you
> with love
> when really she was protecting her soft skin
> by looking away from the wind.

Letting go of all awareness of grammar, spelling, punctuation and proper form is vital in this writing. None of them matter – in fact, they will get in the way. If you wish to share this writing further later, it can readily be edited into a more readable form.

> The daily log is not an exercise in literature; it is an exercise in our lives. There is no need for us to be concerned about our grammar, nor our literary style, nor the use of polite language. It is important that we feel free to write in everyday language, letting the flow of our words reach the paper with neither editing nor censorship. (Progoff 1987, p.96)

HOW TO DO IT

To achieve this successfully you need to be:

- very comfortable and confident in your surroundings
- happy with your writing materials

- alone or with *very* trusted others
- in a relaxed frame of mind
- not feeling totally negative about your writing.

Then:

- allow your hand to write literally whatever arrives at the pen/cil tip. This might be seemingly unassociated words (not even as logical as a list) or even made up words – nonsense in fact
- nothing is irrelevant. Write it all down
- try not to think about what's happening on the page – if you do, you will influence it and, inevitably, want to make more sense out of it
- don't stop. Try to write as fast as you can. This very speed will tend to prevent you beginning to analyse and attempt to write to a form
- you could try writing with your left hand (if right-handed or the right if left-handed) or with your eyes closed
- write for at least six minutes.

Then:

- move straight on to writing more contemplatively on whatever subject presents itself to you at the time
- write without reading and as quickly as you can. This writing will probably make more sense than the first stage
- stop when it seems appropriate to do so – ten minutes/two hours or when the phone/doorbell rings.

Then:

- re-read with care everything you've written
- try to bring a free-intuitive way of being to this reading, similar to the frame of mind for the writing
- mark anything in any of the writing that strikes you in any way. Don't ask yourself in what way!
- add comments, questions, notes about further explorations you'd like to make in writing

- be alive to any connections there might be within the writing, perhaps between the two pieces
- allow your mind to be open to divergent connections, thoughts and ideas which might appear to be completely unconnected. Note them down
- always be open to connections in writing – but you won't know what I mean until you've gasped 'oh I see!'

Follow up any of these ideas in writing then, if you have time and the inclination. Otherwise, this next stage can fruitfully be left to another time, when you have more energy.

Writing like this *can* take you into deep waters. It is part of the healing process but can feel uncomfortable or even a bit scary at times. If it gets like this:

- only do this kind of writing if you know there is someone you trust reasonably near you can call on or that you can telephone
- if you begin to go deep and become nervous, stay with it as long as you can. Be sensitive as to what is right for *you*
- stop if you feel you *must*, but don't be too weedy or the writing won't give you anything
- writing takes more commitment than talking and needs to be treated with respect. You can't cheat with writing – that's cheating yourself and it doesn't work for very long.

WAYS OF PUTTING THIS WRITING TO USE

Six-minute writing, as I always call it, will provide you with a bank of material to work on. The images you will find you have created may be rather similar to dream images in that it may be hard to work out where they have come from, what they connect with and what use they are (I still don't understand my two-faced woman diary entry – a piece I have never worked on). But it is worth spending time and effort extending and working on this material, both for your own personal development and for creating shareable (publishable?) fiction, poetry or whatever (if that is what you wish).

Many beginning writers use a great number of abstractions. They write about their emotions – happiness, fear, anxiety... You will find on re-reading it that it feels 'empty'. This is because there are no human hooks onto which to attach the emotion. If you find you do this (and I started here too), then rewrite the passage using only *concrete* images. So, 'Oh I do love him so. He makes me feel so happy ...', might become 'Oh I love the way he looks at me just out of the corner of his eye, so no one else can see he's looking at me'. 'His expression was abstracted' might become 'he was looking at something I could not see'.

There are a range of things you can do with this material when you have done your first piece of free-intuitive writing:

1. Continue from the notes you made yourself when you first read through the writing. These may have been to extend or explore some of the buds of ideas within the dense packed text. Don't hurry. Take one of your points at a time. Only move on to the next one when you have exhausted that one.
2. Take a word or phrase you marked as being of interest when you read through the writing. Write it down and use it as a trigger to start more free writing. Write free-intuitively from it and see where you get to. When you have exhausted this, but not your energy, take another word or phrase and start again.
3. Take a passage that interests you and extend it. Try to make sense of it, write some more. Allow your mind to come up with a variety of ideas as to what it might be about. Experiment with them. As you write, remember you have five senses, not just sight. Consider including elements such as the season, what the place was like, details which date the occasion (e.g. calf-length skirt flounced out with petticoat layers, and bobby socks), the exact (as far as possible) words he used – inside speech marks, rather than in the form of reported speech – and so on.
4. Study the ideas in Chapters Five and Six. Many of these approaches will be useful for extending this work.

You may find yourself writing memories from childhood you didn't know you had, about dreams you'd forgotten, fictional stories, lyrical poems about scenes you barely remember, or anything else. Just allow the writing to dictate to you what it wants to be.

Or you might not want to do anything with this writing. It might have been enough to create it and re-read it with interest. At least it covered the page, so you no longer had a frightening blank in front of you. Or you might be quite happy with the diary section you have created, want to leave it at that and continue straight away to write something more focused.

GOOD COMPANY

Virginia Woolf said of such writing:

> I have just reread my last year's diary and am much struck by the rapid haphazard gallop at which it skims along, sometimes indeed jerking almost intolerably over the cobbles. Still if it were not written rather faster than the fastest typewriting, if I stopped and took thought, it would never be written at all. And the advantage of the method is that it sweeps up accidentally several stray matters which I should exclude if I hesitated, but which are the diamonds of the dustheap. (1979, p.233)

The surrealists and Dadaists in Paris experimented with this kind of writing, using it to find inspiration as well as to write finished texts. They also played word games with each other using this kind of free association principle. *The Exquisite Corpse* is a version of *Consequences*, with adjective/noun/verb... in the columns, so each writer would only contribute one word each time. Telling a group story by each person contributing one word in turn is another game they played. It was their idea to write with the eyes closed or with the non-writing hand.

Virginia Woolf herself wrote stream of consciousness writing. Her novel *The Waves* (1997) is her closest published work to this kind of writing.

Cathartic writing

This is when you shout or weep onto the page. You may be gripped by anger, pain, hurt, fear. You may be feeling incomprehension at what life has dealt you, or guilt or shame or remorse or anxiety. Or you may need to shout what you think from the soap-box of your diary. So often there is nothing we can do with these extreme human emotions, except break a window, hurt someone else or knead some bread (this makes excellent bread, since the more it's knocked about, the better it tastes). None of these deal with the feelings; they only release a bit of the pressure.

Talking to the right person in the right place at the right time, with time and energy to spare is really good, *when* they are there.

Your diary is always there. Like this (in huge scarlet capitals):

WHY DO YOU WANT A BLONDE BIG-BREASTED WOMAN? *I* LOVE YOU. ISN'T THAT ENOUGH – THE WAY I LOVE YOU? ISN'T THAT ENOUGH?

WHAT TO DO

The method is similar to that for the free-intuitive writing. You let out onto the page just what you are feeling and thinking, trying not to edit it in your mind at all.

Use the paper in whatever way seems right to you. The example above was scrawled across a big sheet of paper, with other words all round the edges, written in a circle. Right across the writing in the middle were the words 'I LOVE YOU' written even bigger in black, over the top of the other writing, but upside down to it.

Your emotion might lead you to scrawl huge, the pen/cil almost making holes in the page. Coloured felt pens and big sheets of A1 paper can be excellent too. As can coloured paper – how about a blue feeling, a scarlet emotion or a yellow thought? Or it might be the kind of emotion that leads you to write spider script, perhaps on a tiny scrap of paper, with a very well sharpened pencil.

The writing might come out attended by scribbly drawings, called *taking a line for a walk* by Marion Milner (1971). Allow these to come too, as they will express as much as the writing. You will also be able to read them later in the same way (perhaps not quite so easily, since they will be visual rather than verbal images).

Description

This is notebook writing *par excellence.* Every writer uses their journal for this; many carry a little book everywhere:

> O the unutterable darkness of the sky and the earth below the moon! And the glorious brightness of the moon itself! There was a vivid sparkling streak of light at this end of Rydale Water, but the rest was very dark, and Loughrigg Fell and Silver Howe were white and bright as if they were covered with hoar frost. The moon retired again, and appeared and disappeared several times before I reached home. (Dorothy Wordsworth 1987, p.136)

or

> Dry-stone walls with the sunrise behind them look like old lace.

These are visual observations. They might just as well have been aural: (overheard on the bus) we couldn't have put him further down in the cemetery; he had to have a good view; smells: he came to bed with me reeking of patchouli perfume; taste: that champagne had a tang of brazil nuts; and the bubbles burst, exploding straight into my brain and along my nerves. And touch: the satin of floorboards, warm under naked feet.

Describing people and places is a wonderful exercise. It is a way of extending experience: describing a happy one, for example, can deepen, intensify and prolong it. Coming at characters or situations sideways is often a really illuminating exercise. For example, try creating a picture of a friend or enemy by describing only the contents of their rubbish bin (fiction will be more powerful than peeking in their real bin).

Sharpening your senses in this way is enormous fun and puts you in essential contact with the world and others. A sense of cut-offness, separateness, of being blanketed, is one of the symptoms of depression. Observing minutely like this, often finding metaphors or similes to gain as close an observation as possible, can help to put you back in touch:

up from the valley,
gold larch needles edge the lane:
stitching back my heart

Precision and accuracy

The most effective way of building up a description is to use a very few, very accurate images with as few adjectives and adverbs as possible. Adjectives and adverbs are the describing words, for example big (adjective) or fast (adverb). Compare these two sentences: The big dog ran fast. The Doberman charged.

Practice noticing what it is that makes a place or person distinctive. Is it the lack of shoe polish, the expression of the eyes, the quality of the light? Try creating thumbnail sketches until you hit that nail on the head: this is the kind of precision which helps you make real contact with those inner workings of yourself, as well as the outer environment.

Tristine Rainer (1978) (drawing on Milner) describes an exercise for discovering joy in ordinary moments, ordinary things, which uses, perhaps, an opposite skill to my thumbnail sketches. She calls it 'the here and now exercise'. You write down exactly what you perceive (remembering all your senses) about where you are at a particular time. It doesn't have to be a special time or place, in fact it shouldn't be. Try and record the very minutest detail with as much loving care as possible. Try it, you'll surprise yourself. Here is Berlie Doherty, an established novelist, speaking of her journal:

> Writing is such an important part of my life that I find it very difficult not to write. There is always something to write about!
>
> There is a down-side to this compulsive writing, of course, and that is that you never really manage to take a holiday from it. When I go away I don't always remember to pack a camera (in fact I find it quite liberating to be on holiday without one) but I always pack my journal. If it gets left out I have to buy another, or I'd never relax. Something, I don't know what, makes it necessary for me to record things – the meal, the sunset, the mood, the strangeness, the people, the wait in the airport... I think there's an element of challenge there somehow – can I describe this scene just as it is, with all its sights and sounds and smells, can I describe how I feel about it right now, can I recreate this exotic, extraordinary/ordinary/friendly/aggressive stranger just as they are at this minute?
>
> But why? Wouldn't you think I'd be happy just having a glass of wine in the sunshine and leaving my work behind? The answer is, I suppose, that it doesn't feel like work. It's personal, and it isn't intended for anybody else to read.
>
> Yet, sometimes, it does become public.
>
> I actually think journal writing is the point at which writing for oneself, just for the hell of it, and writing for a public begin to overlap. There is a you to whom the journal is addressed, whether or not the writer is aware of it. This you makes you pause to seek the exact word and the perfect phrase, yet at the same time there's a fluency about journal writing that makes it quite different from the writing of a piece that is originally intended for publication. Writers rarely find that immediacy of subject matter of response to it, because usually we're writing in a study, at a desk, imagining or conjuring up from nowhere. There's something very potent and therefore valuable about the writing that comes as an immediate and unsolicited response to what is actually there.
>
> Now sometimes I go back to my journal to support a piece of creative fiction. Although at the time of writing it was something written for its own sake, it's still there for reference if I need it. This isn't deliberate, it's serendipity! For example, I have pieces of fiction set in a town in Italy, or Malta or Ireland, on a rough sea crossing, on a railway station, describing a potter at work, and many more, all of which have been made authentic because I've been able to refer back to that real experience of being there

> and observing detail which I could never have made up. I often use the exact language that I used at the time. This helps me to make the writing more vivid. If it helps me then it must help the reader too, and what else does a writer do but invite her readers to walk in her world with her?
>
> (Berlie Doherty)

Reflective

This is the kind of writing that can tell you what you think. If you can allow yourself to put your ideas on a particular subject down on the page, you will discover a great deal. Try to allow the thoughts and ideas to flow in any order. If they are so jumbled that you can't make sense of them (or if you need to present them to others), you can reorder them easily afterwards. Reflective writing is an excellent way of sorting out problems. All the sides of the argument, or the bits of the dilemma, can be put down and then sorted and weighed (see Chapter Eight). Or you may want to do this to explore an issue or a conundrum which fascinates you:

> I think the night is loving and warm, like a blanket. It's so safe at night, I can take my masks off and nobody can see the real me, just resting, just being me. I don't understand why the light is always thought to be good, and the dark bad. The dark protects me when I go out – I can go anywhere (as long as there are no street lights) and no-one can see me. And then there's the beauty of the moon, and Orion the protector, with his dog, and Leo about to leap, and Jupiter like a hole punched right through the sky, and all the others.

Points of view can be experimented with, and different attitudes attempted, in an open exploration towards discovering your own. You can try writing down one thing and then its opposite – just to see how it feels and what it looks like. Normally, in life, we are expected to be consistent. We have to present a whole character to the world. But it doesn't feel like that inside. There are muddles and inconsistencies. The diary is an utterly private place in which the mask of coherence can be dropped. A few pages of illogicality, of expressing completely opposite opinions, can help enormously towards working out what you do think and feel.

Switching from 'I' to 'she/he' in writing (altering the person) is a powerful way of playing with diary writing. It might be possible for 'he' to say something which 'I' would find impossible (for example, the writing of a therapy client in Chapter Thirteen). On the other hand, writing in the voice of your lover, mother, patient, enemy can help enormously in understanding the way they are thinking and behaving. I normally do this in the form of a dialogue or a letter, which we will come to in the next chapter.

Altering the tense is a useful thing to try. The present tense makes writing seem much more immediate and, well, *present.* Writing about a past event as if it is happening now can bring it much more vividly to life. Writing about a very present and painful event in the past tense can soften the emotional impact sufficiently to allow one to face it in writing.

There are some starter words/phrases which can be useful. Eleanor Hall (1990), a counsellor of gifted children has called these 'journal jumpers'. She suggests: 'I get along with people best who are...; when I am bored I...; people don't like me because...' John Calvi (1988), a therapist, uses the following headings (clients write freely about times when they've used these phrases): 'I love you; thank you; I'm sorry; I need help; that's not good enough; No! Stop! Bug off!' I have used simply: 'I am...; I think...; I want...; I believe...; if only...; what if...; and so on.'

How about: 'Write down three secrets you have kept for years; from whom have you kept them?'

Structured journalling

Ira Progoff (1987) has developed a complex form of journalling. Adherents learn how to write under a range of headings in experiential therapeutic workshops. They then keep their personal journal with all its set sections:

> The intensive journal process plays an active role in reconstructing a life ... It establishes a person's sense of his own being by enriching his inner life with new experiences of a creative and spiritual quality. The intensive journal workbook is specifically designed to provide an instrument and techniques by which persons can discover within themselves the resources they did not know they possessed. (p.96)

The journal is divided into a range of different sections devoted to different aspects of life. Journallers write on their own as well as members of a group; they are guided in their writing, re-reading and reflecting upon their writing and further related writing. The work is deeply contemplative, arising from silence, rather like in an active retreat or Quaker meeting.

Simona Parker has brought this method to Britain and has adapted it as non-linear structured journalling. Here are some of her creative journal sections (adapted from Parker 1993):

Time dimension	
Period review	Reconnecting to the most recent past
Recycling the past	Re-exploring the more distant past
Crossroads	Exploration of untaken life-paths
Here and now	Recording feelings, thoughts in the moment
Interpersonal dimension	
Relationships	Exploring relationships with key people
Body	Ways of connecting to our bodies
Recurring patterns	Ways of exploring significant events, situations
Events, situations	Recurring feelings, emotions, life riddles, fate
Work	Ways of exploring meaningful outer activities
Environment	Ways of exploring and connecting to our culture, social and political issues
Symbolic dimension	
Dreams	Recording dreams
Symbolic contact	Record of imagery, intuitions, intimations
Wisdom dialogue	Inner dialogues with mentors, guides on our path for meaning, truth and wholeness
Transpersonal dimension	
Positioning	Review and exploration of changing beliefs, values
Unitive experiences	Record of belonging to a greater reality
Concerns	Exploring issues which have most meaning to us
Credo	Statements of what we believe/what has meaning.

A bit of history

Journal writing is a centuries-old form of self-expression and examination (Simons 1990; Blodgett 1988). This private form of expression and communication has been considered to be a particularly female one, presumably because men have usually been able to express themselves verbally.

But the kinds of explorations suggested above for exploring deep into oneself (the journal intime) are all recent ways of using a diary. Diaries have been used in the past to record public events and persons, family matters, travels and spiritual journeys. People have been a primary focus – behaviours, attachments, opinions and fates. English women have been diarists since the sixteenth century, probably because they were uneasy about their writing skills. This kind of private writing would be less open to criticism than any other. It was a form of self-expression they could use in their deeply restrictive lives. Women diarists did not tend to express themselves freely in the past, however. They tended to be reticent about personal matters, particularly intense experiences, and most especially those which involved the opposite sex. Perhaps they were afraid of their writing being read (Beatrix Potter's was very circumspect and in code: she lived with strict parents until nearly 50). Perhaps there was no precedent for expression of deep feelings. In her book about diary writing, Blodgett points out that the habits, training and expectations of women led them not to think of themselves but of others, and not to express discomforts and woes. Also, there would probably have been no psychological support if they distressed themselves in their explorations.

Anaïs Nin made the journal form well known, or, perhaps, notorious. Tristine Rainer, quoted above, was her pupil. She outlined how to write a truly therapeutic diary (Rainer 1978).

Spiritual writing was a very strong tradition among Quaker women who 'Travelled in the Ministry' in the seventeenth to the nineteenth centuries. Here is the beginning of Elisabeth Ashbridge's journal (1713–1755):

> My life having been attended with many uncommon occurrences, I have thought proper to make some remarks on the dealings of Divine goodness with me. I have often had cause, with David, to say, 'It is good for me that I have been afflicted,' and most earnestly desire that they who read the following lines may take warning, and shun the evils into which I have been drawn. (p.1)

And here is an extract from the journal of Katherine Evans and Sarah Cheevers. These women had a leading to minister in Malta, where they were imprisoned in the Inquisition for three and a half years:

> The tenth day of my fast, there came two friars, the Chancellor, the man with the Black Rod and a physician and the Keeper. And the friar commended my dear friend to go out of the room and he came and

pulled my hand out of the bed and said, 'Is the Devil so great in you that you cannot speak?'

I said, 'Depart from me, thou worker of iniquity, I know thee not. The power of the Lord is upon me, and thou call'st him Devil.'

He took his crucifix to strike me in the mouth... (Graham *et al.* 1989, p.121)

Medieval Japanese Ladies of the Court wrote Pillow Books (journals). *The Pillow Book of Sei Shonagan* (born about 965) is a gem of historical and reflective material. Sei Shonagan wrote about all kinds of things and loved making lists (more about listmaking in Chapter Eight):

Things that should be short:

A piece of thread when one wants to sew something in a hurry
A lamp stand
The hair of a woman of the lower classes should be neat and short
The speech of a young girl

Things that give a clean feeling:

An earthen cup
A new metal bowl
A rush mat
The play of light on water as one pours it into a vessel
A new wooden chest

Things that make one's heart beat faster:

It is night and one is expecting a visitor. Suddenly one is startled by the sound of raindrops, which the wind blows against the shutters. (Morris 1967, pp.58, 161, 201)

Here is an account of an annual diary:

The oddest material on which to write a diary must surely be that used by an Italian peasant woman, Clelia Cmarchi. It was a sheet – not the A4 but the linen bed variety – which she covered with long lines of tiny handwriting and edged with poems in red ink. She had been married for 40 years; her children had been born and her husband died in similar sheets and she found this the most appropriate medium on which to express her life history. A couple of years ago she was able to see the sheet displayed in the village of Pieve S Stefano, now know as the Citta del Diario, in Tuscany. (Cleveland Peck 1995)

Early novels were all written in diary form; the existence of the book was authenticated and the reader expected to join the heroine/hero in the fiction that the novel is a genuine diary. Bram Stoker's *Dracula* (1897, quoted above) is a late Gothic version of this conceit.

Conclusion

Here are two golden rules of journal writing, from Christina Baldwin (1991):

1. Date your entries as you go;
2. Don't make any other rules.

And a comment from a healthcare worker at the end of a Therapeutic Writing Workshop: 'The diary I have is therapeutic and feels like a friend that I confide in… But the style and method of writing in my diary will be very different and hopefully more useful from now on. *I'll be taking the thinking out of it!*'

CHAPTER FOUR

Writing Openers

Unbuttoning; Opening the Box

The Captain unlocked his word-hoard.

(*Beowulf*)

I have written, therefore I must have existed.

(Joyce Carol Oates)

Writers end up writing about their obsessions. Things that hurt them; things they can't forget; stories they carry in their bodies wanting to be released.

(Natalie Goldberg, *Writing Down the Bones*)

Buttoned

Opening the button box can be taking the lid off the 'Box of Delights'.

No one has button boxes these days, I'm told – worn clothes are thrown away. I have two. One contains practical all-sorts and lives near needles and cottons. The other button tin is kept with my work equipment, alongside shells, skulls, bird's nests and so on (if you can imagine what such a 'so on' could be). Its use is to create magical journeys – whether out into fictions of who could possibly have worn such outrageous glittery things or inwards, perhaps, towards memories of the clothes Mother made.

An unbuttoned writing group

At the National Association of Writers in Education Conference (Bolton 1997), a group of writers (both sexes, mix of ages and background), who had decided that they were interested in my writing therapy projects and wanted to experience some of this writing, joined me for a workshop. I wanted us to write from something special, something which would, in itself, leave a lasting impression. Objects can be facilitative when they are handled and then the experience written up.

I took my tin of buttons, collected lovingly over several years with the help of various people. Quite a lot of them are antique. Buttons are everyday dull things; or are they? Buttons belong to the province of women; or do they?

I tipped the tin out onto the table between us. Immediately, every pair of hands dived into the gleaming mass. I didn't have to tell the group to play with them, to choose a few for themselves. I had planned what to suggest the group did with these buttons, but jettisoned the plan pretty quickly. The ring of faces were absorbed, one man giving a running commentary of his choice and why. Comments were made like: 'this reminds me of playing with grandma's box'; 'what a childish pleasure, I'm grabbing all the ones I like best. This is unabashed childishness!' 'these buttons have a history just like people'; 'they reflect a variety just like my life'. They enjoyed the immense diversity, from British Rail uniform buttons, to delicate jewelled ones and a huge fur coat button. 'Who would have thought they would be such a pleasure', one exclaimed, 'They're only buttons!' Yet they seemed to have the power to conjure up every aspect of life.

Then everyone chose a selection for the person on their left, in each case a stranger. Each person, therefore, received a selection from one neighbour and passed on another to their other neighbour. We only had about three minutes for this, so a quick but careful scrutiny took place. Then we wrote (quickly too) anything that came into our heads, whether it seemed connected with the buttons or not.

Leslie Davidoff was so delighted to receive a beautiful handful from his neighbour that he wrote: 'For a brief moment I am in love... I love you momentarily, whoever you are.' At the same time, the donor, Shahzadi, was writing:

Unbuttoning

Why did I give you these buttons? Little things about how you spoke. With care, sensitivity about your daughter. And your own collection. A person of 'taste' I thought, individual, and a sweetness.

Why did you give me these buttons? I don't know... It unnerves me to have someone else's buttons here among mine. But I'm unable to refuse. Somehow I want to. Perhaps put them somewhere else, a trial period in a little box of their own till we can see if they're going to behave the way the rest of us want them to.

Hell, where to now? NOW I FEEL I OWN THESE BLOODY BUTTONS. And I know what's going to happen – you're going to make me let them go.

(Shahzadi)

Here are a few more of the writings:

Button Choosing

The diversity of choosing, the diversity of liking,
the occasional rejection; so much spread out for us.

What would I really want, starting again;
before the big shop window with my
only sixpence, and the Parent rushing me
tugging me on…?

(Ted Burford)

The lion remembers to roar. Only a small lion, but a king of the jungle nevertheless. In this haven, this zoo, protected from the dangers of the jungle, I remember my roar. My roar is love. It shoves aside fear. I remember it. I used to roar a lot.

(Leslie Davidoff)

I would have to wear a suit. I don't wear suits. My alter ego might? She would be able to wear linen all day without it looking crumpled, her hair caught up on one of those elegant, stylishly slightly dishevelled looking chignons of the Edwardian era, her white shirt front crisp even at 6 pm…

(Gillie Bolton)

Then we read them to each other with no time for comment, unfortunately. There was little relationship in the writing to the *function* of buttons. But there was a sense of excitement in the reading. One person said: 'a great deal more poetic writing has come out of these buttons than out of the "poetry" workshop earlier!' Much surprise was expressed that something so mundane should create such personal delvings and satisfying products.

Buttons with others

When a group of nurses used these buttons in a workshop, they thought about first impressions of people and how right these are, or not. 'Some lie unnoticed and then you turn them over and see their brighter side.' One midwife said that was unlike her first impressions of mothers and babies, which are usually right. Another nurse wrote about the diversity of belly buttons.

In another group, one woman remembered her first pair of jeans, bought by herself aged 13. Many of us wrote about childhood clothes on that occasion. One man explored feelings of being buttoned in, buttoned up in his work. Another woman wrote about the way buttons connect two halves together temporarily, as in sex and love.

A group of teachers and lecturers on the Isle of Wight was fascinated at the idea of using a button box to open up images, having read my article about the NAWE conference workshop. One of the group, Pat Murgatroyd, took along her box for a writing session and later sent me their poems and some of their thoughts. The memories captured in the poems are vivid:

Buttons

Splashing onto white cotton cloth
The cascade of buttons returned us
to girlhood; fastening images
of mothers and maiden aunts,
Of friends in summer, sisters in suits,
With court shoes and gloves to match.

I touched a navy blue one
Four eye holes and a rim,
Unmistakable – gabardine mac'.
And there she was after 40 years,
Spinster of the parish,
Mannish, lonely, walking the lanes
All seasons round in thick boots
And that mac'.

Fascinated I would watch her
Through the steamy window
Of the one cafe in town where
She lingered for hours
With a single pot of tea and a library book.

Eccentric, cultured, mad so-say,
Undone by her own past.

(Pat Murgatroyd)

After they had written and read their poetic memory journeys to each other, Pat offered the idea that someone who had had an unhappy childhood might have very different memories, thoughts and feelings brought up by the buttons. The group discussed this and Pat captured their ideas:

Beware of buttons

Whose idea was it then, this open button box?
Smug and cosy memories of mums in floral frocks,
Maiden aunts in cardigans and babies in white smocks.

For me remembering brings back fears
Of childhood, awful teenage years.
Just writing this – I fight back tears.

Take care, beware you culture gluttons,
Untold harm; undone by buttons!

(Pat Murgatroyd)

Care with unbuttoning

The message is clear to the facilitator: opening up images for others may be the 'Box of Delights' for some, but 'Pandora's Box' for others. The kind of exercises suggested for writers to undertake with image-making material must be planned with care. The group, and paired discussion work, described in these button sessions helps hold the writers so they do not fly too far off into solo mental journeys. What they were asked to do and think about with the buttons also affected the directions they were likely to go. Choosing a set of buttons for a partner, for example, is a warming and positive initial activity. It helps the writer feel more confident and trusting within the group.

The word 'button' derives from one meaning 'strike' or 'thrust', oddly enough, for a female-associated and feminine-shaped object. I certainly find they have a surprising impact. It doesn't need much to set people writing. Really just the permission to express themselves to themselves. 'How can just buttons make me think of so much?'

Some more objects

All sorts of other objects, as well as buttons, make good openers for writing, whether with a group or on your own. Precious mementoes can bring back memories; picture postcards can take you to all sorts of places if you creep into the picture. Seashells can take you back to childish times, collecting them on the beach. They can also encourage you to think of what it would feel like to be inside one, like a hermit crab.

Old photos can really take the lid off. Try leafing through an album and stopping at the first one that seems to arrest your attention. Don't question why, but start writing whatever arrives on the paper. Then you might like to imagine what the characters are saying or what has just or is just about to happen. Who was the invisible presence, the photographer? Write in his or her voice.

A tune isn't really an object, but can be treated as one. Some people always have a tune on their mind. I occasionally do. When this happens, try and remember what the words are or, at least, what the title is. This will set you off on some interesting writing. If no words come to mind, write free-intuitively from the tune – there may be memories of when you first heard it, for example.

Some techniques

Letters

At a writing weekend I ran, one of the group, Dave Dight, developed a very bad shoulder pain and asked if I had any pain killers. I didn't, but suggested he write a letter to his shoulder, and one in reply. He looked considerably startled: this was clearly very far from how he expected to deal with a pain, but went off to have a go:

> *To: The right shoulder, from Dave*
>
> Are you a broken male? Did someone stab you from behind? Is the pain coming from deep within? Is the wound old or new? You pain me when you relax, when you tense there is no pain. Why do you not accept surrender?
>
> You throb with the beat of my heart – is your pain a message from a heart-wound? The language of broken love? Or are you from outside: a resonance from someone else's hurt? I need to know who you are and where you're from.

I trace the contours of your outline with my mind; I follow the movements of the pain through the biceps, down the arm, into the palm. The right, male, side of me is hurting. With awareness, I chart the rise and fall of intensity of the agony, experiment with different positions. You know I want to heal you. I give you my love; I breathe through you. I will you to melt and yet you torture me. Please yield your secret to me. It's not for me that I want peace from you. I want us to be one again – like before.

I don't want to play the bully, threaten you with my power – use violent exercise or injected relaxants to impose my will. I don't want you to belong to me by force; I'd rather you yield of your own free will and whisper me the secrets of your distress , so I can heal my heart with your help. We are one, we shouldn't fight one another; we need one another.

From: The right shoulder, to Dave

You never pay any attention to me! You only hear me when I scream at you! You're too busy thinking of yourself! Who do you think you are? God or something? I have feelings too! I don't want anything from you, just recognition. Do you think I enjoy this? This isn't a game: a mind game or power game. I really want freedom: just to *be.*

You may think I'm just part of you, that you're in control, but this pain is to tell you you're not! It's you who have to surrender and relax, not me. You've pushed me around for too long. I've always done everything you've demanded without complaint. I've tried talking to you, but you just won't listen. Well now I'm having to scream! I need your respect and your awareness of me – you're not just going to use me like a tool any more, forgetting my existence when it suits you!

You're right, we are one – we'll never be separate; but it's up to you whether we live in harmony or at war. (Dave Dight)

Dave commented that 'the response from the shoulder was rather reminiscent of my ex-wife…' The physical problem, he later discovered, was a trapped nerve in his neck, possibly caused by a (very masculine) game of playing 'horse' for his two sons. He did muse on whether the real cause was stress at work, where there were those in authority who were definitely a 'pain in the neck'.

The next letter is from a writer on the same weekend. I had suggested the workshop theme of writing about someone who had been important at any point in the writer's life. Jackie Bartlett had been very distressed. Writing, which had been her comfort from being a little girl, had deserted her. She was overwhelmed by a sense of how the adults who should have guarded her had abused her instead. Then an island-gem of a memory shone out. She asked what she should do with this memory and I suggested she write it in the first person, the present tense, and creep back into the memory, filling out the details as much as she could using all her five senses and memory observation. Jackie intensified the experience by writing it as a letter:

Dear Miss Carlin,

I'm in the classroom, the big one with the partition that rolls back to make the school hall. It's afternoon and the sun's coming in through the high windows showing all the dust on the glass and the floor. There's a pot of yellow flowers on the teacher's desk and all of us kids are stretched out in six long lines of desks right across the room. They're the sort of desks with a hole in the top corner for a pot of ink and a lid that lifts up to show a big space for books and papers and stuff. Behind the teacher's desk the stock cupboard door's open and I can see rolls of card and blue sugar paper. We're having a craft lesson and we're making boxes by ruling lines on paper and then cutting and folding. I like doing this because I'm good at it even though the box is a bit wobbly when it's finished.

Everybody knows that there's spelling tests today and sure enough, you come in and beckon me to go with you. I follow you up those twisty stone steps to the top corridor which we call the turret, to where your office is. I see your brown shoe heels going up the stairs in front of me and your thick brown stockings. Your hair is in a big soft bun at the back of your head.

The corridor has windows all down one side and doors down the other and we walk down to where your room is at the far end. Inside, there's a big desk and bookshelves and a large photograph on the wall of a young woman in academic dress that must be you when you were younger. The room smells of polish and papers and your scent which is like flowers.

I sit on the chair in front of your desk and my feet don't touch the floor. It's a hard chair and I'm facing the bookshelves and trying to read the titles on the spines of the books. I enjoy reading. I have been able to read for as long as I can remember and I know I can spell too because the difficult words in books don't stop me. I can work them out. I'm better at reading quietly to myself because I have a stammer and sometimes it takes me a long time to say a word and I feel a bit afraid now because I don't want to do badly in this spelling test; I want to show you what I can

> do. I know you like me and I know you won't be impatient with me and tell me to 'get on with it!' like some of the other teachers do.
>
> The words I have to spell are easy. You read them out to me from a card on your desk and each time I spell the word back to you you make a mark on your card and smile. I feel scared when I have to spell NECESSARY but I get it right and you look at me and say, 'well done, Jacqueline. Now, do you know what it means?' I tell you and you nod and tell me I'm a very good girl and that I can go now. You come with me to the door and when we reach it you open it for me and say, 'Well done dear.' (Jackie Bartlett)

This memory of an excellent teacher offered Jackie the reassurance she so desperately needed. It was an oasis of a memory in the middle of the desert of the rest of her recollections of her childhood at that time. Writing the memory as a letter put her directly back in contact with Miss Carlin; she wrote it *for* the teacher rather than *about* her. All the loving detail increased that contact. This is not a letter Jackie would ever have had any intention of sending, any more than Dave could have done.

Letters are marvellous vehicles, whether they are sendable or not. The journalist Fergal Keane wrote two letters when his son was born. One was to his father who had been an alcoholic, the other to the son, Daniel. The letters, occasioned by the birth, are a way of making contact with the dead father and a way of expressing sadness that he will never see his grandson. The letter to the father ends: 'I remember you had sent me the collected stories of Raymond Carver for Christmas. I had sent you nothing, not even a card. Now I would send you a thousand but I have no address' (Keane 1996, p.34) (see Chapter Thirteen for another letter).

These are all unsendable letters. Some therapeutic letters *are* sent. Here is an example from my Therapeutic Writing in General Practice project. A GP patient was very anxious and depressed. Her relationship with her parents was clearly problematic. Her doctor suggested she write about it. The girl wrote a very angry letter to them, which she didn't send then but redrafted and redrafted until she had a letter she felt she wanted them to read. In it she was able to write things she could never have said, like 'I love you'.

Another time letters were written carefully and therapeutically, and then sent, was when a nurse helped birth mothers write letters to go with their babies to their adoptive homes to be read once the children were old enough. In yet another case a woman dying of cancer in a hospice wrote to her husband (whom she saw every day) saying things she felt she could not say to him, such as how much she loved him and still wanted to be cuddled.

A hospital nurse suggested a patient write to her husband. He visited every day but she was so poorly she couldn't talk to him very well. So she slowly wrote letters to him through the long days and nights when he wasn't there so she could give them to him when he came.

People feel they can say things to others in writing which they couldn't bring themselves to say in speech. This is partly because the words can be mulled over and redrafted, partly because it is not a face-to-face communication and partly because the letter will endure with time, as spoken words cannot. Fergal Keane's son will treasure those letters when he is adult – as will the cancer patient's husband after her death, and the adopted children.

In the USA a suicidal woman wrote to a local psychiatrist she had read about in the paper, telling him about herself, thinking her case would be useful for his research (Jacobs and Mack 1986). He responded promptly; she was hospitalised and, later, wrote to him: 'I owe you my life… I think of all the beautiful things in life I would have missed if it weren't for you. Prior to discharge (from the psychiatric hospital)… we discovered I was pregnant. If it weren't for you taking time out for somebody you never met I would have ended my life not knowing I was carrying another.' This woman would probably never have *asked* for help.

Dialogues

These are as good as letters and rather similar. Instead of writing a letter to your child self, or from your everyday self to your spiritual self, or to the cancer, or to your dead elder brother, write it out like a script. This method will be dealt with at greater length in Chapter Six.

Linking

This is a way of locating where seemingly inappropriate strong emotions belong. For example, I have a huge dread and fear of the end of holidays, quite out of proportion to the natural sadness anyone feels at the end of a happy and comparatively care-free time. This is so strong after the summer, at the beginning of the academic year, that I used to go into an annual depression. I asked my writing when I started to feel this and my pencil took me directly back to my hated and feared boarding-school days when I was so desperately lonely.

When you are experiencing a strong emotion, allow your memory pen to wander back in your life. Can you write about when you started to feel that emotion or felt it forcefully some time ago?

One more kind of object

Another collection of things I have used to set writing off is containers. Here is a description of a day workshop with a group of trainee counsellors who were also healthcare workers (Bolton 1995).

The table between us was covered with all sorts of containers: an egg, a policeman's helmet, a shell, a Victorian ink bottle, a tom-tit's nest, a basket, a tin, a box and a tiny alabaster jar. Everyone had to choose something and begin to write straight away – continuing the free-intuitive style of the six minutes free-intuitive writing with which we had started (see Chapter Three). First, we described the look, feel, smell of the object, any sound it made and anything else which came to mind. Once pens slackened off from this, we moved on to write about what it would be like to be inside it. Joan Dickinson felt the empty coffee box would be straightforward:

> Why did I pick the bright box which had held coffee? Well, I used my 'ordered' mind to realise we were going to be asked to write about it. Then, Gillie has told us not to be 'ordered' and let our thoughts and feeling rule the writing. Very difficult sat round a group of tables with thirteen other pens all scribbling at the same time!
>
> The box is bright, descriptive and instructional, like parts of my life, the decoration is ornate but represents, for the coffee maker something they wish to impart to everyone. Are we like that? Do we have a part of us that represents to the outside world what is acceptable and what we think it wishes to see? Yes, of course.
>
> And what happens when I open the lid? That it's plain inside, dark grey and empty. There is a side to me that is like that, unfulfilled dreams and hopes. How can I respect or think that anyone can cope with death better because of my input! How clever do we think we are that we can be trained to make things better. Walking alongside is what we can do best. having someone to walk with is so important. What about the Franks of this world who had no-one and died with only the love of us to save his loneliness? Second chances. We don't get one really. Life is like the box, looks bright, descriptive and has instructions, take it off the shelf and claim it as yours, and the brightness will dull and the instructions fade if not preserved and loved… (Joan Dickinson)

After reading this, Joan felt amazed, shocked even: 'I didn't even realise I'd written about Frank (a patient) until I read it back.' She thought this death had been thoroughly dealt with at the funeral, in supervision. She enjoyed writing, despite her emotion on reading it out.

Sue had also written, and written breathlessly, only to realise how vital it was on reading it back. She wrote in her summative evaluation: 'I was shocked by the impact the exercises had on me. There are a number of issues I realise I have not dealt with as well as I'd thought'.

The group were astonished that writing had offered such accurate expression; they'd felt able to share it and even shed tears; the group had offered support and interest and it even 'gave me permission to be human.'

The writing, moreover, had been so enjoyable! The reading aloud had brought the shock of the content. The urge or need to create is strong in us all. It doesn't have to be perfect but it is our own. Joan Dickinson, the coffee-box writer, said:

> As a carer you have to give 80–90 per cent of yourself. So you have to protect that last part of you, keep that bit back. But that didn't happen with the writing. And then when I started reading that back I thought 'hell, did I write that? Oh yes I see, oh gosh that's interesting'. What happens when I open the lid, and then off I went...
>
> When you said ten minutes (writing time), I thought ten! Give me two! But by the end of the twenty-five minutes I wanted longer. It isn't until you actually do it that you realise what it costs the writer. You realise counselling's deep and important and might think writing is easy and cosy, but it's not! Did I write that? Was that really me? When you sit and role play in the training you can pick something safe, but you can't with the writing. I suppose it's because you're not listening to yourself as you write.
>
> Writing takes you out of control. It should be trained for like the counselling. Opening the box – it's like a jack-in-the box isn't it? (Joan Dickinson)

CHAPTER FIVE

Images: How to Find, Create and Use Them

Echoes

Other echoes
Inhabit the garden. Shall we follow?
'Quick,' said the bird find them, find them,
Round the corner. Through the first gate

(T.S. Eliot, *Burnt Norton*)

Sunlight's a thing that needs a window
Before it enters a dark room.
Windows don't happen.

(R.S. Thomas, *Poetry for Supper*)

Cut doors and windows for a room
It is the holes which make them useful

(Lao Tsu, *Tao Te Ching*)

Background

Images are windows created in order to illuminate the dark passages of our text of life. To cope with daily life, we normally only allow ourselves to look straight down a narrow corridor. All the perceptions and experiences beyond are ignored or glossed over. We rush along, pleased with our efficiency and effectiveness at being fathers, workers, bosses, wives.

Things happen: frustrating, incomprehensible, abusive, painful, agonising. We are told, or tell ourselves, 'boys don't cry', 'you'll get over it', 'have another baby/kitten as soon as possible', 'time is a great healer', 'get out and join the golf club, meet new people'. A professor of physics told me six months after his mother died, 'I haven't had time to begin to grieve'. Or, perhaps, shame prevents the event (rape, incest, harassment, financial difficulties) being shared in the first place.

We think these elements can be ignored; we tell ourselves they're unimportant; then we forget them. But there's forgetting and forgetting. Why does the incest survivor obsessively wash and scrub herself until her skin bleeds? Why does she starve herself to blueness, each bone etched through her skin? What is agoraphobia, claustrophobia, stammering? Part of us forgets, part of us displays the problem affectively – we gain a symptom.

The bravery of not listening doesn't prevent feeling. It merely pushes it down to where it festers and swells. It is far harder for the grown man to cry because as a little boy he threw the bone china teacups and saucers into the pond instead of taking them into the kitchen to be washed up. Yet the weeping had to be done. It was the exploration of the significance, through writing, of such precious things as his best dinky toys disappearing irrevocably under the water lilies that brought this university lecturer to face the grief and begin to come to terms with his relationship with his parents to a far greater degree. This helped him begin to tackle problems within his own marriage.

Sometimes we have to listen to things from that ignored area because such things have caused big problems some time later (perhaps quite a long time later). Sometimes we want to listen, in order to fill out our habitually 'cabined cribbed and confined' life.

Not everyone can use this route to their inner self, however. Victims of extreme trauma and even their children, can live in a 'world beyond metaphor' (Herzog 1982), a world of 'concretism'. Presumably, the trauma is too great to be faced in any way. This has been particularly reported by psychoanalysts of holocaust victims and their children (Grubrick-Simitis 1984). But for those for whom this route is open, the process can be illuminating, surprising and, above all, *playful!*

A practical understanding of an image

Once an emotion, feeling or experience is pushed away or left disregarded, it can rarely be brought back simply in the same form. Our minds play tricks on us: offering it back in seemingly irrelevant bits and bobs, like jigsaw pieces of a window, or in code, as in puns or metaphors. These are images.

The murky bottomless water, even the little boy's dinkys and the teacups are unimportant in themselves. An image *is* unimportant in itself. What would seem to be perplexing is the way such a simple little thing can carry such a depth of emotion. Why expend storms of tears over such things so much later? It's because of what these images signify. Behind this seemingly trivial image there's a huge hinterland of emotional problem that hasn't been dealt with at all.

Image exploration in writing can offer the necessary time and space to return to old pains – relatively safely. It can pierce the seeming blankness of depression, make more comprehensible the clutch of anxiety. Even though depression feels like black nothingness or anxiety seems out of all proportion to the events of the sufferer's current life – there isn't nothing there. The mind is never empty, there are always images carrying code information about past trauma. Here follows two examples from poets. Their poems, reproduced here, are the result of long processes of redrafting and crafting; the writing of them was just as useful to their writers as any therapeutic writing is to any writer. The pinpointing and graphic reproduction of a childhood traumatic event was powerful for both writers.

The poet John Latham has explored the image of 'my father's painting the gate at the end of the drive a different colour, thereby eliminating its capacity to protect me from the terrifying outside world':

Orange gate

He painted my orange gate away. He, my father,
enfolded in whose jacket – sawdust, barley, ash –
I lost all fear of quicksands,
draughts that blew out candles,
cobwebs trailing in the night.
Painted black, the gate on which I'd always swung
peering through its slats at big children off to school,
empty sleeves, splayed trousers on the rag-and-bone man's cart
steam roller that squashed Ann's cat just sleeping, Mummy said,
though what, I wondered, were its dreams?
– and him, in overalls, sprinting back from work
to whirl me, draw me in,
toss me high and always catch me.

My orange gate, whose blaze in sudden sun
discolorations, crevices and blisters I'd conjure up in bed
to calm my struggle against sleep's black yawn.

Hard, smooth; nothing to hold on to.

I scratched at it until I bled: no orange.
I scratched his face that night
when he bent to tuck me up.

Even now, as we huddle round his bed, swap stories
from fifty years ago, hoping their warmth
is seeping to him through his coma
russet, yellow, orange into black...

Even now, I can't forgive him for painting out the gate.

(John Latham 1996, p.13)

This poem has two power bases: the first for the writer, the second for the reader. The first is that Latham was able to recognise and come to terms with this significant growing point in his young life through the exploration in writing and redrafting of that initially puzzling image. The second is that the poem is a powerful *read*. The reader is drawn to empathise through her instant comprehension of this simple image. This might lead a reader to picture a turning point of her own. Latham has used this poem many times, and very effectively, to encourage others to remember, and write about, similar 'turning point' images. For example: 'One teenage girl taking part in this exercise described how, when she was four, her mother – without speaking, and never explaining subsequently – entered her bedroom carrying a saw, cut the girl's favourite teddy-bear in two, put one half on a high shelf where she couldn't reach it, the other half on the fire' (personal communication).

John Latham was not present to know about the long-term image explosion which may have followed this memory. The environment where this workshop took place was such that he was assured of any follow-up support required. He did trust that girl was able to explore the troubling image in writing and work out some kind of explanation for herself.

An endogenous depressive poet, Roy Blackman has used the image of a soft toy to take him back to an enforced separation which he realised caused him lasting damage:

Donkey

It was wartime. She was only doing her duty,
that Ward Sister,
who wouldn't let you in to see me
once, when I broke my leg at twenty months.

There were rules.
She couldn't have unsettling mothers
wrinkling the covers on her beds.
Instead you made me a little grey
stuffed felt donkey with harness and saddle,
a girth strap round his fat middle,
a tail and mane in nugget-brown
flat, slightly irregular cut strips
whose free ends were more rigid
than the bends hugged tightly to his neck.
Four firm legs, of comforting turgor,
sprang back when forced apart; he sat
on the rail at the foot of my bed
until they took him away.
There were rules.
He never came back.
The leg healed.

(Roy Blackman 1996, p.9)

The unwritten line *I didn't* at the end says it all.

Image as window

The image is unimportant in itself but is a vital element in the process. Its vitality lies in it being accessible. The image cannot describe – it is not the emotion, feeling or experience – it can only give access to it.

This transference from abstract emotion to concrete image takes place in order to give us something graspable and relatively safe to work with. The memory of a sundappled pond, an orange garden gate, a grey felt stuffed donkey or the picture of a trapeze artiste seem innocuous. We can more readily look at hidden things unflinchingly in imagery than we could if we told the emotion. This is also why the poetry we read (in addition to that which we write) can enter the heart – our armour is off, we don't block its entry and impact. Poetry presents the thing in order to convey the feeling; TS Eliot (1951) called this the 'objective correlative'. Or, as I have heard the doctor-poet William Carlos Williams put it, 'no ideas but in things'.

Our lives are full of images. Or, rather, we can readily perceive them as such if we open our eyes, ears, noses, mouths and nerve-endings. There is no need to worry about time being wasted creating mental pictures which take us nowhere. If we explore openly, the vital image will appear like a flash of lightning. 'There is always an element of recognition in making an image' (Thomson 1989). If that recognition is not there for you, you are probably attempting to short-circuit the process. It is unlikely you are a duffer at image creation.

Howard Brody (1987) gives two examples of healing images: 'A boy whose father was missing in Vietnam, assumed dead, had difficulty accepting this. The researcher took him for a walk, they happened to see a dead tree with a sapling growing nearby. The boy stopped and said: "That tree makes me think of my father. You know, I realise now that my father is dead. I think he's that big tree and I'm the sapling. As it dies the big tree loses its leaves, and that lets the sunlight though so that the sapling can grow"' (p.188–9).

The second example is of a cure effected by one sentence. A patient had a terrible skin condition, for which no cause could be found. The doctor finally asked for more personal information and the patient reported a very destructive relationship with his boss. The doctor commented: 'It sounds like he really gets under your skin.' The patient went and did something about this relationship and his skin condition disappeared (Brody 1987, p.191).

Window not cypher

The connotations of any image are varied and intensely creative. There is no one meaning in any image. The image is a window on a whole other world, not a two-dimensional picture. So, the process is not one of interpretation, more one of exploration.

If images are *created* and not discovered, the gaining of understanding from them must also be a process of creation, of connotation, rather than interpretation. Interpretation suggests denotation, the finding of a one-to-one correspondence between the image and the personal material. The process is not one of uncovering a correspondence with the truth but more like playfully trying out stories.

The image is not standing for anything but offering a route for understanding. Not an easy route. Its relationship with the hidden personal material is diffuse, requiring lateral thinking leaps.

The image and the leap

The window that is an image is often a frustrating, locked, filthy glass pane. Breaking it might cut your hand. So you need to feel round it, find the key to the lock, put it in the right way up, unstick the years of spiders' webs and old paint. It's a fiddly job in which you trust your fingers. Written image creation and extension is a process of trusting your writing hand, slowly, cautiously, sometimes frustratingly, sometimes painfully.

You have to trust yourself in the process and allow yourself to 'accept chaos as a temporary stage', having set yourself up in 'circumstances in which it is safe to be absent-minded' (Freud 1950). You have to have the confidence to dive into uncertainty. It is only in this uncertain, 'absent-minded' frame of mind that images flash fire. Or, to use T.S. Eliot's words from later in the *Four Quartets*:

> In order to arrive at what you do not know
> you must go by a way which is the way of ignorance...
> And what you do not know is the only thing you know
>
> (Eliot 1936, p.201)

The positive side

The emotions or experiences suggested by images are not by any means always negative. The recognition of this will gladden the path of therapeutic writing. The poet is always aware of this:

> There are in our existence spots of time
> Which with distinct pre-eminence retain
> A fructifying virtue, whence, depressed
> By trivial occupations and the round
> Of ordinary intercourse, our minds –
> Especially the imaginative power –
> Are nourished and invisibly repaired.
>
> (Wordsworth 1985, p.51)

Wordsworth later says how 'rememberable things' are recollected through 'quaint associations' or:

> Collateral objects and appearances,
> Albeit lifeless then, and doomed to sleep
> Until maturer seasons called them forth
> To impregnate and to elevate the mind.
>
> (Wordsworth 1985, p.56)

The image and visual art

Visual images are explored in art therapy. A visual image is formed in a similar way to a poetic one, but using a different medium. Art therapist John Henzell (1995), however, feels that there is an essential difference between the use of words and the use of paint or other plastic materials. He has said that spoken and written language uses a limited code which is transparent – the meaning can be understood very quickly. Whereas, he says, the painted image, because of its *thinginess*, is opaque – it has myriad potential meanings which are different at different times. He uses the example of 'a tall blonde woman called Jane' which gives nothing at all to the reader, whereas a picture of Jane would offer the viewer far more. The whole aim of this book is to encourage potential writers to create word pictures of Jane, every bit as graphic as a visual one, if not even more so, as we can include evidence from *all* the senses. A cursory look at literature (poetry, fiction, drama), moreover, will tell the reader how powerful word images can be.

An example

The poet Jacqueline Brown offers this poem and commentary to illustrate the use of imagery (particularly metaphor):

Miss Lala at the Cirque

These days when the men below heave
on the oiled rope to hoist her
like a dressed carcass up to the hot,
spotlit space under the girders,
knuckled front and back by air,
all she feels is fear, and fear of the fear.
Weakened nightly by the wooden plug,
her teeth shed skins –
one day there will be just raw nerve
and screaming and a plummet
through parted air.
Then the impact. The Black.
'Just hold on, darling,' Michael says
at night in the bed in the van
when she wakes shuddered from the falling dream.
'Just one more season. Then no more.'

While he gentles her she watches the cranefly,
fixed by one hinged leg to the lamp's
white shade, holding on,
burning.

There are four strands to the poem:

- the actual Degas painting (National Gallery)
- the emotional content of fear, precariousness in the picture
- the emotional content of me as a writer/person
- the reader's response to the poem. (Only you can provide this!)

The images are layered, to intensify the emotional content. Yet the emotion they carry, as well as the similarity of physical appearance, identify them powerfully with each other. Miss Lala has a nightmare of falling, her teeth no longer strong enough to clench onto the cable bar. While her lover is comforting her, her attention is entirely taken by the daddy-long-legs clinging on to the lampshade, being burnt to death.

(Jacqueline Brown)

Nowhere in this has Jacqueline told of her own emotion. The image carries it all.

The vitality of images

Your hearts know in silence the secrets of the days
and the nights.
But your ears thirst for the sound of your heart's knowledge.
You would know in words that which you have always
known in thought.
You would touch with your fingers the naked body
of your dreams.

(Gibran 1926, p.65)

It is images that help us to touch this naked body, know the words we have always known in our hearts but not in our minds. We can recall such hidden windows; sometimes with the ease of a mouse click, but sometimes, with more of a struggle. Whatever process is used for finding images; they will then throw fresh light and insight on current situations or problems.

Many images that arise seem to be meaningless. Dream or other images can hang about for years until the right time or place for them to be sorted out. Then, when the glass clears, or the disfiguring reflection disappears so we can see through the window, the meanings of the image appear straightforward and simple. I have often thought: oh I see, haven't I been dim!

Images, being vital and vivid, are the stuff of art, once created and developed: poetry, painting, sculpture, dance, music...

They are also enormous fun and very stimulating (though occasionally scary). If you have never played the furniture game, consequences, telling one-word-each stories – then have a go (but with care). Many people put themselves in danger and to great expense taking drugs to conjure images artificially.

When and where

Images are created at the margins of our consciousness when the window glass clears, such as at night, for many, or in the very early morning. We need to feel fairly secure and confident – but not too much or we'd just go to sleep. So it might be on your own or with a very trusted other or group. It will also probably be in a safe place – this might be bed for some or the moor top for others such as me. Sometimes, a trusted facilitator or therapist can help both by offering a stimulus, as well as a secure enough and time-bounded space.

One sure, but fun, way of acquiring a wonderful bag of mixed metaphors is to play a version of the furniture game (a metaphor is a particular sort of image – see below). You can do this on your own or with a group. I must have done it with dozens of groups. My way is for everyone to write the name of a person who is important to them (but not present) at the top of a clean page. They then write what kind of piece of furniture they would be if that's what they were – not what furniture they prefer but what they most resemble. It amuses me how many women write that their husbands are huge crimson velvet sofas with loads of cushions. Perhaps they then follow this up by writing them as a field of thistles when it comes to 'now write as if your person were a plant'.

But that is hurrying us along. If you are in a group, every member should suggest a category (animal, book, vehicle, building, season, weather, smell) with every writer noting down the first item in that category which comes to mind. This should all be done at top speed with no time for anyone to muse over their entries – if they can't write fast enough, they miss a category. My husband, on one occasion I remember, was 'a big cox apple brought down by the wind from the top of the tree, bruised on one side and wasp-nibbled on the other, but the sweetest for having hung on the tree till the end of the season'. These are straightforward images, but don't be misled into thinking there is no depth there. If they are written at speed, you may well be surprised at what you think about some people.

The process

Images have to be explored and extended until they make some sort of sense to our thinking minds. When we look through a window, we have to infer that there are twigs and leaves higher up when all we can see is part of a tree trunk. Or we might see bits of the room's interior reflected at dusk against the tree trunk.

This exploratory process has to be a loose and open one. The reason why this kind of writing (or visual art or other art forms, possibly) works is that it creates a direct link between the writing hand and the feeling heart – our thinking, organising brain is ignored for a change. Thinking inhibits image creation.

There is rarely a straightforward direct correspondence of image to meaning, still less one that can be gleaned from a dictionary, such as of dream imagery for example. Your own images belong to you and to the time and place you are at the moment. The same images could carry very different inferences for different people or you in another time or place. Just to think, for example, *I dreamed of a train journey*, so, therefore, it was about my journey through life or *I dreamed of snakes*, so, therefore, I was dreaming about sex, will narrow and stultify your thinking. Allow the image to tell you what it is about for you, then and there.

An image on its own is of little value, like a window onto a blank wall. It needs to be connected up to the other jig-saw pieces of window or correctly understood as a metaphor, metonym, pun, etc. This can only be done through the kind of relatively safely staged processes that therapeutic writing offers.

The privacy of images

They are for you. Initially, at least, you might like to explore them and see what they offer you, on your own. Sharing them with others later might well be useful in various different ways.

Another's insight into your images can offer a wider perspective. You might do this as a game; by painting, drawing or writing together; or as an in-depth discussion allowing your imaginations free rein. It is important that you both allow your minds to free associate while, at the same time, displaying a caringness for each other's vulnerabilities. Or you might share your writing with them.

Do not allow another's interpretations of your images to dominate your own. Some of the connections they will be making will have no meaning for you. Be aware of this and do not be swayed: one image can have any number of 'meanings'. Take another's inferences into account when appropriate, allow them to colour or illuminate yours, but never allow them to supersede yours.

The images of a close and trusted other might well have a vitality for you. A dream doesn't have to be dreamt by you, to hold meaning for you. One such was a dream of a blackbird, shot by the dreamer while it sat on his hand. The bird sang and sang without a head and would not be killed. This became a powerful image of unquenchable hope for me. Even after bereavement there is life, and even love.

Finding vital images

Images can be discovered or created in as many different ways as there are people and situations. There are, however, some certain places to try. Many of the other chapters contain ideas, such as free associating from buttons, hats, containers, memories and, of course, dreams. Freud considered that there are many happenings in our waking life which can be treated like images (forgetting of names/words/intentions, slips of tongue/pen/computer, misreadings, bungled and 'symptomatic' actions, symptoms, jokes). These 'parapraxes', as he called them, have a similar power to dreams and can offer us windows into our deeper and wiser self (unconscious). Accidents, symptoms, errors, habits, actions are useful: they can be read as texts – as if they were images themselves (I am not here entering into any discussion as to whether there really is such a thing as a genuine accident). Here are some examples:

Slips of the tongue or computer

I kept finding I was writing 'i' for 'I' (lack of self-confidence) and 'curse' instead of 'course' when writing about my teaching (no comment), 'spychiatrist' (again no comment). One man kept writing 'clam' instead of 'calm'. He thought back over the times he was keeping calm and decided it was much more like clamming something up. Another time I was repeatedly unable to remember the name of someone I later realised was almost an enemy.

Symptoms and illnesses

What is she unable to stomach that she was so sick? What's making your skin twitch and itch? (See Howard Brody's example earlier in the chapter.) What burden am I carrying that my shoulders ache so? Why does he always have a little illness so she has to be there all the time caring for him?

Small accidents

These don't just happen, according to Freud. Sartre also said that we are responsible for all our actions. We are fairly cognisant with this in small children, when we say that they are seeking attention. Adults are just the same. For example, he just happened to drop the entire tray of glasses and plates just as the other two began to gaze into each other's eyes; or the man who just happened to leave his love poem about his lover's bottom under the building society papers which he knew his wife was to deal with the next day.

On the other hand, things that really do seem to be accidents can be read as texts. For example, the saw fell from its nail, grazing his head slightly. What sword of Damocles is hanging over him, about to fall?

Habitual losses or mistakes

The man who always loses his keys so he is locked out of house (warmth, safety, company) and car (a getaway vehicle); we always lose the oven gloves in our kitchen, so we burn our fingers (metaphorically and literally).

Everyday occurrences

For example, we threw the old broom head on the fire. Perhaps we had just bought a new one to sweep far cleaner or perhaps we didn't need to sweep at all any more? Images of burning here might have been important ones alternatively/as well.

Or a man who always said he hated ornaments gave his ex-girlfriend a heavy statue doorstop as a wedding present. He clearly wanted her door kept open.

Habitual common phrases

The woman who doesn't meet people but connects with them; or doesn't suggest things but makes overtures. She sounds like someone who needs to distance herself from normal close human contact.

Sartorial messages

What are clothes/hairstyles/jewellery saying? What is being covered up/hidden behind/displayed? What is he trying to protect himself from that he never takes his jacket off, she that she wears so much makeup? What is that scarlet shouting?

Repeated habits/body language

Whenever she sits and talks to me she crosses her legs and folds her arms tightly; what is she trying to prevent jumping out of her, why does she have to protect herself from me? Why are they always so busy that they never have time to stop and just be together; what are they running away from?

Coincidences

I dreamed of making marmalade, now you bring me a jar, and I saw a recipe in the paper today. What's the significance? Something from childhood or, perhaps, to do with preserving golden summer sweetness from a warmer land than our January darkness?

A song on your mind

If this happens, try to think of the words. They are bound to be significant. Free associate from them.

Misreading texts

For example, labels, road signs, adverts, newspaper headings. Often, punctuation is left out, leaving several interpretations of the words – the writer assuming that the reasonable person will read it how it was intended to be read. WARNING HEAVY PLANT CROSSING or SLOW CHILDREN are common ones.

Or how about Keats' idea for a Kelloggs cornflakes advert (needing only the slight change of purple to golden):

> I dreamed I saw thee, robed in purple flakes
> Break amorous through the clouds, as morning breaks.
>
> (Keats 1906, p.149)

Superstitions

Counting the cherry stones – who will the sailor be? Four magpies – what kind of important letter might arrive?

Weathers, objects, phenomena which seem to reflect mood

An object or natural phenomenon can often stand for a human emotion or feeling. For example, a rainbow is a symbol of hope; a thunderstorm can stand for anger or a deep feeling of unrest; the soft thwack of willow on leather (especially when accompanied by light clapping and borne to my ears on a light breeze) or the smell of new-mown hay are peaceful and harmonious. This has been called the pathetic fallacy.

Objects or events noticed for no obvious reason can be milked for significance. The rocking stone on the moor takes a tiny shift of my weight to slip silently and gently yet it is powerful enough to crush whatever is beneath it.

Metaphors

The most commonly used image in writing is the metaphor, in which one thing doesn't so much stand for another as carries over its essence, its smell and taste, to the other thing: my love *is* a red red rose, prickles and all. The original subject is magnified by its association with the metaphorical one.

'Metaphors are more than ways of speaking: they are ways of perceiving feelings, and existing' (Hillman 1975, p.32). Play the furniture game (see above) on your own or just notice the metaphors you use; we come out with them all the time. A powerful one for me has been that my life feels like running up a down escalator. I once said this to my supervisor. Instead of sympathising, she merely asked 'why?' I wrote free-intuitively from this one word and realised that I was responsible for my life being like this: no one but myself is driving me endlessly up this escalator. So I rewrote my story, using the metaphor of running up a mountain stream, which my son and I had done (risking broken legs or worse) in the Dolomites.

Pun

When two words sound the same but have different meaning, such as soul and sole, knead and need. We often write puns inadvertently; they're well worth noticing and exploring.

Contrasts

Unlikely things together: the touch of an angel's wing being like an electric shock, for example.

Sense mixing (synaesthesia)

A scarlet taste, for example, or a symphony of flavours, an abrasive smell.

Pick a vital word from your writing

List every word you can think of that rhymes with it (or begins with the same letter). I have listed and used in my writing: snake, bake, cake, rake, lake; and mum, magic, mirror, music, mud...

Do some research about an intriguing element in your writing

I heavily researched snakes – their natural history and mythical associations particularly.

Other art forms

These can take you elsewhere too. Music is great for suggesting images, as is studying paintings or sculptures, watching ballet, expressive dancing...

Engaging the senses other than sight

This can be a trigger. Smells are very evocative (mother's perfume, hay, engine oil, etc). The smell of new-baked bread is supposed to be one of the most evocative smells there is. Sounds, such as water, are useful too. The feel of silk, teazles, and so on can open up images, as can tastes – cloves or vanilla, curry, strong cheddar with the cloth rind round it. How about these: 'The sound of fox-paws in the snow/... the language of flames dancing along a blade' (Warren Wilson 1997, p.23).

Guided fantasy

You can go on a mental journey, led by a facilitator, in a group or with a friend or on your own. If you do it with a friend, be careful to bring them back to the here and now afterwards.

I shall never forget being guided to a beautiful garden. But my garden had a high wall around it. However hard I tried, I never got over it, remaining on the moor with no fountain or trees, only heather flowers and the tumbling stream. When writing about it, I realised, to my delight, that I didn't want to be in a walled garden anyway. Give me the freedom, wind and wild streams of the moor any day!

Objects used for stimulus

Any object can connote a range of images and meanings (also see Chapters Four and Ten, and Catherine Byron's workshop description in Chapter Nine). With groups, I have used a bowl of bread dough, loaves of freshly baked bread and some flour and yeast; or a sprig of each of the two dozen or so herbs from my garden; or a miscellaneous collection of matchbox toys, a baby's hairbrush, a silk sari, a Victorian button hook...

Rewriting those powerful culture-carriers

Myth, legend, fairy story, nursery rhyme, folk story, Bible story, Shakespearean story and so on. These well-worn and well-loved stories are vital to our psychological well-being. Jung (1963) wrote: 'myth is the natural and indispensable intermediate stage between unconscious and conscious cognition' (p.343). Our mythologising self is in contact with, or is a part of, our dreaming self – that wise self who knows and has experienced so much more than our awake self. Bettelheim (1976) considered fairy stories to be vital for the developing child, helping them to come to terms with the impossible array of emotions and relationships in the adult world and to sense for themselves justice, fidelity, love, courage and so on:

> There is a right time for certain growth experiences, and childhood is the time to learn bridging the immense gap between inner experiences and the real world. Fairy tales may seem senseless, fantastic, scary and totally unbelievable to the adult who was deprived of fairy-story fantasy in his

> own childhood, or has repressed these memories. An adult who has not achieved a satisfactory integration of the two worlds of reality and imagination is put off by such tales. But an adult who in his own life is able to integrate rational order with the illogic of his unconscious will be responsive to the manner in which fairy tales help the child with this integration. To the child, and to the adult who, like Socrates, knows that there is still a child in the wisest of us, fairy tales reveal truths about mankind and oneself. (p.66)

Listen to this wise voice inside you. Take the first tale which comes to your mind – do not question why – and rewrite it in your own way. Who is your Bluebeard/Wicked Stepmother? What happens if you become Cinderella or the Prince who followed the third feather? Try recreating a minor character, such as the spoon who was run away with or Lot's daughter. Or retell the story with a different twist or from a different point of view.

Image expansion (or explosion)

In the expansion (explosion sometimes) of an image, energy is released and understandings occur. This realisation feels to me like the sound of Gerard Manley Hopkin's thrush: '… and thrush/Through the echoing timber does so rinse and ring/The ear it strikes like lightenings to hear him sing' (1953, p.28). This doesn't just happen, you have to make it happen, as RS Thomas pointed out in his poem quoted at the beginning. There are various simple techniques to be used.

Free-intuitive six-minute writing (see Chapter Three) is the first one to try. Write the image (rabbit warren, for example) at the top of the page and then scribble, without stopping, whatever comes into your head.

When this dries up, try some of the other writing ideas in this book, such as the exploration of the Sleeping Beauty story in Chapter Six. You do need to write in the same spirit as the free writing: without stopping to think, just as far as you can.

A word of warning

Images, because they are windows onto areas of our lives we have chosen to forget or marginalise, are immensely powerful. I have spoken of playing with them. That's what it feels like nearly all the time. If you are feeling reasonably balanced, and are using writing as your medium, your mind is almost completely unlikely to offer you a glimpse through a window at a view you can't cope with seeing.

Writing is gentle and kind: the hand/heart connection which seems to exist is incredibly trustworthy. There is time between writing and re-reading for the mind to adjust to the content of the writing. Then there is plenty of time for considering if any of the material can be shared with another.

Thinking and playing with images in your mind, without writing, is even safer – usually too safe. Images and ideas slip and slither the other side of the glass. The power of writing is to stabilise them so that you can look at them, like fixing a photographic print. You need to take them out of your mind and put them on paper or as a 3D art image. 'The image is ... often an external expression of some unconscious internal state which has yet to emerge into consciousness.' Putting them on paper helps this state to emerge into consciousness (Waller and Dalley 1992).

However:

- If you are working with someone else, things can be said which can never be unsaid. Your own mind can pace things to an appropriate speed when you are exploring alone. This can't be the case in an interaction between two or more people. There are so many examples of therapeutic damage (particularly in groups) that I don't need to underline this point.
- If you are feeling vulnerable, yet wishing to engage in exploratory writing, ensure there is a trusted other at the end of a phone or near enough for you to contact.
- If you become nervous as you delve deeper and understandings (perhaps even memories) begin to clarify, pace yourself carefully. Only go as far as you wish to go. One of the amazing things about therapeutic writing is that you can reach a barrier of fear and stop for that time. When you return to the work, refreshed and emboldened, you will perceive other, less frightening ways of opening the window and letting in the fresh air.
- Mind-altering drugs (LSD, mushrooms, hash, etc) might seem a simple route to image finding. In my experience, the mind can offer you quite exciting experiences enough without these.

But don't be too timid – stay with the fast-beating heart and whirling images as long as you can. Allow yourself back to that place again later (not too much later). It is worth it. Trust yourself with another person (if you are working with another) if you think they are trustworthy; just always remember they aren't an extension of you, nor godlike!

This all sounds a bit stop and go all at once. In answer to your bewildered 'but how do I know when it's therapeutic and wonderful and when too difficult?', I can only reply with what is really the motto of this work: trust and listen to yourself. You are worthy of your own trust. After all, your images are yours.

CHAPTER SIX

Dreams Which Put Us in Touch with Ourselves

'The Royal Road'

Every poem happens in sleep.
How outrageous sleep is!

(David Hart, 'A child, the earth sends postcards out')

I write in the morning. In fact what this means is that I begin writing at night, in my dreams.

(Helene Cixous, *The 'Double World' of Writing*, p.18)

The interpretation of dreams is the royal road to a knowledge of the unconscious activities of the mind.

(Sigmund Freud 1959, p.608)

It is so important not to have any preconceived, doctrinaire opinions about the statements made by dreams.

(Carl Jung, *Memories, Dreams, Reflections*, p.343)

Sleep is outrageous because our dreaming selves know so much more than our waking selves. They're wiser, have a breathtaking sense of humour and lack the inhibitions of our socialised daily selves. Dreams are 'the royal road' to understanding ourselves, simply bursting with useful images, stories and references to myths, puns, jokes... They give us a side of ourselves which we tend to squash or ignore.

'Ask your dreams' is what I often say to people who feel stuck with a seemingly insoluble problem or a matter they don't understand about themselves. A man had just realised his physical problems were probably irritable bowel syndrome. 'That's a nervous complaint', he said to me, 'yet I'm more happy and stable now than I've been for years. What on earth can I do about it?' He asked his dreams; that night he dreamt about his car exploding. Now what has that to do with irritable bowel syndrome? Well, nothing obvious: but he was able to write free-intuitively from that image of the car and gain much more self-understanding. Dreams are rather like a treasure hunt or asking the *I Ching* for advice. This latter is a Chinese divination text, the oldest book in the world. The kinds of answers you get to mundane questions involve dragons, rivers, mountains, ice. But it's worth the puzzling around to understand the connotations.

There are many examples of inspirations taking place in sleep, such as the discovery of the benzene ring in 1865. Kekule con Stradonitz visualised the correct chemical structure in a dream of snakes biting their tails. One novelist always asked his Brownies to solve his current plot problem before he went to sleep at night. It's a failsafe system, but needs time and patience. Below are plenty of ideas for clues in the treasure hunt.

'I never dream' is a comment I quite often hear. According to tests done on sleeping, we all dream. It's just that some don't remember. It is possible to train yourself to recall dreams, or bits of them at least. The main element of this training is to respect, and be willing to work with, fragments. I once invited dream authorities Lorna Dexter and Leslie Davidoff to breakfast. We decided we'd all bring that night's dreams to play with while we breakfasted. I was very apologetic – it had been my idea and all I had was one image, a tiny pair of red shoes. But I expanded and expanded that image, allowing myself into several bursts of free-intuitive writing. That one image became a four-page poem, a vital self-illuminating piece of writing which took me usefully back over past traumas I thought I had thoroughly sorted. I am so glad I didn't say: 'no, sorry I didn't dream last night'.

Lying quite still in the same position in which you woke, without moving, taking the mind back over the night's activities while you are still half asleep, is the best way of recalling those elusive images. Remain in that position with the story, or the scenes, as long as you can. Then write or tape-record them.

Write the dream down verbatim in the present tense in order to keep the immediacy of the images and story. Fill in as much detail as you possibly can – colour, animals, objects, quality of light, exactly what was said and in what way, where the 'I' was in the dream, the placing of everything, relationships, what things/people remind you of. Nothing is insignificant or unimportant.

An example of this is a dream I once dreamed of reaching up to open a high cupboard, which proved to be empty. I think the dream concerned aiming high, but fearing failure. That's a glib interpretation – useful – but not taking me very far. I did, however, write free-intuitively starting from my first half-awake thought: 'Mother Hubbard'; her cupboard was bare, much to the discomfiture of her dog. I put myself in the place of the dog who was told to search a seemingly empty high shelf. The poem which resulted was about being sent back again and again to search a dusty, cobwebby high shelf, and eventually finding a fragile-seeming but powerful 'pair of wings / just my size'.

Now move on to rewriting the dream, expanding it, pushing out its edges. We are not concerned here with the literal dream, or with any set denotation or interpretation such as a dictionary could offer, but in exploring connotations, what the dream means to us at that time and place. Any notion that dreams mean set things will hinder understanding. Dreams are fluid, elastic, intangible things. Any attempt to force them into a mould will ensure they cease working for you. Dreams are like Tinkerbell, they need to be believed in and respected before they are willing to be seen and played with. If you possess one of those dictionaries of set meanings for dream images, put it straight in the bin or burn it. Don't by any means give it away.

The following is a series of suggestions of ways to write about a dream or dream fragment. Additional ways of extending dream images may be found in Chapter Five. I have, for ease, chosen a dream which uses a story we all know as my example. It has a very clear structure of beginning, middle, end and characterisation. I had a vivid dream about a very grand occasion starring twin babies and their very stiff regal mother. I retold the story of Sleeping Beauty's christening with two very different little sisters and then the rest of the story with one protagonist, Beauty.

- Choose a title. That was easy: Sleeping Beauty.
- Run through the five senses as a check-list. There's the dull and dry as sawdust taste of the christening cake under the fancy icing. Smell is one of the most evocative of our senses – this was a hot stifling room reeking of bored or frightened bodies. The huge double doors blow open bringing the clear wild scent of the moors as the Wicked Fairy stalks in. The endless sound of tinkling voices saying nothing at all, followed by the abrupt and breathtaking silence as the fairy enters. The babies' sense of being trapped in tight jewelled bodices in a hooded cradle set about with lace, ribbons and bells. Fill out your account by adding vital tiny details. What time of year was it/hot or cold/inside or

outside?/What words do the characters actually use: '"GET OUT!" the Queen screeches', rather than 'She shouts to the Wicked Fairy to get out'. Colours and numbers are important. Be precise: it is not just a grand gleaming room, it is a long gallery with huge gilt-framed looking-glasses opposite long windows; crystal chandeliers reflect light, the mirror-like sequins among the ribbons and lace of frocks and the babies' far too tight bodices; the mother/Queen's eyes are hard and bright – no maternal warmth there.

- Identify the genre of the story. Is it romantic, horror, science-fiction, farce, sitcom, melodrama, soap, detective. I feel quite drawn to writing Sleeping Beauty as either a soap or a horror story.
- Explore the main character. The difference between the two babies was a vital element here. I sat in different chairs (couldn't manage two cradles) to write in each of their voices, writing what they had to say. List all the characters. And this includes animals such as the Wicked Fairy's frog; objects such as the castle, the cradle, the spindle; and colours such as the scintillating white of the gowns, lights and adornments in the great room, and the black of the men and the Wicked Fairy, the jewel green of her frog.
- Dialogue, as if you are writing a play script. This might be between you and one of the characters or between two of them together. I wrote scripts of each of the girl babies talking to each other and of me with the mother/queen (see Chapter Four for more dialogue ideas). Write a letter to one of the people you have been writing about. I wrote to the Handsome Prince, speaking in the voice of Beauty. I haven't yet written his reply back to me but I can see it will lead to some very interesting results. That answer will, of course, be written by the Handsome Prince within me. Our personalities are multi-faceted and these different facets can be represented as different voices. In our everyday lives we are used to some of the voices within us – such as the teacher: 'now you'll get into trouble if you do that!' or the anxious child: 'I'm not going to do that I might be hurt!' or the determined adult: 'I don't care if I have a sore throat and sneezes, I'm going out into that

snow!' This kind of writing merely expands that awareness and offers a wider variety of intriguing facets of ourselves.

- Rewrite the account from a different point of view. How does the castle itself feel on being surrounded by brambles and filled with dust, mice and sleeping/rotting royalty? Or what might the mother/queen's own story be? She was a very unhappy lady in my dream. I wonder what her background was.
- Rewrite the story as a film blurb or treatment. In this, of course, you are looking for the dramatic visual images.
- Alter an essential ingredient of the account, even trying the opposite. I have already indicated that, in my rendering, Sleeping Beauty is desperately unhappy as a princess and the Wicked Fairy (alias Lilith) comes as a breath of fresh air. In my initial story there were twin babies.
- Change the tense. So far, the story has been told in the present tense (Sleeping Beauty lies in her glass coffin). Trying the past (Sleeping Beauty lay in her glass coffin) can make a surprising difference (see Chapter Three). It might make it easier to put in elements which are vital to you psychologically if the story is at a distance in the past. I found the Queen quite frightening (as indeed I might, I was just a baby). It was less daunting if I gave her her say in the past tense. She couldn't get at me from there, 'the past is another country' (Hartley 1953).
- Change the person. Tell the story of Sleeping Beauty as if you are the heroine, Beauty herself, then retell it from an observer's point of view as a 'she' story. It's odd how much difference this can make. Well, perhaps not odd if you remember that everyone notices different things, relates to people differently, has their own interpretation, draws their own conclusions.
- Write a commentary on your account, as if you were an outsider writing notes in the margin: a village girl crept up and watched from the window…
- Write what a particular character is thinking at a particular time, like thought bubbles. Perhaps the Queen was unhappy and confused, rather than haughty and distant.

- Write about (or in the voice of) a missing character. Like a photograph, an account is always an unreal and slim slice of reality. Try thinking of the area beyond the frame. What about the baby's father, the King? He doesn't figure at all in the classic story.
- Write a diary entry for a character. The baby's nurse for example. She must very much have had her own opinions of the carry-on.
- Rewrite the account with the locus of power or control shifted. What if the Queen was no longer obeyed and Beauty bawled and bawled her head off so they could no longer carry on their glassy chit-chat over her unnoticed head?
- Interview the characters as if you were, for example, from the *Fairyland Echo*. Remember, colours, objects, animals, numbers are all characters as well as the people. They all have something to tell you. Find out about their relationship to each other.
- Take a character who's just left the action. What might he/she be thinking or doing? Aunt-Duchess Mattie is plump and on the shady side of fifty. She notices a great deal but does not say very much. In the carriage on the way home she gives her husband, Archduke Jo, her astute opinion of what is going on at Diamond Palace, where everyone is so hard and bright.
- Continue the story six months/a year after the end of the fairy tale. Did Beauty and the Prince really live happily ever after? In fact, he has an affair with the village girl who had been peeping in at the window of the wedding and leaves Beauty to become a cowherd. Or, in another version, Beauty flounces off with the Wicked Fairy asserting: 'Who needs men?' How would you like the story to end? You are in charge. Rewrite it as you like.
- Turn the text into a play. Then the characters will all be able to speak in their own voices.
- If the waking you were in the dream, who are you and what would you do? You can do anything, remember. At this moment I want to vandalise the whole room where Beauty's christening party is held, with its shining tinkling glass and hardness. No, perhaps I will pull down the wings, exposing it as a sham, a mere flimsy film set, not worth the cardboard it is painted on.

- Who could help you in this? You can take a character who is already in the dream or you can import someone or thing (and remember to use the notion of character widely). I think I will ask the emerald green frog to croak on all these shallow people so determined to impress the neighbours regardless of the hurt to themselves and poor Beauty.
- You are not on your own. You can call for help in your dreams and become powerful, rather than a victim.
- Finally – explore the area or character that puzzles you. This brings you full circle back to the free-intuitive writing again. Write the puzzling image at the top of the page and continue from there.

Of course, this process is endless – goes round and round in circles – excitingly and dramatically, however. But I haven't yet finished with this one dream. All the above exploring has widened and deepened your understanding of the dream. The next things to do relate the dream to your daytime life. It is important to see a distinction between these two. I dreamt my habitual dream the other night – a huge old house which I had bought. It is always quite the wrong house for me – too big, too dark, not enough access to outside, in a city. There are two kinds of answers to my question: 'what can I do about it?' One is within the terms of the dream, such as 'sell it quick!', the other is in terms of my real life set of problems to which the dream relates.

Look for dream images, in the same way as I have suggested you look for them in everyday life (see Chapter Five). Puns (words which sound the same but have different meanings) are common, whether verbal or visual or proper names: gilt for guilt; window blinds may signify blindness; Celia Payne may mean pain. Proverbs and sayings can be interpreted, so a dream of a muddle of people cooking might be an indication that you are better out of that rather tense situation at work – there are too many cooks spoiling the broth. You dream of sewing a small repair – a stitch in time saves nine – what is it you need to do to prevent a situation worsening? Symptoms and body language can be read similarly – Why is the boy child in your dreams always flattened, poorly, disabled – Who is this child? How can you care for him?

Of whom do the characters in the dream remind you? You are still writing free-intuitively. Don't hesitate to write whatever comes first to mind – however surprising it is.

What do the events in the dream remind you of? Do the same as for the characters.

What is the dream saying to you? I think my Mother Hubbard dream was telling me to have more confidence in what I'm doing although I am reaching up to a very high cupboard.

Here is one of my poems from the christening dream:

The uninvited guest

Beauty opens her eyes wide
as the fairies tinkle,
fluorescent with all the colours
of the peacock's tail, and some that aren't.

Her pudgy fingers grab at a stardusted rod,
but her fist closes on nothing,
as each flibbertigibbet kisses like thistledown
and flaunts away to drink more bubbles.

All the princess wants now is Eve, her nurse
and to see the light
reflected from the lake
dancing on the green of the yew tree.

Instead she has to lie still in a sequinned crib
under candles, her breath tightened
by a pearl embroidered gown.
She doesn't want magic gifts,

only the cradle of arms, milk, and a lullaby.
She sighs when the last promise is uttered,
the last iridescent skirt
flounces out in a shower of glitter.

That was the last but one promise.
Now: darkness rushes in as the door slams open;
the candles gutter, and are blown out;
the breath from the moor bursts

Beauty's tight sash, and a baby thumb
edges towards baby lips. A winged figure,
blacker than the night behind her stalks in:
'What use is a handsome prince?'

Lorna Dexter's dream

I am a dreamworker and therapist who works with individuals and groups to explore dreams through art and drama. Although in my workshops writing is only a small part of that exploration (a group provides better opportunities for action and the spoken word), I keep an in-depth dream-journal myself, in which I describe my dreams and work on their significance to me through free-intuitive writing. Here is part of that process.

Some time ago I was asked to take part in a television series on dreams and dreamwork, to allow a film crew into a dreamgroup to film us working. At first that seemed impossible, given the sensitive and personal nature of dreams, but I began to realise that if I could gather a group of experienced dreamers together, their confidence in the process of dreamwork might counteract any inhibitions created by the presence of the cameras. While I was considering the implications of this, trying to decide whether the risks of misrepresentation outweighed the benefits of introducing dreamwork to the viewing public, I had the following dream.

I'm in an ordinary shopping street when I hear singing and realise it's a man in front of me, just singing as he walks, a lovely lilting, wandering, wordless song. Although I am supposed to be joining a group to catch a bus somewhere, I have to follow him and find out what the music is. I catch him up and ask him, but he keeps on walking and singing until he gets to the entrance to an old fashioned menswear shop with elegant curved shop windows on either side of a covered arcade. He picks out a cloth from a bucket and starts cleaning off some white stuff that's covering the left-hand window. Then, at last, he turns to me and names the song – 'Ravel's Rimsky' – but so inaudibly that I have to ask him to repeat it. I've never heard of it, but the music sounded like Ravel.

A dream is like a poem: the meaning of a poem lies not just in the dictionary sense of the words but in the feeling of the sounds and the rhythms, which resonate in the listener's body and soul to set in motion an answering response in the imagination. As poetry catches resonances in its choice of words, so dreams catch resonances in images. It is those images, and their, often, bizarre combinations, which create the strange harmonies that move us to wake and ponder. So it is not easy to write about a dream, any more than it is easy to retell a poem in prose: when I was walking up a hill the other day I saw hundreds of daffodils bobbing about in the wind. It really cheered me up.

Yet when we wake and want to record or share our dreams we must use words, for most dreams are not a single image which can be captured in a painting or a sculpture but a story which has to be told, a narrative of images. The knack is to find words which are as near to the original experience of the dream as possible.

One way to make this easier is to write the dream as soon after waking as possible, while the sensations are still fresh in our imagining bodies. In that half-waking state, words slip out, carrying some of the mystery left by the images, like the glint from a snail trail. It might be a slip of the tongue – like writing smother for mother; or a spelling slip – like writing heroine for heroin in a dream about addiction to bravery; or even, when more awake, a typing error – like repeatedly hitting a particular number key by accident when the dream refers to an important childhood year.

But, even more, so later, when time and daytime concerns have come between us and the dream, we must learn to reconnect with what Gendlin (1986) called the felt sense of the dream. To really honour the dream, to let it speak, one must return to that half-waking, half-dreaming state where the knowing of a thing carries more than its dictionary definition. I think a poet would understand.

So I let myself drift back into this dream, let the music of the dream resonate in me:

Ravel – what do I know of his?
Why am I so sure it's his style?
of course! Pavane for a Dead Infanta
(my adolescent theme-tune) –
the clipped garden, the formal dance,

the stiff clothes, the trappings of the court –
a princess killed by courtesy…

And Rimsky-Korsakov? – that's
much fainter, vaguer –
a whiff of far-off Russia,
wild unbridled, passionate –
The Polovtsian Dances?
A far cry from a courtly funeral
Ravel and Rimsky Korsakov, eh?
Quite a combination!

But it's only Rimsky, a diminutive,
as you'd address a child –
as if he was his brother or a friend –
someone he could be easy with,
not stand on ceremony...

This wandering song – what is it?
I know it, I'm sure, or something very like –
no words, just sounds,
a lovely easy singing –
like wandering on a grassy hill some
soft spring day –
sounds growing and moving air ...

Oh dear! The menswear shop –
respectable suits in subtle greys,
stiff shirts and sober ties –
But wait a minute!
What is this white stuff?
Windowlene?
What are you trying to show me,
Windowcleaner Orpheus,
drawing me with your music?

There's nothing in it,
the shopwindow's empty, the grey
suits gone –

'This space is for you' he seems to say.
For what? Why are dreams so obscure?
'For your song.'

What's that tune I'm always half singing
under my breath, driving friends crazy?
That's Russian – from Scheherezade
did he write that? (Where's
the dictionary?)...

What's Scheherezade to me
(or me to Scheherezade!) –
The sultan's chosen concubine for the night
who like the others has to die the next day
except she tells a story so entrancing

he lets her live to tell the sequel,
night after night – clever woman! –
until he falls in love and marries her...

Aha! That's it! Stories, night after night, which save your life: dreams. That's my song. And the Windowcleaner Extraordinary, clearing the curved glass (of a television screen?), shows me the shop window for those dreams. I seemed to be getting the go-ahead for the television project. Then I shared the dream with a friend.

Speaking preceded writing in our personal and cultural development and speech carries us back to the pre-history in which dreams are rooted. Our story can touch listeners, move their imagination, maybe their heart, and then we have their resources too: to catch our puns before they slip away unnoticed, to share the connections we have been too fearful or too unhappy to make, to hold us to our exploring with their shared compassion (a group, of course, gives us several listeners).

Speaking the dream, I used different words: I said the singer was 'just vocalising'. She said: 'It sounds like Vocalese' and my heart leapt (our bodies really know) – 'he wrote that'. I'm not so sure (I'll check the dictionary later) but that was not important. Much more important was to be reminded of Vocalese, because the whole point of that lovely, lilting, wandering song is that it has no words, it is pure sound. Though my dream offered me the encouragement to show dreamwork to the public, it also reminded me that behind all the words which would be used there runs a thread of wordless beauty through our dreams – as through our lives – which we can only follow. There is no explanation. And although the friend did not know this, the last time I had heard Vocalese I had wept for the lack of that wordless beauty in my life. Television project aside, this dream had come to tell me what I would otherwise forget.

(Lorna Dexter)

* * * *

Lorna redrafted this account, as we both felt her meaning was not quite clear. This was her comment in her letter: 'Writing this – and especially re-writing it – has really helped me clarify what I feel about writing and dreamwork: that although words are important, explanations useful, and writing a valuable tool, the true knowing is a wordless one. No surprise then that I should have chosen this dream as illustration even though I did not fully understand it when I started. Thank you!'

Brenda Mallon's dream

Brenda is a dream expert and writer (Mallon 1987; 1989). The following is some of her own dream writing, showing the way writing about a particular dream helped her to understand and listen to her own body better.

> The saliva glistening in their crimson, gaping mouths was the last thing I saw before the dogs leapt. I had never dreamt of being attacked by dogs before and it disturbed me, threw me off guard and confused me. I restrained them in the insecure kennel that was the back of my mind as soon as I woke up.
>
> Of course, working with dreams as a therapist and writer, I should have known better, considered more, avoided less ... however. I was preoccupied and of course, I wanted to deny the dream violation. Staying with such painful feelings is hard and it was as much as I could do to write the dream down and tell myself that I'd work on it later.
>
> In the dream I was standing in the back garden. It was a dark night and a man, a silent companion, was by my side. The dogs sprang out of nowhere, and I knew with that cold certainty that you often get in dreams that I was to be their victim. In the brief second before they jumped, I said, 'But I'm good with dogs. They're my friends. I never have trouble with dogs...' Incredulous words lost in the darkness as vicious mouths ripped me and blood spurted.
>
> I began bleeding later that morning. The snarling dogs slipped their restraints and the baby I was carrying went with them.
>
> I had taken my body for granted, assumed it would not turn on me, because that is what it felt like, and I was shocked. The suddenness, the pain, the blood, it seemed as incomprehensible as the dream yet every bit as real. Nature, red in tooth and claw, was there in all her power and it hurt.
>
> Dreams tell us more than we know. As I dreamt, my body was already engaged in the process that would lead to the early miscarriage. At the time I had no waking indications or symptoms that anything was amiss. On the contrary, I was deemed to be in perfect health. However, there was another truth, another story being enacted within my inner world that the dream narrates. In a way, the impact of the dream prepared me for the shock of loss and the feelings of vulnerability that followed. Nothing could ever be certain again.

I recalled the dream as the white-coated doctor stood silently beside me after he told me I'd miscarried. The man in my dream had been wearing a white coat too.

(Brenda Mallon)

Coleridge's dream

Samuel Taylor Coleridge was a poet who regularly took laudanum (an opiate) and used dream images in his writing. I think this poem is one of the most famous dream images in the English language:

Kubla Khan

In Xanadu did Kubla Khan
A stately pleasure dome decree:
Where Alph the sacred river, ran
Through caverns measureless to man
Down to a sunless sea.
So twice five miles of fertile ground
With walls and towers were girdled round:
And here were gardens bright with sinuous rills,
Where blossomed many an incense bearing tree;

And here were forests ancient as the hills,
Enfolding sunny spots of greenery …

And all should cry, Beware! Beware!
His flashing eyes, his floating hair!
Weave a circle around him thrice,
And close your eyes with holy dread,
For he on honey dew hath fed,
And drunk the milk of Paradise.

On awakening he … instantly and eagerly wrote down the lines that are here preserved. At this moment he was unfortunately called out by a person on business from Porlock.'

(Coleridge's preliminary note to *Kubla Khan*,
quoted in Smith 1983, p.152)

The moral of this tale is: capture your dream onto paper as soon as you can. If something is in your mind about a dream, note it down then and there. Most writers carry a notebook around everywhere; it's worth cultivating this writerly habit.

There is comfort, however, for the busy ones – for those who have to wait for the right time and space to write. Dreams and the inspirations for writing are infinitely kind. They will come back, if you need to examine whatever they are trying to tell you. They are likely to come back as a different image, however: Coleridge may have got the same message in terms of hoarfrost on oaks and beads of ice bobbing from the end of grass-blades in a rushing stream in his next dream (possibly depending on how large a dose of laudanum he had taken that night). This might have been just as helpful as the stately pleasure dome with whatever psychological problem he was trying to sort out but would not have enabled him to finish the poem *Kubla Khan.*

Stevie Smith has her own views on the *Person from Porlock.* She is clearly feeling here a desire to stop an endless self-examination in writing and would welcome the interruption of a visitor!

> Coleridge received the Person from Porlock
> And ever after called him a curse,
> Then why did he hurry to let him in?
> He could have hid in the house.
>
> It was not right of Coleridge in fact it was wrong
> (But often we all do wrong)
> As the truth is I think he was already stuck
> With Kubla Khan.
>
> I long for the Person from Porlock
> To bring my thoughts to an end,
> I am becoming impatient to see him
> I think of him as a friend.
>
> (Stevie Smith 1983, p.152)

Using dreams to help understand our inner selves has been around a long time and over the world. Hippocrates (1983) believed that they could be used for diagnosis. 'When the body is sleeping it receives no sensations, but the soul being awake at that time perceives everything; it sees what is visible, it hears what is audible, it walks, it touches, it feels pain and thinks ... A correct appreciation of these things implies considerable wisdom' (p.252). If we listen to our dreams, we will hear the voice of our soul as well as our body. He carries on to list a considerable number of good and bad portents in dreams, including: 'It is a sign of health if a star, which is clear and bright, appears to fall out of its orbit and to move eastwards' (p.255). This particularly interests me, writing as I am in mid-December.

There are many instances of dreams being used for foretelling, such as the way Joseph's interpretative skill won him his many-coloured coat (Genesis 4:1). And there have been many many theories of dreams. Freud (1959) believed that they were disguised wish fulfilment and full of sexual imagery, and that we could decode them like a 'picture puzzle'. He said that they are 'the guardians of sleep' – the unfulfilled wishes would disturb our sleep otherwise. Jung (1983) felt that some dreams connect us to the collective unconscious, an area which belongs to all of us and goes right back to our primordial past. He felt that dreams compensate for aspects of our lives we have not fully developed and that they can be used to solve problems or can be premonitions.

Fritz Perls was a psychologist who developed a whole new approach to working with dreams in therapy. Although my suggestions are drawn from eclectic sources, they owe a great deal to Perls' theories of gestalt.

Australian aborigines believe dreaming puts them in touch with their mythological ancestral spiritual heritage, which is set beyond time and space, 'The Dreamtime'. The Senoi of Malaysia have dreamwork knitted into their culture. Children from a very early age are encouraged to remember and recount their dreams, making sense of them in terms of their daily life and using them to help them. Nothing is wrong or shameful about dream life, even bizarre sexual exploits. They are then taught how to take a more active role in their dream life: they ask their dreams to help them with particular issues. They also learn how to affect the outcome of a dream while still in it. For example, they learn how to confront and subdue a dream opponent. And they ask for gifts which will help them, to bring back to their waking life to share with family and friends. They ask a dream place, enemy, or lover, for a gift.

> When you dream of a figure you really dislike, hang on to it – that's the one with a gift for you, the one who can teach you something valuable. (Anne Wade 1993)

CHAPTER SEVEN

The Power of Poetry, Autobiography and Fiction

'Something Hatches'

Writing

A startling crack
and something hatches:

blue membrane skimmed
over eyes' brightness – milky blind yet;

thick yolk-sticked
wing-stumps wag like thumb ends.

There's work to do:

to splay out wing bones;
chisel feathers
skin the eyes allowing vision;
hook the claws;
balance the wing tips.

to dart out – beak sharp – meaning.

and then let it go –
and see if it's a bird or no.

(Lesley Glaister)

People's lives are told as stories: over the kitchen table, the bar and the GP's desk. Your life is reworked as poetry: you create and recreate poems about death, childbirth and love – on the bus and when the doctor visits. Our life is a re-enacted as a drama. We do this in order to make some sort of sense of our lives. And this involves making creative leaps to interpret metaphor; to create links between disconnected parts of the narrative; to perceive the interplay between plot, character, place, time; and to diagnose from an unrhymed lyric. Writing all these down helps even more.

Writing to a form, such as poetry, fiction or autobiography, can channel the healing nature of writing, enabling it to be even more illuminating and helpful to the writer. One of the ways writing is different from talking, and similar to the plastic arts such as painting, is that a piece of writing is an object which is separate from the writer's mind. As such, it can, therefore, be related to, and worked upon, as a separate entity. In this way, therapeutic writing is similar to art therapy (Seth-Smith 1997).

Crafting the writing into a form seems to make it even more of an object, increasing its power to communicate back to the writer. The fact that poetry, fiction or autobiography might also be able to communicate to others (in a way journal writing is less likely to) is a happy by-product.

Poetry

> Long before there were therapists there were poets, and from time immemorial man has struggled to cope with his inevitable inner turmoil. One way of so coping has been the ballad, the song, the poem.
>
> (Molly Harrower 1972, p.7)

> Every poet starts from his own emotions.
>
> (T.S. Eliot 1932, p.136)

> Poetry is the spontaneous overflow of powerful feelings: it takes its origin from emotion recollected in tranquillity.
>
> (William Wordsworth 1976, p.22)

> String
> Is a very important thing.
> Rope is thicker,
> But string
> Is quicker.
>
> (Spike Milligan 1968, p.11)

Poetry is very like string. Its comparative thinness and quickness enables it to reach the parts that prose cannot, leaping straight to the heart of the matter, whether anguish or joy. Poetry is an exploration of our deepest and most intimate experiences, thoughts, feelings, ideas, and insights: swift but minutely accurate delineations of these and our world, distilled and pared to succinctness, are the soul of poetry. Grammar, spelling and prose form are out of the window, so the writing is not hindered by such niceties as a sentence needing a verb. Poetry is also lyrical: the absorption required, listening with the mind's ear, is healing.

These, allied to the free-intuitive writing process (see Chapter Three) – the initial stage of a poem – take the writer into areas they didn't know they knew, thought, felt or remembered. This is therapeutic because the writing hand not only knows what the thinking mind doesn't but also knows how much that mind, as well as the feeling heart, can bear to face.

This section takes the work of poets for its examples, not because these are better than raw therapeutic writing but because these poets have been able to reflect on and express their own experience of writing. Here is Catherine Byron, telling of her own writing:

> When I started writing seriously, in my mid thirties, I was fascinated to observe from how far back in time the subject matter was coming. It seemed that any autobiographical material that was surfacing, as if from a source deep underground, was from at least fifteen, and usually more, years earlier; laid down under strata that had compressed it, pressurised it, given it both urgency and a new form. A sort of oilwell of the heart.
>
> I know, looking back, that my first 'flowering' of poetry was therapeutic on a psychic level, though in a way hidden to me at the time. It proved to have a wisdom, a clear-sightedness, that was not available to my conscious mind. I thought I was writing about landscape, my Irish grandmother's life, archaeology, but on a deeper level I was writing a slow realisation I was in a marriage which was unravelling beyond repair. Once that particular poetic seam was worked out, I began to write, rather more directly but still 'telling it slant', about the ending of that marriage. It was still a sort of recording, an examining: still a sorting through of what was already over, my own and others' pasts. (Catherine Byron)

A vital element of most poetry is, furthermore, the use of image, particularly metaphor. The use of metaphor opens windows in the mind onto seemingly inexplicable matters, as already described in Chapter Five. 'The image is the constant in all poetry and every poem is itself an image. Trends come and go, diction alters, metrical fashions change, even the elemental subject matter may change out of all recognition: but metaphor remains the life principle of poetry, the poet's chief test and glory' (Day Lewis 1974). (Metaphor and image are here seen to be the same.)

This leads to poetry having layers of meaning, some of which are subtle. The uncovering and understanding of these layers offers great insight to the writer. I once found that I had used the word 'gilt' with an implied understanding of 'guilt', an effective but simple pun which my writing hand supplied without the help of my thinking brain. These happenings of the hand tell me something I didn't know, or had forgotten, about myself, my past, others in my life. I often find I have included references and meanings which will only be understood by few readers, but I know those readers will respond with joyful clarity – rather like finding a clue in a treasure hunt.

Redrafting

The crafting and redrafting stages of poetry writing which follow the free-intuitive are lengthy, slow and deeply thoughtful; poetry has been said to be only 10 per cent inspiration, the other 90 per cent being perspiration. These stages can be intensely therapeutic as the writer sinks into the memory/experience/thought depicted in the poem, as far as s/he can, re-experiencing it (recollecting it in tranquillity) and trying to fit words, and word structures, to what is in the mind and the heart. This process draws to a close with the recognition of clarity and deepened understanding.

But this writing process is not straightforward. It has been likened to 'an artist painting a picture. Instead of working systematically from the top, left-hand corner of the canvas across the to the top, right-hand corner, and then down the canvas, the artist engages in a series of activities: application and reflection, revision and reflection, close-in painting and long range perspective, balance and colour. Each step entails action and reaction without prescribed sequence' (Luidens 1997, p.140).

Another reader can offer valuable insight at this stage (see Chapter Nine). Catherine Byron and I tussled with a constipated sentence in her above piece. We both ended up with far greater clarity about what she was trying to say. Poetry writing was suggested to Anne Sexton by her therapist:

> Creativity, at least that which is communicated clearly to others, requires discipline. For Sexton, the creative process, rather than her psychiatric illness, was able to become the controlling force, and the conscious effort of will involved was a stabilising effect on her.
>
> Anne Sexton illustrates the dialectic in poetry as therapy, between expression and catharsis on the one hand and cognitive control on the

> other. To be sure, because her poems were often based on her experiences and emotions, they were outpourings of her individual human experience. Yet, her intense revision of these outpourings gave them artistic form and structure, and elevated her unique experience to the universal experience of human suffering. As she perfected her poems, she was, perhaps, able to achieve an intellectual distancing from, and control over the emotions that initially stimulated the content of the poems ...
>
> It may be that only when writers are forced to craft their expressive products into formal words of art is there a psychotherapeutic effect. Several commentators ... believe that Sexton lived as long as she did because she was able to do this. Had she not been introduced to poetry by her therapist she might well have killed herself sooner. (Lester and Terry 1992, p.47)

All the stages of writing help create order and understanding out of a mental muddle. A poem is an ordered entity with a beginning, a middle and an end. If an even greater order is required, a poet will often choose to write in a strict form (such as sonnet like Hamberger, below, or villanelle like the one opening this book) or in metre or a strict rhyme form.

> I write poems because they solve a conflict, because I am ill at ease spiritually and want to clarify my thoughts and feelings. I write poems because from some inner chaos, I am driven to create order. I write poems because I am flooded, overpowered by feelings which have been provoked by some aspect of life or nature. This great bulk of feeling can only be subdued or brought under control if I allow some intellectual craftsmanship to work on it, to produce a manageable thought which I can control in the place of the all-pervading emotions which control me ... Much of my poetry springs from the inner need to set thoughts and feelings in order and to emerge triumphant from the difficulties ... One of the functions of poetry is to restore an inner balance which has temporarily been lost. (Harrower 1972, p.53)

Robert Hamberger is a poet who feels writing has helped him create some kind of order when his life seemed overthrown:

> My first thought is that the processes of writing and of therapy have similarities for the person experiencing them. Having gone through therapy and being a writer I would say that (particularly in writing poetry) there's a similar initially wordless almost physical urge to bring something unvoiced into the light. There's that receptive waiting, in

stillness and silence, for whatever words initially come to mind. Then there's the attempt to develop those words from incoherence towards some coherent order which describes the feeling or the experience as faithfully as possible.

In 'On becoming a person' (1961) Carl Rogers writes of observing the searches his clients make through therapy: 'the importance which the client comes to attach to exactness of symbolisation. He wants just the precise word which for him describes the feeling he has experienced. An approximation will not do. And this is certainly for clearer communication within himself, since any one of several words would convey the meaning equally well to another.' So on some level as part of the process of both therapy and writing, it becomes a search for the exact word to describe the feeling or experience, and to convey that feeling or experience to another.

The therapeutic value of writing includes its ways of helping a writer (and hopefully a reader) to discover what Rogers calls order in experience. He writes: 'It seems inevitable that I seek for the meaning or orderliness.' I can think of three crucial points in my life where I have consciously tried to use my writing as a means of helping me to make sense of what I am experiencing. These were the nine months leading to the birth of our first child; the months leading to the death from AIDS of by best friend Cliff, and the months after the break-up of my marriage. These experiences led to three poetry sequences: 'Journey to a Birth', 'Acts of Parting' and 'Die Bravely'.

It is important to make a distinction, however, between the process of writing and its end-product. The fact that the experience led eventually to publishable poems which have some correspondences to other readers' experience is a bonus. But the initial purpose of writing is, if possible, to make sense of the experience for myself. If the process had led to nothing publishable that would not denigrate the value of the work to me in helping to understand experience. I read somewhere that Yeats called poetry *an argument with myself,* which sums up that sense of internal debate which probably gives most poetry its initial impetus.

I would suggest that the need to make sense, if possible to find some order or meaning in experience is a basic human drive. Although I worked instinctively at the time, I now see it as significant that part of my structure for the 'Acts of Parting' and 'Die Bravely' sequences involved alternating sonnets with free-verse. When starting the sonnets for 'Acts of Parting' I half-instinctively chose the Petrarchan form, in my view the most difficult rhyme-scheme, as if attempting to put order on the chaos

> of my feelings, and at the same time – in the mess of my emotions when my best friend was dying – almost to set myself an intellectual challenge as a way of keeping going or even distracting part of myself from the horror of what I was feeling and seeing. I wanted to turn the scream I refer to in the poem '*Muscling In*' into an art. In so doing, I also wanted to honour both my experience and my friend. I remember thinking at the time that if Wilfred Owen can play with sonnet-form rhyme-schemes in the trenches, I can try the same.
>
> (Robert Hamberger)

Some other poets

There is a great deal of poetry, the writing of which has clearly been therapeutic. Douglas Dunn's elegies to his wife (1985); Jacqueline Brown's award-winning charting of infertility (1993) and Mark Doty's sequence about the death of a lover from AIDS (1996), are examples.

Atlas, Smith and Sessoms (1992) encouraged hospitalised adolescents to write poetry. They considered that this writing gave the young people a space not too frighteningly close to other people (their therapists primarily), where they could enter the internal poetic world and '"suspend" critical appreciation of reality while letting her or his awareness plumb depths of experience of memory that are typically unconscious' (p.279). Judith Fuchel (1985) had a student patient who was able to express memories and thoughts in poetry which she could not say. David Tooth (1990) has reported of a woman suffering intense low back and leg pain who wrote poetry as a means of self-expression. She received physiotherapy, regional local anaesthesia and psychotherapy to help her come to terms with her new lifestyle. And she wrote. The article includes extracts of her writing, clearly charting and expressing her feelings – the final one a triumphant paean of acceptance both of her current situation and of the help of others.

> Poetry is therapy and is part and parcel of normal development. Poetry therapy is a newcomer. Long before there were therapists there were poets, and from time immemorial man has struggled to cope with his inevitable inner turmoil. One way of so coping has been the ballad, the song, the poem. Once crystallised into words, all engulfing feelings become manageable, and once challenged into explicitness, the burden of the incommunicable becomes less heavy. The very act of creating is a self-sustaining experience, and in the poetic moment the self becomes both the ministering therapist and the comforting patient … The writing

of the poem seems to provide comfort when external solace is lacking. (Harrower 1972, p.56)

Spiritual writing

Our culture has great difficulty sharing spiritual matters. Yet somehow it is permissible in writing, particularly poetry (which is seen as a secular form of spirituality, divorced from that sensitive area – religion). This is of particular value for the very ill, particularly the dying. Their minds are turning naturally away from this world towards their relationship with whatever they perceive is beyond us. At the same time, they wish to go back over spiritual experiences from the past: brushes with the eternal at whatever stage of their life. They may well find this kind of writing helps them to see previously not-understood incidents in this light. This can offer both patient and relatives support, encouragement and acceptance.

Writing is a secure and unembarassing vehicle for exploring our spiritual journey. Images such as darkness and light, a gift, fellowship or guidance from a special person along the way are all sources of inspiration that have been used (Bolton 1994, 1995a and b).

The arts do tend to generate moral questions too, in a way which can too easily otherwise be neglected. Reflective writing can raise questions and challenge assumptions (Downie and Charlton 1992).

Autobiography

> But now I only know I am – that's all.
>
> (John Clare 1997, p.90)

> Our own stories are always a symbolic representation of ourselves.
>
> (Gersie and King 1990)

> The Fancy [imagination] is indeed no other than a mode of memory emancipated from the order of time and space.
>
> (Samuel Taylor Coleridge 1975, p.167)

We tell the stories of our lives all the time: telling ourselves and others who we are, what we think and did, where we went, why we did so, how we created things and when. People are social beings, they function together by showing themselves, and each other, that their stories knit into the pattern of their culture. Creating an artefact, a piece of writing, out of this essential communication must reinforce even more strongly the sense of the 'I' at the centre of all these coherent accounts. A rational and purposive kind of 'I', moreover, who is the hero/ine.

> Suffering is produced, and alleviated, primarily by the meaning that one attaches to one's experience. The primary human mechanism for attaching meaning to particular experiences is to tell stories about them. Stories serve to relate individual experiences to the explanatory constructs of the society and culture and also to place the experiences within the context of a particular individual's life history. (Brody 1987, p.5)

Brody carries on to explain that healing can take place, with no drugs or other treatment, 'when the meaning of the illness experience is altered in a positive direction'. Positive change has three components: the illness experience must be given an acceptable explanation; the patient must perceive herself surrounded by caring (I would add trusted) individuals; the patient must achieve a sense of control over the illness experience. 'Storytelling heals by restoring a disrupted connectedness.'

One of the best ways of achieving this sense of control is by writing some of these stories down. The process of writing, as I have said above, clarifies, orders, creates illuminating connections and makes contact with fresh psychological material. Once written, the story is an object outside of the writer and can then be related to in a developmentally fruitful way.

Each of us has a unique story, even if, as Humpty Dumpty pointed out to Alice (Carroll 1871), we are all fundamentally identical in being human. There is a sense in which if we do not control our stories, they will control us. If the story we are currently telling is a 'sick' one, the self-respect will be lowered and the sense of control lost.

Older people or those near to death, in particular, gain great value in rediscovering they are the same person who had their pigtails pulled by the boy in the desk behind, fell in love, lost their job. Writing can connect us up to the person we always have been, because there can be no pretence. This unifying process can offer the writer eventual peace of mind, security and confidence, once they have overcome any difficulties (sometimes, abreaction) the writing brings up. It can also be a precious way of saying goodbye, and of reconciliation and healing old wounds, before the intervention of death (Frampton 1986, p.1594). It also offers the satisfaction of a lasting memorial or testimony. The benefit of this should be rescued from the now almost derogatory term 'reminiscence work' (Birren and Deutchman 1991; Bornat 1994).

Autobiographical accounts can be angled in different ways – generally positive or negative, for example rather like a glass can be described as being either half-full or half-empty. The vital element to work towards is a positive sense of self. But, clearly, this has to be authentic. There is no point in forcing autobiographical writings into a positive tone. The negative, if it is there, may need to be thoroughly explored before the positive can be arrived at. The hero/ine of the autobiography may be a victim (for example) initially. The writing and rewriting of life stories enables the writer to examine and begin to understand the forces on them which have made them see their life in this miserable way. If the writer, however, becomes stuck and unable to redraft with a fresh vision, another reader (friend, doctor, nurse, therapist) may be able to help.

Healing narratives

Peter was my creative writing student at a college for people who had missed out on education first time round (Northern College – see Chapter Twelve). And how he had missed out, having spent seven years of his childhood confined to a hospital bed with only *one* visit from his parents and no tuition. I happened to give the group a piece of advice from a publisher of romantic fiction: 'You may put your bleeding heart all over the page when you write for yourself; but you must take it off again if you want to publish'. The reader is not interested in the writer's bleeding heart. But it is this smearing over the page which is the stuff of therapeutic writing.

Peter was not interested in publishing, it was the first part of the sentence he heard loud and clear. But it was slow: he would write a small paragraph and I would comment and suggest certain areas were far too interesting to be expressed in one sentence. He would write another paragraph and I'd do the same again. He was, justifiably, immensely proud of his writing, commenting one day how 'opening the pus-filled wound and allowing it to drain through the writing' was altering his life. Then it was the end of the course.

Years later I received a self-published booklet with Peter's picture on the front and a clear, unemotional description of the hospital: 'You dare not move in your bed, it had to be kept tidy at all times. You would be laid there like a corpse and everything had to be in its place.' This was followed with an account of the roving life of an illiterate. Peter was a loved and respected member of that course, despite his booklet's title *Scarred for Life.*

Medical Monitor has published an account by a GP about two of her patients who have written themselves out of their bad psychological situations (anonymous author 1995). The author says of one of the patients: 'I have gradually watched her change until she has once again been able to return to work'.

There are many examples of novels, stories and plays written as therapeutic journeys. Mary Karr (1995) has written about her childhood abuse in a slum in Texas through the eyes of a child: 'I would write and cry and write and cry'. Anna Reynolds (1996) battered her mother to death with a hammer. Hilary Mantel (1996) had half her insides, including her ovaries and womb, removed when she was nineteen. Linda Hart (1995) is a schizophrenic. Howard Wilson (Campbell 1995) is a bank robber turned novelist who shot dead his former colleagues. John Berger (1995) and Isabel Allende (1995) have both written about the death of a child. Irene Ivison (1997) was not a writer, yet has written tellingly about the murder of her teenage daughter. Jean-Dominique Bauby (1997) wrote *Le Scaphandre et Le Papillon* (*The Diving Bell and the Butterfly*) through a series of eye blinks, dictated letter by letter.

Narratives of sickness and mental illness have become quite a genre, since about 1950, in diary and letter form, publications and on the internet (McLellan 1997; Hudson Jones 1997). These narratives offer insight into suffering and treatment, as well as some hope, to both medical and nursing practitioners and to other sufferers. Some of the writers have published in the hope of supporting reform in the treatment of the mentally ill. There is evidence of practitioners altering their treatment having read such texts.

How to write autobiographically

Writing the story of your life is an excellent place to start writing – as long as you don't hold yourself to writing it all *just* as it happened. You'd be doomed to disappointment if you did. The line between autobiography and fiction is very slim and the truth is probably impossible to remember, let alone convey. You won't remember it all. What you do remember might come up like the jumbled pieces of a jigsaw, half of which you've lost. Write the bits you feel like writing then go back to fill in the gaps which don't interest you so much, if and when you feel ready:

1. Start – with the six-minute free-intuitive writing to get the pen moving, the mind clearer and also, possibly, find a focus for the sustained writing.
2. Endings – do not come in neat story forms in life as they do in fiction, whatever the King thinks (see below). Don't worry about a proper beginning and an ending. Your account should be all:
3. Middle – Write about 'A Time When' ... begin with the most vital experience which comes to mind. Write about a person who has been really important to you. Then have a go at some of these:

that was the Christmas/birthday/... when

the blowing of the pressure valve

a time I learned something vital

the hand on the doorknob

a parting or beginning

a missed opportunity

a misunderstanding

a path I did not take

a clash of interests

a memorable time

a celebration

taking care

a dilemma

in control

conflict

a joy

4. List – things you love providing/hate providing; what your rituals are, and why you do them; the times I forgave someone/myself; the times I was amazed.

Try drawing your lifeline, including on it all the important things which have happened to you. This is a line like a graph, going up for the up times and down for the down (you may need several sheets of paper stuck together lengthwise). You could write a vignette for each memory you want to depict or draw it (one woman I worked with used a montage of cut-out pictures from magazines).

When you write in this way, remember the following:

- nothing is too trivial to write about
- write exactly what occurred – detail and feelings, direct speech
- try not to censor or judge
- write in the present tense if possible (*I am*, not *I was*) and the active voice (*I threw*, not *it was thrown*) but choose between first or third person (*I am* or *she is*).

Re-read carefully, allowing your mind to pick up chance connections, fresh avenues and additions, however odd.

Use the way of re-reading and altering writing as suggested in Chapter Three. These are really important stages, certainly before the writing is shared with anyone else. A good area for expanding and rounding out your memory is to check you have covered as many of the five senses as you can. The sense of smell, for example, is powerfully evocative and can conjure up experiences which can involve the other senses. Here is John Lyon's smelly workshop:

> Gather a variety of smells in small bottles with firm screw-on lids: e.g. cotton wool saturated with liquids, oils, essences, or any smelly matter you wish.
>
> Invite the group to sniff one or several of the bottles. They must make notes of anything which comes to mind no matter how far-fetched: associative ideas, words, phrases, events, etc.
>
> They must now attempt to describe the smell, not by trying to identify what it is, which in some cases may be pretty obvious, but rather in terms of what it reminds them of, or makes them think of.
>
> From the brainstorming of ideas and the emotive descriptions, the memory of some incident or event ought to be jolted, or the imagination stimulated to come up with a first draft of a poem or story. (John Lyon)

Writing as a child

> I don't know whether you have ever seen a map of a person's mind. Doctors sometimes draw maps of other parts of you, and your own map can become intensely interesting, but catch them trying to draw a map of

> a child's mind, which is not only confused but keeps going round all the time ... nothing will stand still. (Barrie 1967, p.19)

We *can* pass through the looking glass to meet that self we *didn't* lose in those stormy adolescent years. That little child is still here: you are the same person you were at four and fourteen. We believe too readily in progress, that we need to move on and discard old illusions and fantasies. In medieval times people listened to ballads and *knew* there were dragons – somewhere. It is still surprisingly simple to shake off adulthood and get lost on some of the 'zig-zag lines that are probably roads in the island (of Neverland)'.

Writing in your child's voice is an invaluable thing to try. You will be surprised how much is remembered and expressed once this child gets hold of the pencil in your hand. Ask the child to write an account of events, in the way outlined above. Or write a letter to yourself as a child and then write the reply, or write a dialogue (see Chapter Three). Try writing with your left hand or use a chunky pencil/felt tip: the handwriting will be clumsy, the words short. The adult could be on hand to respond with a normal pen.

Or you could write to any of these beginnings:

- what kinds of questions did you ask?
- what were some of the answers you remember receiving?
- what kinds of things were all right to question; what not?
- who were your childhood heroes/heroines?
- what about their lives did you admire?
- what real people in your life turned out to be your guides? (Baldwin 1991)

There has been a great deal written about the inner child and the value of getting in touch with her/him (Parks 1990). Children's writers have always known about this, since they have to write in a child's voice. You can't fool a child audience, you can't write down to them. You have to grow down, join them in their world, and write from it. There are other advantages gained by children's writers: 'Many, including myself, have a need to redress the balance of their childhood – to create in their books the world they wish they'd had – a world in which kids have the power, rightness prevails and everyone gets tucked up at night full of milk and biscuits' (Novotny Hunter 1995, p.10).

Fiction

> 'Begin at the beginning,' the King said gravely, 'and go on till you come to the end: then stop.' (Lewis Carroll, *Alice's Adventures in Wonderland,* p.104)

Fiction differs from autobiography in that the writer knows they are concocting a story, even if it is based on their own life – and fiction probably often is. I asked novelist Lesley Glaister where her extraordinary characters came from and she answered: 'from me, they must be all me mustn't they?'

Fiction can leap over the boring bits of life and be dramatic; conflate fascinating bits from separate events into one story in a chosen order; sidestep problems of confidentiality; convey multiple viewpoints; merge traits from different characters; set the account in just the right place and time rather than prosaically where and when it really happened. Real life events can be depicted with essential ingredients altered, such as a happy ending supplied or the right thing being said and done rather than the very wrong one which caused you so many sleepless nights. Above all, fiction can be presented with a beginning, a middle and an end, unlike real life which dribbles on in an unsatisfactorily imprecise way. A crafting of structure creates an impression of wholeness which is supportive.

Fiction can be enormous fun. Since it is a creation, you can let your imagination go and write what you want to write. Well, I say that, but any fiction writer will tell you that a story has ideas all of its own – there's no point in trying to tell characters what you want them to do or say, they know their own story best.

Writing in fiction can be oddly illuminating. Once a character has a name and a particular place and time to be in, they take on a life. This person is part of you, yet separate from you, and you can relate to their unfolding adventures without feeling responsible or threatened – after all, this is a fictional character! We say a great deal more about ourselves in fictional writing than we might realise. I well remember one group member on a health professional course who decided to write a wholly fictional account as she felt she didn't know the group well enough to expose an episode from her real life. The group learned a great deal more about her from her story than if she had written autobiographically.

Fictional writing can help us to look in from the outside and it can enable us to try out all sorts of things which are impossible in life. It can enable us to see events from different angles and in different lights. Events in life can too often seem immutable, unchangeable. We can't change things which have happened, clearly, but we can change our story of them. And, often, it is our story which is at fault rather than the actual incident (see Chapter Eight for rewriting ideas which help to reshape our view of ourselves).

Fiction can be used to go on fantasy journeys too, enacting events which seem to be totally different from our own lives. If, as Lesley Glaister says, all these characters and events are within me, these fictions are the roads I never went down in my life (perhaps never could have gone down). They won't all be fun, exciting adventures. Some of them may be unpleasant – but necessary.

Theresa Tomlinson, an author for young people, wrote a story to help her with the trauma of breast cancer. She wrote it for herself but her editor wanted it. Theresa was uncertain if publication was right for such a story out of pain, but, now, the book, *Dancing Through the Shadows*, is a fable of hope for young people and a way of helping them to tackle thoughts and experiences of death and life-threatening illness. She ends the book with:

> 'I know now what the most precious thing on earth is.'
> 'What?' I asked.
> 'I think it's just ... being alive,' she said. 'We mustn't waste a minute of it.'
> I leant my cheek against hers. 'No ... we won't,' I said. (1997, p.104)

CHAPTER EIGHT

Writing to Help You Take Control of Your Own Life

'This is *My* Decision!'

> Emotionally charged events no longer make me gulp and bottle things up. I now tend to write about what has happened and what I feel about it.
>
> (Moira Brimacombe, *The Emotional Release of Writing*, p.32)

> Writing things down in itself sharpens perspectives, breaks things down into clearer 'elements' and brings up further questions which facilitate learning.
>
> (Liz)

> Reflective writing helps to prioritise, organise and give direction to actions.
>
> (Anna Stanford)

> The periods when I undertake this (writing activity) can be unsettling just as much as they can be therapeutic. They are vehicles for me to test out the very basis of my assumptions and re-evaluate significant portions of both personal and professional life.
>
> (Sonya)

Writing helps the writer to see things more clearly and to act in the knowledge of that clarity. Bringing a specific problem to the pen and paper can enable the situation to be seen more from different angles and as if through fresh eyes. There are various methods for writing in this way, depending on the way you like working, your mood and the type of problem. A range of ideas are discussed below. Some of the examples are from people in their professional roles and some from personal; both can be applied to either.

Listing

This sounds really obvious, but listing is marvellous. It:

- is straightforward, quick, easy and everyday. We all make lists all the time – nothing fancy or creative writingish about it. Anyone who can write or dictate can make a list
- cuts through the muddle of stuff in the head, picking out the important points as list items; these then can become headings for further thought
- is a good first stage for thinking a problem through. The items in the list can be sorted, reworked, expanded upon; the writer is brought gently and unthreateningly into writing expressively or exploratively.

The nurses in my BA module group found list making to be very useful to their patients. Patients listed feelings and issues such as:

- 'why I am afraid of going into hospital' (practice nurse)
- 'things I would like to put straight before this operation' (Macmillan nurse)
- 'things which make me feel warm and comfortable' (hospital nurse)
- why I can't sleep (oncology night nurse)
- positive and negative feelings about bereavement (hospice social worker)
- pros and cons about whether to be sterilised or not; this helped her decide, as well as relieving some of the anxious pressure (health visitor)
- fears, anxieties and frustrations about caring for a frail, immobile, incontinent mother (district nurse). This last patient concluded, as a result of her writing, that if she didn't find some help she would neither look after her mother properly, nor attend to her own life.

Lynn Longmuir, a midwife, invented a variation on listmaking called 'Fear in the Hat'. She asked all the members of her parentcraft class to list their questions and fears and put them in a hat anonymously. This proved to be a very effective way of covering all the topics the members of the group were anxious about. Among the issues raised have been: sleepless nights, breastfeeding problems and stillbirth. Lynn felt that not all of these would have been raised if the parents-to-be had had to expose their fears verbally in front of the rest of the group.

Gyll Marples, an oncology night nurse (see also Chapters Ten and Eleven), reports:

> If a patient I knew well was awake, I made a cup of tea and sat with them for a chat. Using my intuition as to why they were really awake and if I believed it was appropriate, I asked them to write. I began asking patients in list formation why they couldn't sleep, negatives and positives. With the lists together the client and I discussed the problems and tried to solve them. I found this interesting, not threatening to the patient, beneficial and did not feel nervous at all. It felt quite a natural process. So natural, I began to wonder why I had never done it before. It was something concrete, something they were finding difficulty in doing, eg sleep at night. A problem solving exercise. After I had used it with two patients, a nurse colleague did the same with a patient who couldn't get comfortable. I felt very pleased, particularly when this man through the list making process became comfortable in a chair and actually slept for four hours, a record for him.

Anything can be listed. Sei Shonagan, the tenth-century Japanese courtier who wrote a pillow book (Morris 1967), has already been mentioned (Chapter Three). She listed all kinds of wonderful things, such as things which have lost their power; unsuitable things. How about trying these:

- list everything in your life you like and would want to keep
- list everything you'd like to change
- from these two make a positive list of choices.

Spider/clustering/brainstorming

Put the vital word in a box in the middle of the page. As the ideas come, jot them down in an appropriate place on the page. They will begin to cluster helpfully. This very clustering will trigger more ideas:

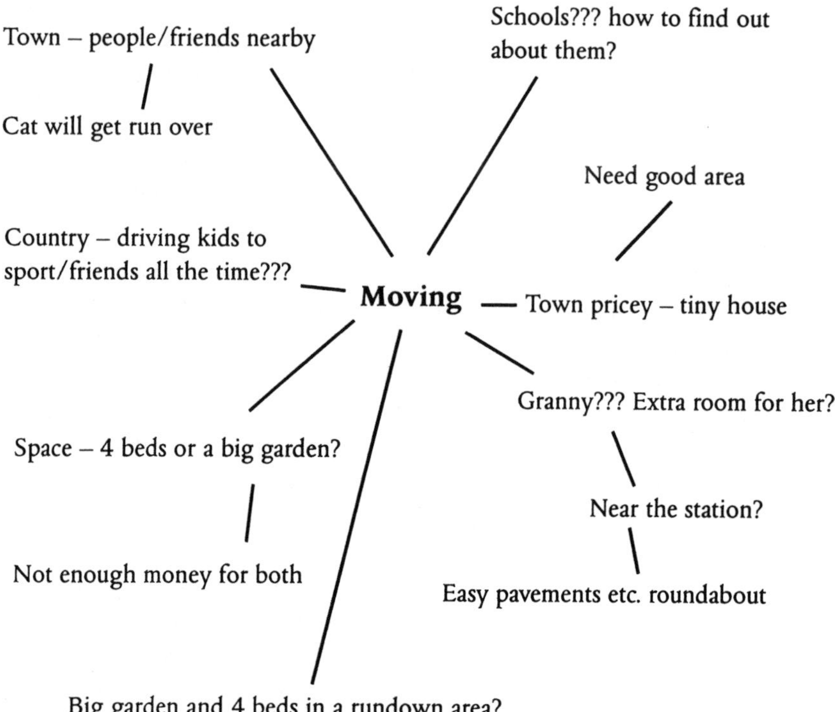

Tom carried on with this and covered an A1 sheet of paper. Then he found that the dilemma really lay along the town/country axis, so he abandoned the spider and tried the following method:

The dilemma

For this you set up two columns: Town and Country, and list the thoughts and ideas as they occur to you under the appropriate columns. It still wasn't clear to Tom when he'd finished what was important to him, so he weighted his points. He gave each item a score between one and ten. Then he relisted them in order of importance.

The answer then was clear in front of him, not in black and white because he'd used green and red pens. He discovered that it would be logical and rational for him to move to a neat little house in a good part of the town, near to schools and facilities for granny.

He bought a house with plenty of space, but in need of a great deal of attention, with a rambly garden in a village with a railway station on a line to the town. They were all very happy, despite having made the illogical move. At least they did it knowingly. It was the house and area they fell in love with; they coped with the attendant problems of granny, driving the kids about, and so on. He afterwards decided that the red pen was the colour of the cat's blood, which would probably have been fatally spilt had they moved to the city.

Stephen also used this process to decide whether to apply for a deputy headship job in a primary school. He spent a great deal of time, paper and ink; like Tom the logical decision was clear – to apply for the school job he was likely to get. He didn't apply, is now an academic, and never regretted not taking the logical step. The working through enabled him to see where his heart lay.

Writing spiders and listing pros and cons can be used for all kinds of purposes. I came across the spider first when it was described to me as a method of gathering ideas for sermons. My students have used them for the initial drafting of essays; others have used them with children to help them capture and organise their thoughts (as Gyll did with her daughter Beth, see Chapter Ten). This is not offered as a surefire method for working out what you should do. It is a process for helping you find out what you think, feel and know. As you have already seen, Tom and Stephen worked out what they wanted to do, but it was the opposite of the logical conclusion which the exercise seemed to suggest.

Just write it out

My mind is too loopy for anything as organised as spiders, pros and cons or listing. I just write and write (free-intuitive writing) and then read through the morass and write again. I use a great deal of paper but the thinking in the writing gets more and more organised and clear. Sonya, a NHS Senior Nurse Manager, used this kind of writing and commented afterwards: 'this seemed to spring from no-where and resulted in me actively seeking a new job! All based on a few minutes' thought!' Now, six months later, Sonya is in an extremely good, more suitable, new job.

Here is a piece from Anna Stanford, an asthma liaison nurse (see also Chapter Eleven), whose patient, Anne Parnham, used a similar technique:

Anne is a patient who became very severely disabled with asthma about four years previously, following a chest infection. She had been put on steroid tablets (Little Red Devils) which helped the asthma, but had severe side-effects. She had a major debate with herself one morning as to whether to take the steroids or not. Anne Parnham used writing to help her. Here is an extract:

> *Little Red Devils*
>
> I woke this morning and even before I opened my eyes, my heart sank to my boots. Oh no! the thundering headache and raging sore throat, those damn streptococci are on the march yet again… This morning was going to be *THE* battle of the 'Little Red Devils'… I am in this terrible cleft stick of: my lungs are shouting please increase the dosage of the 'Little Red Devils', and all the other parts of my body are screaming back, *NO* please don't do this to us… Now let's sort this problem out logically and weigh all the pros and cons sensibly.
>
> OK body! Put your best foot forward, and give me all your reasons as to why I should not increase the steroid dosage.

Here follows a lengthy, humorous, but harrowing response from her body parts, describing what the steroids do to them. For example:

> Skin's not at all happy with the 'Reds'… I wouldn't mind a penny for every hour I have had to spend in the local A&E department having the tears stitched back together, and the poor nurse trying so hard to put skin back that isn't even there any more…
>
> Lungs, you have heard all the arguments and evidence put forward by the rest of the body for not increasing the dosage of the 'Little Red Devils'. Now, what have you got to say for yourselves?
>
> Not a great deal except this: we are not ready to meet the Grim Reaper…
>
> THINK ABOUT IT!!
>
> I did, and counted out the 35 mg of steroids. After all, life is sweet.

Anne concluded with what her three wishes would be if a genie called. The first two were for her husband and family, the last:

> To be nut brown, wear short shorts, a skimpy T shirt, and pink satin sneakers, astride a gleaming Harley Davison. With the wind in my hair, and the sun on my back, tramming down a motorway on the Spanish Costa.

An opener for this kind of writing has been suggested by Leslie Davidoff. He uses it with clients who feel their problem is intractable. It works like magic with his clients; its very simplicity, perhaps, ensuring success. He asks: What's your problem? If you could solve it, how would you do so?

The aim is to encourage the troubled writer to give their problem to a fictional character and stand back and see how that character deals with it. More about problem solving using a fictional or storying approach is explained later in this chapter.

Writing can be a supervisor

Caroline Wilson is a writing therapist (her contact details are in the Appendix) who has developed a method from her own professional need:

> I worked in a drug and alcohol rehabilitation unit for a while, and at the end of a session or shift would write formal notes to be read by colleagues and clients. These notes gave the bones, but left me with all the flayed flesh which I had to heal before I could re-enter my world.
>
> I felt in need of supervision after nearly every shift – so I would write to my inner supervisor, telling her about what had happened and how I felt about it. She would write a letter back, commenting on how I had handled the situations, suggestion other things I could have done. She was tremendously supportive and encouraging, though she often saw things that the conscious Caroline had missed. Both letters started 'Dear Caroline' and ended with a lot of love.
>
> That inner supervisor was always great to me – I hope you can find yours. If she is grumpy or critical, tell her that is not what you want from her. Tell her what you do want and I expect she will oblige. (Wilson 1997)

Reflective or fictional writing

Write a story about the problematic situation. The story may be painfully true and autobiographical or it may be fictionalised. Both have their impact. Write it as 'a time when …' – just as suggested in the autobiography section (Chapter Seven). Don't expect this to provide answers. Instead, as one group member, Jenny, commented: 'just as we had been told, this process raises more and more questions'. The suggested approach and guidelines for this kind of writing are very similar to those for journal writing (see Chapter Three):

1. Start with six minutes of free-intuitive writing.
2. Turn to your particular problem area. WRITE IT AS A NARRATIVE, 'a time when ...'
3. You can't write the wrong thing. Whatever you write will be right for you.
4. Don't stop to think. Thinking will inhibit the flow.
5. Forget about grammar, syntax, spelling for now. They too will block the flow. Correct them later, though you may find you don't need to – this writing often creates clear, graphic text.
6. Do not stop to think, just write. If your problem is large and unrelated to any particular incident, choose the first event which comes to mind. Do not question it.
7. Nothing is too insignificant or silly to write about.
8. You may find it useful to limit yourself to a length of time in which to write. This will prevent you from fidgeting and wasting time or thinking too much.
9. Allow your pen/cil to notice exactly what occurred – detail and feelings. As you replay the experience chronologically, details begin to emerge which were ignored at the time of the experience or only noted in passing.
10. Try not to censor reactions, emotional responses or feelings.
11. Refrain from judgements at this stage.
12. Try not to force the writing into a set good story form (or poem, if that's how it seems to be coming out). Write it as life is, all muddly middle, rather than having a proper beginning, middle and end like a story. Let it come out with the same sort of glorious muddled format as it originally had when you were living it. You may well find at this stage that musings on the event (what you should/should not have said, for example) will interrupt the narrative flow. Leave this kind of writing until a later stage. Writing is endlessly plastic and can be altered and tidied up later, before anyone else has to make sense of it or, embarrassingly, read your innermost feelings.

Then when you have finished your first dash:

1. Re-read all (including the six minutes free-intuitive) you have written with attention – for content rather than form. Be open to perceiving divergent connections – things previously perceived as separate or inappropriate together. Be open to such underlying links and to fresh understandings and awarenesses. Add in aspects you have missed out, or alter anything.
2. Return to fill out the narrative. You may want to check that the observation is sufficiently detailed – perhaps smells and sounds as well as what things looked like. You may want to tell about time of year, discomforts, intuitions, the actual words people used – in speech marks rather than reported speech. *Everything* which occurs to you is significant.
3. Share it with another if this seems appropriate. They may suggest things you haven't thought of and help you to take the reflection deeper. And set the problem in a wider context. A note of warning: select your reader and sharer with care. Do not automatically choose the seemingly obvious one. For example, your marriage partner might be a very wrong one.

This writing may be done for a group set up for the purpose. The value of doing this with a group is that it is possible to share problematic material which would normally be felt to be too threatening to expose to the possible ridicule or censure of others. Yet instead of loss of face, there comes from the other members of the group a capping with similar experiences, a compassionate understanding, and an offer of support in creating a strategy for future action built on experience (see also Chapter Nine).

Reflecting in this fashion can open the writer to feel uncertain about issues they had thought they felt certain about. This uncertainty is one of the indications that very real change is taking place. Change cannot happen without a degree of discomfort accompanied by a sense of vulnerability. Try and stay with this; it is a vital stage – write your way through it; accept help from your group if you belong to one.

I run groups for health workers who have to cope with the sticky end of life every day of their working lives. And it's stressful, requiring life-and-death decisions. Moira Brimacombe (1996) and Tom Heller (1997) (who wrote the quotes at the beginning of this and Chapter Nine) are both members of my Reflections in Writing for GPs continuing medical education group. The other groups I refer to mostly in this chapter are a module on a BA in nursing and a module on a masters degree in primary care.

Here is an extract from the writing of a group member, Ann, a health visitor and experienced educator. She is reflecting on her writing about a disastrous session with a group of young disadvantaged mothers which she had facilitated many years ago:

> When I began to write this incident I started with a series of descriptive words. They mostly related to emotions, both mine and those I had felt from the other people involved in the incident. Then I began to write the story. As I began to write I was unsure about why I had chosen this incident. It had happened some years ago and I felt that as I had discussed the incident with a number of people at the time, that I had understood and analysed it sufficiently. Perhaps that was why I used it – perhaps I felt I had the answers ready to be neatly inserted into the story.
>
> Nevertheless I had been instructed to write about the first incident which came to mind and this was the one. As I wrote, the situation was re-created before me. I could see the room, feel the atmosphere, although parts of the sequence of events were hazy in detail. What I did remember and what hit me again was the emotional force of feeling, both those of the women in that room on that day, but more particularly my own feelings. As I wrote I couldn't believe how much there was to put down. I had to force myself to stop after all the others had finished. When I read the piece to the group I was overwhelmed by the emotional force and couldn't complete the reading. All those emotions. And I thought I had 'dealt with' this incident.
>
> I surprised myself with both the subject of what I wrote and the power of emotions it provoked. I hadn't realised I had so many unresolved feelings about the incident despite having talked about it to others many times. On reflection I feel that Gillie is right: there is something in the writing that gives another dimension. Seeing the words on the page gives an added intensity to the power of the feelings. There was a lot of honesty in the group this week, although some people understandably chose to use a far less problematic incident than others. I feel I have learned a lot from hearing the others in the group talk through their incidents ...
>
> (Six weeks later) I can see that I had still not been able to put this incident behind me and therefore was cross with others for trying to help me to do that. I feel rather embarrassed now by my reactions to the group. It was, of course, not about them but about me ... I can now

forgive myself for this incident, understand it and accept that everyone gets it wrong sometimes.

(Ann)

Lynn Longmuir, a midwife, wrote a heartfelt account of visiting an extremely distressed mother who had consulted her GP as her week-old baby had cried a great deal in the night (this mother was not Lynn's client; the midwife who normally attended was off duty). The GP had informed her that she was 'starving her baby' and that clearly her milk had dried up because her breasts weren't 'squirting milk' all the time! Lynn, restraining her fury when responding to the mother, assured her that 'a starving baby does not put on eight ounces in weight in only four days', that colic is extremely common and that if there was a problem with poor weight pattern, 'the midwives would have been the first to inform her'. Lynn did not keep her anger back on the page, using several-four letter words. She clearly did not feel she had any right to tackle the doctor (partly because he was not the GP with whom she usually worked), however much she would have liked to do so, but used the writing not only to vent her feelings but also to explore the rights and wrongs of the situation.

Developing the reflective writing

Writing such a piece is illuminating and helps the writer move onwards and outwards from a stuck situation. Rewriting the same episode – writing a companion story – can be even more enlightening. Here are a few suggestions for how this can be done:

- ask someone else who was there to write about it and note the differences
- write the story from the point of view of one of the other characters
- write from the point of view of the opposite gender to your own
- write a commentary, or ask another to write one, either as yourself or as one of the characters
- retell the story with a different ending or focus, for example both parties experiencing a positive result (see Elaine's writing below)
- write what a character is thinking at a particular moment
- write a diary entry for a character

- rewrite the story in a different style/genre – a newspaper article/fairy story/narrative poem/children's story …
- rewrite the story with the focus of control/power altered
- interview a character from the story
- take a character who's just left the action; what might she/he be doing/thinking?
- write the next chapter
- you are a reporter, what questions would you like to ask the main character(s)?
- write a letter/transcribe a phone conversation from one character to another
- list the objects/colours in the story; are they significant?
- write a film/dustjacket blurb for the story
- explore the area that puzzles you
- continue the story six months/a year later; ask: what if?

The primary care group made a range of suggestions for re-storying every piece each of them wrote. Liz wrote hers again as a series of thought bubbles – thoughts which had not been expressed, and, therefore, not explored, in the original writing. Elaine wrote a depressing piece about an event which she felt she had handled badly and not helped the other person at all, but allowed herself to be manipulated. She rewrote it as a 'win: win' account – changing the picture of the events to show herself as having managed the occasion as well as she possibly could, while leaving the client still in a good position too:

> I was amazed at the reduction of anger when I wrote the win: win situation towards the client and myself. I was also struck by the lack of centrality of my position in the clinic compared to the wide complex circumstances of the client's life… Writing a *win: win* situation enormously reduced the overall anxiety and power which caused both myself and the client to OVERACT and OVER-REACT.

One of the most enlightening is to write from the other person's point of view (fictionally, of course). GPs and nurses have often rewritten an event as if through their patient's eyes. It helps them to understand the events and the patient's reactions. I well remember one midwife writing an absolutely furious and hurt account of a hospital birth which had taken place years before. She came back the following week, having rewritten the story as if she had been the mother, looking rather penitent, and certainly no longer angry and hurt. She didn't *know* exactly what had caused the mother to be so cantankerous but she made a jolly good guess. I suspect she was much more able from then on to empathise with the mother's point of view. Here is Juliet's writing, rewriting and reflection on the writings:

A meeting of the new Mental Health Magazine Management Committee

Handling D is very difficult – defusing the situation of choosing a title by putting it off is not going to work for very long. D says he has talked to lots of users and they all like it (his choice of a magazine title), can it just be because he bulldozes them? The black and ethnic minority groups do not like it …

S made me think about the way I was managing the group – I feel we are all learning together – but at the same time it is obviously my responsibility to produce the minutes and what we agreed as a group. I learned that it is useful to stand aside and listen when other people have an idea, which may be a very good one even in stressful circumstances where you are prepared for a verbal battering and feel you must not give way on an important point. It is hard to be open to suggestions from one reasonable person, without giving in to a verbal bully. D is very dominating in this group and I wonder what the others really think. If he gets a bee in his bonnet about something he won't let up on it, and he won't listen. He often prefaces his remarks with 'I don't want you to take this the wrong way but …', which makes me edgy before he gets to the difficult bit.

D's point of view (possibly!)

… I like the idea of a user-led mental health newsletter, but I don't want any participation by health service professionals. It should be just for us; it's such a brilliant group and doing so well … It should have been called UP YOURS IN MENTAL HEALTH, which is what I originally wanted, and now I have thought of three more titles and every time I think of something, the professionals just tell me I can't have it …

I want a proper training course as well … to tell us how to run a newsletter and then we can do it without any help. Then we can get jobs on *The Star.*

(My point of view again) Some weeks later …

> At the last management group meeting D asked me how to handle a very difficult group member he had! What a contrast with how I felt at the beginning…
>
> I think the way I used to feel about D stems from a feeling of inadequacy in handling the situation, and therefore of holding it in very tight because otherwise it feels as though it will spin out of control. Now I am more confident in my dealings with the group and they have come to trust me, at least partially … I am sure I shall have lots more difficulties with this group as we set up the newsletter, but I feel much more confident of my ability to solve the problems. The course has made a real difference here – I had no idea about any of it, and had never worked with this sort of group when I wrote a business plan last summer, and I don't believe I could have done it without the learning opportunities that I have been given.
>
> (Juliet)

Here is Ann with a final comment:

> The writing has been a real eye-opener for me … The very act of writing down an incident makes you reconsider what was really happening. Further sharing of that writing leads you to exercise further the reality of what is described. The suggestions about re-writing pieces from other angles then gives another dimension and views of their 'reality'.

This chapter covers an array of thoroughly practical suggestions for altering your life by writing. So often when I go and give a talk or run a workshop, people say enthusiastically afterwards: 'Oh I thought it would all be writing poems about flowers and things. This is practical: I can use this!' The next chapter is just as down-to-earth and concerns how to make the best use of a group – whether as a facilitator or member.

CHAPTER NINE

Writing and Groups

Laugh and Cry with Each Other

> I felt like I'd been given something – real parts of other people.
>
> (Liz)

> Somehow the process of being part of the reflective writing group has helped me to dig down to new layers of depth and understanding within myself. It has been a journey rather like an archaeological exploration through ancient layers of protective and professional gubbins. I knew there was something stirring deep down, but never gave myself the time, or quite found the mechanism to bring it into the light of day.
>
> (Tom Heller 1997, p.29)

> Reflection is a real key to change, but facilitating good reflective learning experiences is probably more difficult than many anticipate.
>
> (Ann)

Relating to a piece of paper and a pencil on one's own can be lonely, frustrating at times, puzzling even, or become unproductive. Mixing the solitary activity with a bit of being with like-minded others will be perfect for some. Bramley apples are good for you; mixing them with brown sugar and putting them under crumble to eat warm and gooey with yoghurt or custard is even better – for your soul as well as your insides. A therapeutic writing group can provide a trusted ongoing forum for the sharing of writings, hopes, fears, ideas, anticipations, tears, laughter...

We learn from our tutors, teachers and lecturers; we learn far more from our peers – colleagues, relatives, lovers, friends and those with like interests. As Catherine Byron makes clear at the end of this chapter, it was the writing of one student, and her response to that writing, which enabled an understanding 'of what writing is about' for the other members of that group. The response of others to our own writings can also help us with what our writing is trying to tell us. Robert Hamberger, in Chapter Fourteen, describes his poetry as telling him things about himself he didn't know. The group with whom he shared his writing could sense the presence of deep problems, and were able to be tacitly supportive.

A group needs to be set up and facilitated with care, however. Writing in this way, and sharing it, can be deeply personal – feelings and emotions can be raw and exposed. This kind of writing brings out confidences which are only drawn forth by therapeutic or counselling processes. So the group needs to be handled as a therapeutic group: both the writings and the writers need to be treated right for it to work right. The guidelines below are the result of therapeutic and teaching experience, and many years of trial and error. A clear understanding of the way the group might work is as useful for the group leader as it is for the group member. Those in either role want everyone to gain as much from the group as possible.

A closed group, that is a group with the same members at each meeting (allowing for occasional absences of course), will be the most effective. The group will test the boundaries during the first few sessions and decide how they wish to function and what it is they wish to do. If you are the facilitator, it is your job to guide them in this process. Trust, respect and confidence will increase in each meeting, if the ingredients are right and mixed carefully.

Groups have ends as well as beginnings, however, and will not continue to get better and better; the duration will vary for different groups. One way of handling this is to set a time limit, say six sessions, review the situation at the end of that and decide on a further six, if appropriate.

Function of the group

A therapeutic writing group exists to support the writers in their own personal explorations and expressions. A group can gently lead a writer to understand the import of their own writing more clearly; to think of fresh writing avenues to try; enable them to discuss issues with involved and caring others who are on similar voyages themselves, yet are 'disinterested' (are not family, personal friends or other 'interested' parties). A group can also reinforce the self-confidence and self-esteem which writing tends to bring ('what a lovely piece of writing' or 'you've moved on such a long way since you joined') and help a writer out of the occasional inevitable bog of depression and lost way.

The group members need to be clear before they start, more or less what they are there for. To an extent, of course, the group will (and should) be organic: develop its own specific working aims, objectives, patterns and relationships over time. But clarity about the basic underlying aim from the start is vital. A great deal of hassle, disappointment and, possibly, pain is avoided by having a fairly clear idea of an aim and some objectives, as well as the extent to which group members are expected to create the agenda themselves.

Deciding what the group is NOT can be useful. It is not:

- a writers' workshop in which writings are constructively criticised in order to help the writer improve the text (story/poem/etc) with publication in mind. The focus is on the form; the content of the writing is not considered in such a forum
- a professional development group, where the content of the writing is analysed to help the writer work more effectively or information/experience is exchanged
- a chat group where the writings are read out and the response is such as: 'how nice, now that reminds me how my Auntie Gwen used to...'

Principles

Respect, shared responsibility, confidence and confidentiality are vital cornerstones (I will return to confidentiality under 'ground rules'). There will be a wide range of different abilities, interests and confidence in the group, as well as possibly nationality, ages, types of social background and both sexes. Respecting these, and respecting the contributions of everyone, is vital and will ensure that the group will gain from variety. Some people readily talk a lot, others are naturally quiet; encouraging a balance of contribution is also important.

I often think of a group as being like a warm island in a stormy sea. The members arrive out of the wind and dark, clutching their precious papers; they smile tentatively and shyly at each other, wrap their chilled hands around a cup of tea and settle into a circle with their papers between them. If the group members can take each other as they experience them within the closed social system of the group, if they can relate to and support each other through a discussion of the writing without seeking to question beyond the boundaries of that writing, then the group can be powerfully facilitative.

It is this last which helps the members to lay bare some of their most secret places to each other. They are not actually exposing themselves, but their writing. This is the vital difference from a group which relies on talking rather than writing. They will have had time to write, re-read and think about the sharing of that writing before they do so. I always ask people to behave as if each writing was a fiction. The discussion will then remain relatively safely focused on the writing rather than on the hinterland of the account. Questions like 'did they *really*? …'; 'And what happened next?…'; 'Why did you perceive your mother like that?…' can lead the writer to say far more than they intended when they brought the piece.

If the writing is fiction, there isn't a 'really', nor is there a 'what happened next': characters don't walk beyond the page and do anything. Occasionally, in my experience, a question will be asked which strays beyond this rule but is accompanied by such as: 'I'm going to ask you this; please don't answer if you don't want to but I think it would help.' A group will always respect a 'no' answer, just as they will respect a decision not to read a piece because it feels too personal.

Group management

Groups don't happen, they have to be created and nurtured. These things are vital:

- Everyone knowing everyone's name from the start. Beginning the first session with a game to learn names is a good icebreaker. Beginning the second session with a name check is useful. I often just ask those who don't know a name to ask across the circle – it's quick and leads to laughter and companionship, rather than embarrassment, as we are all doing it at once.
- A formative evaluation at the end of each session. This is a simple check to see if members are getting what they want from the group or have any other ideas.
- Timing is vital. Each member must have a share of time for their piece: running out of time so one writer takes their piece home unread could be disastrous. The session must begin and end when expected: this time boundary helps create the sense of a safe island.
- The silent as well as the dominant members need to be respected. If everyone takes a responsibility for the running of the group,

they will attempt to ensure the drawing out of the quiet ones and the restraint of the voluble.

- Listening to, commenting on, and eliciting comments on the writings of others is a skill to be learned. I have been told by group members that this can take several sessions to begin to feel confident. Other chapters of this book offer ways of looking at, and extending, writing, any of which can be suggested in a group. Learning how to take the comments and discussions of others, about one's own work, equally needs practice. People, to begin with, do not know what to expect. I have often been asked: 'now are you going to psychoanalyse me?', the writer expecting to be a passive recipient of my judgement. Quite the opposite: it is the role of the group, and the facilitator, to support the writer to extend and clarify their *own* ideas about themselves, not to offer their views.
- Who comments first, and when, after a piece is read? In my groups it is never me – as the leader I can so easily dominate, and always have quite enough to say about a piece, so I speak after everyone else. I ask for someone to respond quickly: waiting after you have read can be an agonising time – seconds seem like hours – while you imagine everyone thinks your writing is awful and you are a pig.
- Arrangement of furniture affects a group. Will you have the security of a table between you? King Arthur's idea of sitting in a circle helps everyone to feel equal. Having just the right number of chairs for everyone makes the group feel complete. If fewer people arrive than expected, it is worth removing the unneeded chairs, though if the group is a strong, gathered, trusting one, leaving the chair of the absent member can retain a sense of their presence within the group. I had a lovely experience of this with a group of primary healthcare workers (health visitors, GPs, nurses, etc). Jenny was expected, but not present, so we left her chair. The group referred to her empty chair as if she was there. Then, when she came in apologetically late, slipping into her waiting chair was a warm and wanted experience.
- Ground rules. This deserves a section all of its own.

Ground rules

A sense of the group's confidentiality fosters the development of trust, of this being a safe forum. Belonging to such a group, hearing stuff from the innermost selves of others, is a privilege and must be treated as such. The writings belong to the writers and the discussions to the group, neither should be shared outside the group without express permission.

A sense of the group's boundaries helps create confidence that probing questions will not be asked in order to extend the information given in the writing. The viewing of each writing as a fiction is useful here. Some groups create further boundaries for themselves; many professional groups with which I work, for example, choose only to write about, and discuss, work issues. I always create a further boundary by outlawing apologies: many want to point out that they know their writing is not a perfect poem/story because they are nervous at exposing their creation (I am among the worst for this). Instituting an imaginary £5 fine for any apology about a writing defuses this effectively and humorously.

This is the handout I sometimes give groups about ground rules:

Workshop guidelines

This writing will have been expressive
(of something the writer knows they feel or think),
and explorative (using the process of writing to find out
what the writer feels, or to recall forgotten memories).

We will be sharing this writing in an open questioning way,
supporting the writer in their search to express and explore.
This might mean responding to other writers by:

Helping draw out related, underlying themes
of concern to the writer and the group
sharing from one's own appropriate experience
suggesting future directions.

While you are listening
be formulating your discussion queries/points
which will probably be provisional, and tentative,
and might be:

- something you like
- something the writer could develop, or grasp more closely
- a question
- a suggestion
- a comment on connections, themes, issues ...
- a response from your own experience.

A thoughtful silence often arises after a piece has been read.
But someone must break the silence.
If it lasts too long
it can prove unnerving
to the waiting writer.

Everyone's thoughts are of value
yours *and* theirs must be heard.

When you read you may feel hesitant.
The group will not perceive your writing's imperfections as you do. They will be interested and involved.

Remember
The discussion and each writing belongs within, and is confidential to the group, and must not be shared elsewhere without permission.

The use of fiction preserves confidentiality
even if some pieces appear to be true.
We will maintain the fiction that it is fiction.
It is up to the writer to share as much as they wish.

Content

What is the group going to do? There are two basic things: to discuss writing which has already been written; and to generate new writing. The former will clearly always be undertaken and has been discussed; the latter sometimes. It can be wonderful to write together in a group, though some can find it threatening.

Writing here and now on a set topic can be liberating: things can really happen in such a workshop. Creative writers tend to be addicted to these. I must have run hundreds and participated in a fair few exciting experiences. There are so many creatively facilitative stimuli to use with a group, far more than I have been able to include in this book. Care is needed to tailor the stimulus to the sensitivities of the group. A group of nurses coming together for a dayschool should not be asked to write about 'The worst experience of my life', for example. But 'A turning point' or 'A person who influenced me beneficially' can be excellent.

When we write during the group, I always begin with the six-minute free-intuitive writing exercise detailed in Chapter Three. I do, however, stress that this writing is NOT for reading out – this gives permission to write anything. The exercise puts something on the white space of the paper, captures fleeting inspirations and stores those distracting thoughts (horrible traffic getting here/what shall we eat tonight?). I then move onto a specific stimulus and give time for re-reading, altering, making connections (see the same part of Chapter Three).

People must be given warning that they will be asked if they would like to read some of their writing to the group, but also told they can opt not to read anything or only a tiny bit if the writing is very personal. Ample time must be given for them to read their writing to themselves, make additions, deletions, alterations and decisions of how much or little they wish to share with the group before they are asked to read their writing out.

Being a facilitator

I cannot do better than give you the thoughts of Beth Edge, an experienced facilitator:

Getting the feel of it

Tick the correct statement:

☐ The best workshops are well-prepared.

☐ The best workshops are spontaneous.

If you ticked both, then you know what it's all about. If you think they contradict each other, then read on.

Over the past twenty years I have led writing workshops for all ages and types, from infants (who couldn't write yet but certainly knew how to put words together), to senior citizens. Along the way I have been into all kinds of institutions, including prisons, and not once have I gone in unprepared. Yet the truth is that I hardly every use my preparation.

The first, and most important thing, is to get the feeling of the group. You need to know what will work for them, and invariably it will not be what you thought was necessary for the fantasy group you had postulated while preparing.

How do you do this? Simply open your mind, forget about yourself and think about them. find out what it is they need, and then give them a practical exercise to do, preferably where they can work together in a supportive, not competitive way. Watch what happens and answer the questions that come out of it. It goes without saying that you should take part in the exercise yourself.

Remember, always, how easy it is to demolish confidence, and how difficult it is to build. Encouragement is the key word. Find the good in the writing, and help the writers to see for themselves where they can go from there. Show them how to help each other. However much you think you know about writing, never lecture. Draw conclusions out of the group, and answer their questions if you can. Be prepared to learn a few things yourself.

So, you may be asking, why bother with preparation? There are lots of reasons. One is, that in preparing work you clarify your own thinking. Another is that if you don't prepare, you are likely to waffle, and there is always the million to one chance that your group will not respond. That won't happen, but what if it did!

My personal reason is that I need a crutch! I need it to help me walk into a room full of strangers. It's a great feeling to realise that, once again, I can throw my crutch away because I am being supported by friends.

(Beth Edge)

Housekeeping

These small details are much more important than one might think:

- Numbers: the size affects the group dynamic considerably. I think eight is a lovely number; twelve is the maximum I would take for this purpose; four is too few because there will be times, especially in winter, when one or two may be unable to attend.
- Funds: who pays what, when, how, how much, to whom?
- Venue: is it the right one?
- Coffee time: important because people get to know each other. But when, where, how, how long, who pays, and how much?
- Word processors/copying: libraries have these, some shops are cheaper; sharing advice is really useful.

Publication and reading

A group anthology of shareable redrafted pieces, which can be given to family and friends, can be a wonderful affirmation. A sense that these booklets should reach a wider public, or that writings could be published nationally, is NOT useful for this kind of writing, however – it would force a self-conscious hothouse type of writing (I return to this in Chapter Fourteen). An informal reading to the rest of the patients and staff in a hospice day-unit, for example, could be a heart-warming occasion also.

Some examples

Here are three examples of groups to give an idea of different ways of working. The first is from a member of a Reflective Writing Course for Nurses, a BA module. They had discussed euthanasia at some length as a result of some of their writings. Anna Stanford recorded her response to both the writing, and the discussion which followed, in her portfolio log:

> I'm not very comfortable being present during this discussion. This surprises me, my personal feelings overriding my professional ones.
>
> It has evoked memories of a close relative's painful death over eight years ago. What surprises me is that I thought I had worked through the grief process but what has probably been more difficult to deal with is the consequences of death on the family which triggered major changes to my life. The discussion exposed a vulnerable part of me that I thought

I had dealt with but maybe the very painful feelings have just been suppressed waiting to be acknowledged and accepted so allowing me to move on with my life.

I have very vivid memories of my father-in-law's painful death from bone cancer and the thin line between pain control and euthanasia … As the 'nurse' the family looked to me to make decisions and take responsibility about his care … [He] did appear to have a peaceful death but I still worry that it could have been managed with more compassion and dignity.

As the discussion carries on around me I'm conscious that I'm the only one who hasn't contributed but no one seems to notice as it's a subject that all the group without exception feel strongly about.

I remember as a junior staff nurse on night duty having a moribund child wrapped in a blanket, thrust into my arms. This was a child with severe physical and mental disabilities who had deteriorated … A junior doctor and I worked on the child only thinking about saving her life, and she recovered. I'll never forget the father's relief and joy at seeing his daughter respond and the scepticism of the senior medical and nursing staff as to whether we felt we had taken the correct course of action. I still have no doubt that we did.

This is a very personal reflection and I am reminded that reflection if not dealt with a degree of empathy could have the potential to be destructive. A bit like lighting the fuse and missing the fireworks. It was obvious to me only when listening to the group discussion that I had not in fact dealt with certain experiences as well as I thought I had. I was interested that just by highlighting this has helped me to come to terms with and accept the effects of the grieving process on the family relationships.

(Anna Stanford)

The next is an example of how *not* to lead a group, how *not* to respond to a group member, from Stephen Wade, an English lecturer who runs creative writing classes:

Never rubbed out a line

The problem was not with .Trevor's imagination; it was not his enthusiasm. With Trevor, it was the fact that no-one could ever read a word of what he had written. I can laugh about it now, but on our first meeting I was, of course, very polite and did what no tutor should ever do – pretend that something is fine, when quite clearly a lot is very wrong.

You see, I waffled on about the importance of letting your imagination go. I set a free exercise as an ice-breaker. We brainstormed, then people went away suitably inspired. They returned with a page or so of prose and the keen ones read aloud. Trevor was a keen one, alas. He read a chaotic, surreal account of what was probably a trip to another planet, but we were not sure. It could have been Wigan or Nether Wollop. Let's just say it was vaguely classified as science fiction/fantasy.

But the shock came when he handed me the piece to look at. It was a mixture of some oriental script and psychobabble from beyond the Internet. A little voice inside me said, 'Tell him you can't read it' but another very stupid voice argued against it as I smiled, said how good it was and hoped he would go. I thought that was the end of it.

Then, a few days later, the saga of Nagakapkin the Grindod appeared. At least, that's what it seemed to say. This lasted for three instalments, until I gave in to the voice of reason. Diplomatic to the last, I gave it all back and said my migraine prevented me from reading any more.

(Stephen Wade)

And here is an excellent example of tutoring, from Catherine Byron (see also Chapters Seven (poetry) and Fourteen), another lecturer, writing about her English BA undergraduate group:

Opening trapdoors without warning

When I run poetry workshops, I always prefer the ones that aren't one-offs. If I have a series of meetings in prospect, or a whole five days such as an Arvon residential course (see below), I feel much happier doing what I do best: creating an initial, brief sense of security, and then dropping the writers into a messy chaos. I want to help each of them to tap into their own teeming material, to let a bucket down into the brew of memory, obsession and association that is so efficiently lidded over in everyday life. I choose my stimuli and writing 'games' with this prime intention. But in a one-off session this approach would be too risky.

If I induce what I intend to be a fertile chaos, I run the risk that individuals will haul up shocking material in their bucket that will be hard to deal with in the context of a writing class, especially one that will finish in an hour's time, with no follow-up. Memories of deaths and other losses, forgotten incidents of violence and abuse: in the context of a longer group-life, such discoveries can not only be taken forward in terms of writing – the prime purpose of my being there, after all – but the growing strength of the group, the intensity and generosity of sharing that can develop, will enrich everyone in it, and support the wounded sharer in particular.

Last year I gave my Introduction to Writing students one of my favourite starting points. It was our third meeting in a thirteen-week course. I told them to close their eyes, and be ready to receive an object I would place in their hands. They were to explore it with touch, smell, even taste if they so desired, but were not to look at it. After they had held their objects for about three minutes, I collected and carefully concealed them, before telling the students to open their eyes and, in continued silence, to record the memories, journeys and/or associations that their object had evoked. My bag of objects is the fruit of years of beach- and skip-combing, and none is easy to name unseen. Many are impossible to name even when seen. Immediate identification hampers the imaginative interaction I am after. Year after year I am astonished by the shapeshifting abilities of the same object held by different hands. On this day, a stone that has previously become the rubber grip on a racing bike's handlebar, or a lump of beeswax after the honey has been extracted in granny's kitchen, or numerous other incarnations, became a whole shingle beach for one young woman. As she talked about the place to which the stone had taken her, she suddenly burst into tears.

'We went there every summer, but this was the last time we were a family. My dad died that September.' She then rushed from the room, and disappeared into the maze of corridors and doors.

I had to think fast. Never had a workshop member actually run away before! And the group left behind were very distressed. I decided to talk calmly with them about what had happened – in terms of writing. Writing was risky, I told them, and needed to be if it was going to be any good. And that applied as much to light verse as it did to literary fiction. I explained to them, more explicitly than I would otherwise have done at that stage of the course, what I was trying to do with such open-ended stimuli. I told them how differently the same object works on the individual imagination, and about her stone's previous lives as a handlebar and a lump of wax. Some of them spoke about her courage, or asked me for clarifications, but they were mainly silent. Eventually I felt I could leave them for a few minutes, and gave them a simple writing task. I didn't want them to leave the group's sad but singular circle, not yet.

I was scared that the girl would be far away by this time, but no, she was coming out of the loos just a corridor away. She was still sobbing, but she said it was shame rather than grief that was upsetting her. She felt that everyone in that room would laugh at her, despise her, for her breakdown and flight. I tried to reassure her that this was not any part of the reactions of the others, that they were full of compassion and admiration. And I talked to her, as soon as I could, about practicalities. What did she want to do next? Come back straightaway into the welcome that I assured her she would get from the group? Leave it until the following week? I arranged an informal tutorial with her one-to-one later in the week. Then we went back in together, she quietly collected her things and left, and I resumed the class with the rest of the group.

This young woman did have the courage to return the following week. And she used the rest of the writing course to explore that long-suppressed show of grief for her father – as well as other preoccupations, of course. At thirteen, it had not been possible to grieve openly: she had been expected to be 'brave', so for her the outcome was clearly therapeutic. But when I read the required reflective 500-word piece on what the students felt they had learned about their own writing processes and practice in the end-of-course portfolios, I was astonished to see how therapeutic it had been for several of the others too.

Not only had this whole group been creatively and humanly supportive to the student who had broken down, in the weeks that followed, but her testimony had had an extraordinary effect on their own writing. Two said they too had lost parents at a young age, and that their unseen objects had dropped them back, like her, into remembering that grief, but they had not felt able to speak about it then, or later. They wrote wonderful pieces that in an astonishing variety of ways came out of their complex responses to her disclosure. Another wrote about imagining such a bereavement. This narrative was, like hers, set on a shingle beach, but in other respects the scenario was entirely different. Nearly every student referred, in their reflective commentary, to that painful but illuminating moment in the third workshop, and said that it had changed their understanding of what writing is about.

(Catherine Byron)

Many years ago I was privileged to be a member of one of these workshops of Catherine's. And I have collected my own drawerful of odd objects now. The last time I used them, at a taster therapeutic writing group, in much the way described above (only preceded by the six-minute free-writing exercise and another simple confidence-building one – probably similar to the warm-ups Catherine used), a group member ran away crying part way through reading her writing to the rest of the group. She did come straight back, however, and finished reading her piece. This painfully honest piece deeply affected the whole group (who had all written moving but much safer pieces) and helped them to see, as nothing I could have said or done could, what writing can do.

There are few places where one can join a therapeutic writing group in Britain, unfortunately. But there are writing groups or classes where this is undoubtedly an aspect of the proceedings. The Arvon Foundation mentioned by Catherine is one such. Five-day intensive residential courses are run for 16 people with established writers as tutors. The address is in the Appendix.

In a group we listen intently, laugh or cry at each other's stories. Everyone comes thinking only writers, academics or very clever people can write. They go home clutching a new knowledge to themselves – they can write vivid accounts. These stories have not only created intense interest and response from the rest of the group but have opened up fresh avenues of thinking and feeling, fresh experiences. 'Creating and sharing writing seems to improve and increase self-disclosure, self-actualising behaviours, and self-acceptance of feelings and experience ... A focus on writing in a group therapy environment may elicit new and significant insights and feelings that may not surface through other therapeutic modalities' (Wenz and McWhirter 1990, p.38). Philip Lyons runs writing groups for people with mental problems and thinks belonging to an effective group, and relating to others through writing, is vital: 'Writing is one of the ways by which we become human. And being human means being in relation with others' (1997, p.4). Writing and belonging to a writing group is not a pastime or even merely a therapy, it is a way of life.

CHAPTER TEN

Writing Out Trauma

A Bobble Hat, a Pair of Jeans and Grandad

Race
(for Janna)

This girl will run against the odds.

Her child's heart lost control of counts
it oozed, not pumped;
it gave no promises
of seeping into adulthood
or anything like that.

She went in her nurse's uniform
with her Ladybird book of Florence Nightingale
and her grandma's real nurse watch
measuring last moments
how well we played that game
my girl and I.

Someone took me inside the tent where
she was held between air and nothing
on webs as fine as breath,
cradled in nothing
but the flow of oxygen and blood
nothing more,
nothing to say the heart of her still lived,
nothing in all that silence save
the slow sucked gasp she gave
and the screen to chart her passage back to life.

Now she practises sprint starts
and each burst is a birth
a charge of sap and strength
that flows in the living swing of her hair
and in the mysterious machinery of her limbs.

(Berlie Doherty 1993, p.40)

It was about half past eight on a summer's evening that tragedy changed our lives. On Thursday, 14 August, 1969, my husband and I were in the garden of our Hertfordshire home, collecting washing from the line. To this day, as I gather in sweet smelling clothes, I am transported back to the moment when I heard my daughter Hilary's frightened call that two policemen were at the door.

(Myrtle Yeoman 1995, p.17)

Myrtle Yeoman's autobiographical book (1995) details how she gave over her life to care for and promote the rehabilitation of her son who was brain-damaged in a motor bike accident. He recovered much of his mental and physical powers, despite medical predictions, and lived for fourteen years.

Writing can be invaluable in supporting sufferers of extreme trauma, whether at the time (as in the second and third of the accounts below) or on reflection later (as in the first account below). The three accounts are: a fictional story by myself, the true story of a poem by Averil Stedeford, and a piece about the work of Gyll Marples and her family.

Just a bobble hat:
The story of a 'writing as therapy' counselling training workshop

Extract from Jo's journal, Friday 16 February

Story telling is what counselling is all about. The stories aren't always expressed in words – sometimes they're physical, sometimes painted or in coloured mosaics, even occasionally in grunts, shouts and screams. The difference between these stories and the ones we heard at our mother's knee is that they don't necessarily have proper beginnings, endings or even middles and certainly all too often stop with the characters not living happily ever after.

But we want so much to make them work as stories, to reach some sort of an ending, even if it has to be one of acceptance rather than sailing off into the sunset. That is why we come to counselling to have a go at dealing with some of this unfinished business. Even so, what we tell are stories – models of our experience; and it's important to recognise them as such.

We all write as part of our daily lives, even if only reports and lists. But somehow we have lost our ownership of the writing of stories in this age of expertise. It's not true that only writers can write. There are so many ways of discovering for ourselves the revealing and self-illuminating power of writing journals, scrapbooks, specific lists of vital things, stream-of-consciousness wanderings, dream notebooks, unsendable letters and their replies from the person within, and so on.

Writing is more powerful than speech or thought for, among others, three reasons: the writing process draws on a deeper personal well, perhaps because it is solitary yet connective and self-absorbed; writing can be staged – the first drafts being formless and sometimes seemingly senseless; a piece of writing has a life of its own and the writer, and her colleagues if she chooses, can interact with it – continuing the creative, critical process indefinitely.

That should cover the introduction to the day-workshop – enough for me to say, I think. The afternoon will be for developing those ideas and looking at strategies for building them into therapy, as a group. In the morning we'll have a go at some writing ourselves – to experience the process first hand. What about a stimulus for the writing – something with enough lightness, as well as potential for group work, yet something that can be taken much deeper if anyone wants to go that way? I think I'll take the big bag of hats – see where they take us. It needs a careful introduction though.

The participants will all be psychiatric hospital staff. The demandingness of their professional life tends to make them protect themselves so that they aren't open to very much. But the writing could still bring up painful things, so it'll have to be handled sensitively. Also they'll feel strange being the participants, and doing what I suggest. I hope they find release from their habitual roles, rather than this being a difficulty.

Why do I run these workshops? In so many ways I want the members to explore and discover something in themselves, for themselves, as well as find out that writing is a releasing and joyful tool in counselling. I'll be in no position to help with whatever personal material comes up. I must remember to double check at the beginning of the day that they have their own support system and triple check at the end that I'm leaving them with each other and their supervisors.

Why do I do this? What right have I to bring a workshop that I know will uncover sticky stuff for some? But I've been so grateful for what therapists have done for me, in the past. Yes, I have. But I'm not them, I'm only me.

Clear boundaries. Enough security, but not too much or nothing will happen. Not too much spotlight on anyone – this isn't a therapy group but a training day. Respect, but support. What a juggling act. Why do I do this?

Extract from Jo's journal, Monday 19 February

Goodness knows. Was it illuminating, facilitative, or just plain exhausting? Terrifying being in that vast hospital – took me right back to being wheeled around that night in confused pain all those years ago, with a drip by side, having no idea where I was or why. That's what *my* writing was about – not about hats!

What do Janice, silent Harry and the others feel about it all now? What do I think and feel? Quite a lot, but I'm not sure what!

Well, they wrote creatively in order to reach a clearer understanding about themselves and their situation. Perhaps I can do the same with my jumble of experiences from yesterday. Writing certainly does get to the heart of the matter in a way talking doesn't seem to. It also seems to uncover tricky thoughts, feelings and memories.

Also, I might want to share this next writing with others – that might help me further clarify what the issues are for me. If I write in fiction I won't have to worry about what Janice and the others feel about me writing about them – no problem of confidentiality. I'll use their real names for the draft, just for myself. Anyway, I'd probably get bogged down and bored with myself writing about the day as an extended case study – that wouldn't help at all. If I write it as a fiction from Janice's point of view rather than my own, I might begin to understand how it might have been for her. I will start with the writing she did during the session, and then carry on with my story from there:

Janice's writing

'Watch.'

She tipped the bowl with its pregnant mound of glistening proved dough upside down above the table top. Slowly the bread belly extended, tearing against the sides of the earthenware bowl. It began to slip, long strands pulling away until it fell, thud, on the table. The little boy gasped. His eyes, their whites blue-white, were wide open, his mouth an O.

He wasn't interested in the blob of dough gradually settling and creeping on the table. He'd been called to watch too often for that. His gaze was on the inside of the bowl where the rest of the dough still clung. The upended bottom and sides of the bowl had become a cave. The sticky dough hung down in threads and tendrils, light and airy from the action of the yeast.

'It's a fairy castle, Tommy. Can you see them flying there?'

She glanced down at the top of his head, hair springing into titian curls from his pale scalp. She could just see one sock, as ever, wrinkling above his shoe.

He put his head on one side, forehead creased, his skin so translucent she could almost see him thinking. He looked right up at her and made a long statement, all in incomprehensible toddler scribble. He paused on the upturn of a question mark, clearly waiting for her reply.

Jo's story of the workshop

The reader stopped and reached for her handkerchief, shoulders shaking. The circle of faces around the room were attentive, holding this weeping woman. Her neighbour put her hand over hers and held it still.

'I, I'm sorry. I can't carry on. He ... he died, you see – meningitis. He had a little bobble hat just like this, only smaller of course.'

There was another pause as she gasped for breath, then a comforting murmur from a group member was taken up by the tutor, Jo.

'You're all right. Don't worry. You've shared something really important with us. We feel honoured you have, thank you.'

But Janice's mind was confused between the old memories flooding back and her shame at having broken down in front of the group. Her thoughts jangled. How did I come to write such a thing? Why did I come on this course – I'm a psychiatric nurse, not a writer. Why on earth did just writing about a silly thing like a hat bring up all that? I can see why she, Jo the tutor, wanted us to write first and then talk afterwards about the ways in which writing can be therapeutic.

I'd forgotten all those little details of how Tommy looked. I thought all that had healed up – that I'd forgotten and moved on. I'll have to talk to Barry about it when I get home – wonder if he'll remember the little hat. I think I'll get all Tommy's clothes out again, tomorrow.

Her chest twitched again, but feeling the warm squeeze of Joan's hand on hers once more, she was jerked back to the present by Jo's voice.

'Thank you for telling us, Janice, and thank you for reading your story. I'm glad I heard it – but I can see it was really hard for you.' And then after a little while the group attention moved to listen to the next writer.

'Oh good,' Janice thought, 'nobody'll look at me any more, they'll all be listening to what Tim's written. I hope he doesn't mind if I don't, I'll ask if I can read his later.'

Extract from Jo's journal, Wednesday 21 February

Well, that wasn't really fiction! In fact, I've more or less told the story as it happened, and with the real names. Never mind, that's only what my students do most of the time. I expect I can redraft it more fictionally before I share it with anyone. I wonder if Janice has continued to write? I wonder how she is? I do hope that her partner and her supervisor support her so she can deal with some of the complexities of her grief and bereavement that started to come up on Saturday. I do find these day-schools so unsatisfactory and worrying in that way. If she is writing, I wish I could see it and talk to her. One of the problems of my role is having to let go all the time. I'll never know. Just hope.

Extracts from Janice's journal, Tuesday 20 February

Will the remains of this exercise book do? She said that what mattered was the writing of a diary, not what it was written in.

So here goes. It feels a bit daft sitting here in the bedroom, I'm glad no one can see me. She said no one need ever read what I've written – just as well.

Tommy, oh Tommy.

I'm not getting very far am I? I've only written that much then stopped for so long to cry again at the sight of his teddy, here on the bed beside me.

Start again. My teddy was called Cuddly. I cuddled him so much that he lost all his fur and I had to knit him a suit that covered him from eartips to over his leaking feet. Only his little black nose and beady eyes showed.

Though the nose was a replacement too, I'd embroidered it in wool. Poor Barry – when we first married – 'I'm not having that in my bed. It's either him or me.'

Tommy's rag. His teddy didn't really matter that much, but that old cloth nappy – trailed in all the dirt, one comer rubbing his nose as he sucked his thumb.

Why did it have to happen? Why my little Tommy? And I only had him. Joan has her three, Harry two – they show their photos, talk about their little sayings and exam successes. Tommy would have been … Would he? Could I have coped with everything as he grew up?

If only I hadn't taken him to that party. If only I'd called the doctor sooner. If only Barry'd …

Extract from Janice's journal, Thursday 22 February

Why did you have to bring all this up? Why, Jo? Everything was all right until you came along with your stupid writing idea and that bobble hat. I think you're an interfering manipulative cow and this ridiculous exercise book is going in the bin. So much for your bloody ideas.

Extract from Janice's journal, Monday 26 February

Teddy bears. Teddy bears everywhere. My dreams are littered with bears. They're mutilated, hanged, tied up, they've been mauled and mangled, savaged and half devoured. There was even one in the dustbin when I went to empty the bin. One on the butcher's slab when I went to buy the steak and kidney. It's eyes were oozing blood – crying blood. I waited to see if the butcher would bring his great cleaver down on it and sever an arm or a leg, or separate those eyes. He didn't – perhaps he was waiting until I went. I had to leave, I was blocking the shop and people wondered what I was waiting for.

Teddy bears. Every child that I pass is carrying one. One hand clutching a bear and the other clasped firmly and safely in its mother's hand. But these bears are smiling. Mine aren't. Some are grimacing as if they know something that I don't, something I'll eventually have to know.

Extract from Janice's journal, Wednesday 28 February

Today I went into Tommy's room. I haven't been there for months (years?). His teddy was lying on the pillow, Barry must've put it back. I picked it up and ripped it. I yanked out the stuffing and spewed it round the room. I shredded the skin and unpicked the embroidered claws with my nails. I ripped out the glass eyes and threw them down the toilet. They won't stare at me any more. They rattled as they went down. Not like real eyes. Real eyes are made of goo and jelly. They're not eyes that I want to look at any more. I want you Tommy. Not some remembrance of you.

Extract from Janice's journal, Thursday 1 March

Barry says I need help. He says I need more than you, diary; and him to talk to. I say I'll need more than the few days I've had off work. But I don't want a stranger. Not yet.

Extract from Janice's journal, Tuesday 27 March

Pages and pages of it. I had no idea I could write so much in only a little more than a month. You were right, Jo, when you said that anyone could write. Funny I didn't throw this book away when I was so angry.

Most of it's rubbish though, some of it unreadable. Funny though to think of the way it led me to see things differently – just writing them down as they came to me – in their red hot heat.

Extract from Janice's journal, Monday 2 April

At least I'm an aunt. Sally and Kate were so pleased to see me, I hope it wasn't just the sweets I took and stories I read. Perhaps there isn't enough time for cuddles and trips to the swing and bedtime reading now the new baby's on the way and everything to be thought of and done. I can't think why I haven't been there more often. Yes I can. I know exactly why I haven't wanted to see my sister so cosy and happy with her babies. I'm glad I went now though.

Extract from Janice's journal, Friday 9 November

Barry's agreed! Sally and Kate here for a whole week! I can't wait! Oh dear, what'll they want for their breakfast? What can I do to make it different yet homelike here? I do hope they'll be happy with us, but I'm not sure I know what children like best any more.

They might cry for their mum, especially at bedtime. I won't be the right person for that special time. I never will be that just right everyday yet special person for a little one again. How painful will it be remembering Tommy as I button up their coats? Perhaps I'll remember the wonderful bits of having Tommy as well.

Extract from Jo's journal, Monday 26 November

What a blaster to get in the post.

I never thought Janice would get in touch, let alone send me her writing.

When I started my journal entries about that session, I never thought she'd let me know what happened to her and all that grief. I'm so glad and grateful that she's let me in, wanted to share it all with me in this way.

I wonder if she's knitted Sally and Kate bobble hats, like she did for little Tommy?

* * * *

That whole story is fictional, using my experience of encouraging both those in distress, as well as their carers, to write, and training those carers to use writing with their clients and patients. *Just a Bobble Hat* was part of a series of writings, the writing of which was deeply therapeutic to me. Averil Stedeford has written this next account. It is completely true and follows the use of writing as a lifeline through tragedy.

The multipurpose poem by Averil Stedeford

Why does anyone write a poem? If it is successful it may become a work of art, but it may have many other functions too.

Nottingham five

They knew you
from your driving license.
No-one else could tell
who any was
and only one could scream
in that crushed wreck.

There were five,
you are alive,
but two are dead

At half-past five
a doorbell in the dark:
Policeman. Do you have a daughter?
Name Elizabeth?
The news is bad.
Go quickly, it is bad.

There were five,
she is alive
but two are dead

A rag-raid, round the pubs,
for charity.
Five in a mini
in the driving rain.

Head-on collision
with a heavy lorry.
Lucinda screamed and screamed
but no-one came
and four were silent.

There were five,
three are alive
but two are dead

I rinse the blood
and vomit
from your clothes.
Stripped off you,
I unroll them to reveal
more of the story.
Lumps of pizza,
bits of soggy crisp,
thirty-three p
falls into the sink.
How glad I am that
I can scrub your jeans,
not burn them.

You are alive,
but there were five
and two are dead.

This poem was written within forty-eight hours of the event it describes and was scarcely reworked after the initial hour or so of composition. It began to arrive in my mind while the jeans were being scrubbed, and gave words to the horror in which I found myself. It was the beginning of catharsis. A poem, because it involves discipline and structure, allows the expression of profound and almost intolerable emotion within a framework of control. I dare not collapse and be overwhelmed at that time when there was so much to be done, and yet was bursting with anxiety and grief. Writing the poem met the double need for expression and control.

The poem took me, and takes the reader, through the event to the first inkling of resolution; the first idea that there might be anything at all in this dire situation to be glad about. It provided a container for the pain and a pointer toward hope.

The use of repetition has an important function here. The appallingly unexpected had occurred: I assumed Elizabeth was safely tucked up in bed in hall at college, and in reality she was unconscious and her body was being prised out of a crushed car. 'It was happening to my child and I did not know!' I screamed within myself. To heal this I needed something very predictable, to begin to deal with the element of surprise and shock. Over and over again I recited the poem to myself until I was not surprised any more; I had begun to accept.

The poem made communication of my plight a little easier. I wanted other people to know, but did not know how to tell it while it was so unspeakably raw and awe-full, so I showed them the poem. Then they could comfort me.

The little refrain allowed mourning of the two boys who were dead, and the other two who were injured, and saved me from seeing my daughter's plight in isolation. There is some strange comfort in the knowledge that other parents are mourning too. Two pairs were even worse off than I was; they had no jeans to wash, and only a funeral to look forward to.

Varying the refrain has the literary function of adding interest, but it also allows the first and last versions to be addressed to Elizabeth, and the middle two to be directed to others who will read the poem. And many did.

I sent it to the university chaplains. They had the task of helping the students to come to terms with what had happened. All five in the car came from the same department, so a group of young people was dreadfully bereaved. For some it would have been their first encounter with death at such close quarters. One of the chaplains wrote to tell me how the poem helped those students, and also staff, to begin their own grieving.

The accident happened at a notorious blackspot; a dangerous bend on a hill. Local people had been campaigning for years for something to be done to make the road safer. Somehow the poem reached them, and was sent on to the local MP; so it became an instrument of propaganda.

In my professional life as a psychiatrist I used to work part-time in the local hospice. There I met groups of medical students regularly to teach them about the psychological aspects of the care of the dying and the bereaved. To broaden their perspective and take the subject beyond a clinical context, I offered each group a poetry session to which they were invited to bring poems related to death. I also brought some and usually had this one with me, but what I chose to read depended on what they contributed and the kind of session it turned out to be. They used the time in all sorts of ways. One girl brought a hymn sung at her father's funeral, and thus let me know that she was still grieving. Some used the session for relief of the tension which the course naturally generated, by bringing in the comical, such as Kit Wright's splendid poem *Bump-Starting the Hearse.*

The most remarkable coincidence occurred on a day when I read *Nottingham Five,* and a girl came to me privately afterwards to tell me she had studied for a first degree at that university, and that her flat-mate had been a close friend of one of the boys who died. 'I often wondered what happened to the ones who were injured', she said.

Perhaps you are wondering too. I believe both the others made a full recovery, though I do not know how they have dealt with the memory of what occurred on that October evening. Elizabeth's recovery took three years, and she will always be partially blind. In spite of this, she went on not only to complete her degree, but did exceptionally well in a second one. Now she enjoys her profession as a town planner, is most happily married, and has three splendid little sons.

(Averil Stedeford)

This next account is also only too tragically true:

Trauma writing for all the family

Gyll Marple's father was brutally attacked at work at the post office. He made a very slow and painful recovery from head injuries and brain damage, but later died. This accident happened while Gyll was doing a therapeutic Writing module with me as part of her post-experience BA in Nursing. It was quite natural to ask her family to write through this time of pain and anxiety. She said that the writing offered release of pain and anxiety at the time, helped clarify issues and created a lasting record of what happened and what the family all felt.

There are several pieces by Gyll's father himself, chronicling the slow movement of events in his recovery, including some exciting ones, such as the removal of the nasogastric tubes being 'just like Christmas and birthdays all rolled into one'.

There is a painful piece by his wife, Gyll's mother: 'No premonition of what was to happen on this ordinary Monday. Gordon went to work as usual. I drove him there and collected shopping on the way home …'

A bewildered, angry piece from his 14-year-old grandson, Gyll's son, contains this: 'I want to scream, swear, hit the person who did it … Even if they wanted money, why hit Grandad? He would have given it. They are hard cruel thieves who do not care for anybody but themselves.'

Beth, Gyll's daughter, wrote a stream of consciousness word-association spidergram (clustering) '… brainless at first, aggression, extremely pleased he is responding to us, sorry, hate …'

Gyll's sister (Mandi) wrote a lengthy and very graphic account of the event. It gives a clear and immediate sense of their feelings. '… Abruptly it dawned upon me that the alarm was still ringing incessantly … Slowly I forced myself to concentrate and pressed the numbers, half amazed that I could still remember the combination. Instantly there was silence, the alarm ceased to ring, the noise outside appeared just to ebb away. The silence was awesome, it seemed to give me the strength I so urgently needed.'

Gyll herself wrote: an account of the day; lists to attempt to sort out her feelings; an unsendable letter to her dad; stream of consciousness word-association; agonised questioning free-flow writing about his slow recovery, and reflections on writing about the accident:

> Through writing these articles, it has allowed my thoughts, emotions and fears to be released on paper to allow normality to continue, clearing my mind to be able to support my mum and family.
>
> If it hadn't been for the creative writing course, I don't think I would have written my thoughts on paper because I would have considered I hadn't enough time. But really that wouldn't have been true because most of my writing was done in the hospital when I was sitting next to my dad's bed. When disaster strikes time stands still … Writing became a comfort to me and I have now started a personal diary which I find very beneficial.
>
> Since writing about Dad, I have (re)read the articles about the incident and am amazed by the detail I wrote. If I hadn't written them down at the time I would have forgotten them.
>
> My father has read the articles and has found them extremely beneficial, allowing him to put the jigsaw pieces together from the

moment the accident had happened. If they hadn't been written, he would never have been able to do this.

I asked all my family to write articles which they did. My son's anger felt better having written the unsent letter about his anger. It gave Mum and Mandi a purpose too; I suppose initially to help me, but on retrospect, it gave them a job and time to reflect on thoughts which were suspended in no-man's land.

Not having to write in English form with grammar and punctuation allows the writing to flow from the heart rather than in a stilted essay form. Beth used a spidergram to depict her feelings in reference to her grandad. We had been discussing them because they had been using them in English. A method she found easy, quick, summing emotions together so quickly.

Through writing about Dad's accident, it helped the family to come to terms with the enormity of the situation more easily. I would most definitely recommend this method to other people within a disaster, tragedy situation. Allowing you to come to terms with your own thoughts in your own time.

(Gyll Marples)

CHAPTER 11

Writing at the Doctor's, the Hospital, the Hospice

Writing on Prescription

It is rude to interrupt
(When someone is living)

(Lois Hjelmstadt 1993, p.27)

Memory

The pain returned
and hovered long over the spot
where the wound had healed

(Yana Levieva 1991, p.52)

The writing stopped it going round and round

(Mavis Heaton)

Writing has been offered in some surgeries, hospitals, hospices and other health institutions, supported either by the doctors, nurses and social workers, a writer in residence or a therapeutic writing specialist. Below are examples of all of these, written by practitioners and patients at GP surgeries, hospitals and hospices.

At the GP surgery

Here is Margaret Brothwell with her experience:

A page,
blank, uncritical
... a sponge

soaking up endless thoughts
soothing a tangled mind.
Always available
ready to listen,
comforting, non-judgemental.
A real discovery
... a friend

This poem would not win prizes. but it represents what writing meant to me when I first began writing poetry, twelve months into an illness which was to last a number of years.

I had ME complicated by severe mood swings. I did not want to take anti-depressants. Taking so long to get better I was under pressure to take a decision about my teaching job. All this coincided with the start of the Gulf War. At the time it seemed that the world was falling apart as well as me. It was at this point that my extremely supportive GP suggested writing poetry. At first, I thought he too had gone mad as I had not written anything creative since leaving school.

I remember lying on the floor one afternoon and beginning to write. Some hours later I couldn't believe the three poems in front of me. When I showed them to my GP he was very positive and encouraged me to write more. For the next two years I continued to post the poems I wrote to him. We rarely discussed them but it was enough that I knew he had read them.

Writing helped me to make sense of what was happening to me. In my most severe depressive moments it gave me something positive to do with my feelings. After many months, I was able to stand further away from them as they became less raw. As my poem implies, the page is a safe place in which to explore and diffuse, in my case, what turned out to be years of trapped emotion. Over the course of my illness I encountered psychiatrists and psychotherapists, some meetings more successful than others. Again writing helped. Looking back, it empowered me after my most negative experiences. It gave me a voice in what felt like helpless situations.

Writing became so much a part of me that it came through the illness, out the other side with the new person that emerged. I regularly attend poetry courses and now write from a much broader base. In my core being I have the need to be creative. Writing helps fulfil that need.

(Margaret A Brothwell)

Therapeutic writing from the doctor

Sheffield GPs offered therapeutic writing to anxious or depressed patients, having been trained by me and given suggestion leaflets for themselves and for the patients (Chapter Two) in a project funded by the Royal College of General Practitioners. The GPs found it a useful way of working with such people as the patients were involved in their own treatment and cure, very different from what usually happens when a treatment is handed out by the professionals. It also effectively extended the consultation time as the patients felt in contact while writing. It is impossible for patients to remember to say everything in the seven minutes of a consultation or, even if they do remember, to have the confidence to express everything. Furthermore, as one GP put it: 'you can't mis-hear what's written'.

Another GP commented: 'Dis-ease is when a patient is not at ease with their body. Patients present with many psychological problems, which should not be medicalised. But they feel they need to present with medical symptoms and feel embarrassed to show emotions. This is a way of opening this area out.'

Some patients brought their writing for the GP to see. Some of this was commented on, some not. Several patients only shared their writing with a relative or friend, or kept it private, offering their GP reports of what they were doing. There was a wide range of types of writing undertaken, from exact descriptions of symptoms to outpourings and poems.

All this takes up a little extra of the practitioners' time in the beginning because they need to explain what to do and support the patient initially. But the pay-off for them is quite great. The patient gains greater self-respect, autonomy and self-understanding, and it creates a wider bridge between patient and practitioner, if the writing is shared. One GP also felt that many of his patients like to bring him something in gratitude for all he does for them; a piece of writing feels like a gift.

Peter Nelson's GP, David Gelipter, suggested writing to him as part of this project – much to his surprise. And did he write – there are pages and pages of close-typed thoughts, feelings, memories, angsts, analyses, accounts of symptoms and activities. He had presented to his GP with acute depression and physical symptoms of stress, having been unfairly dismissed from work as the living-in headteacher of a special school.

Peter started by writing a diary on his computer and then widened out to handwriting in different more explorative ways, on my suggestion. He has written lyrical stories from his childhood, drawing on all his senses most pleasurably, and delightful accounts of his life with his wife and boys, as well as bewildered pieces about all the stresses and superhuman strain he was under at work.

Peter wrote that he found it enormously important to choose writing materials with meticulous care and that writing at different times and in different places affected what he wrote and his ease and pleasure in writing. He was very struck with the idea, from me, that access can be gained into deeper material in writing when habitual patterns are altered. So he tried writing in places like by a river – none of which reminded him of writing for work – and with paper and a pen he really really liked, as well as a folder to hold them:

> A silly price to hold a £3 pad but it had quality, yes it was secure and perhaps I did want this facility. The style and quality appeared to be part of giving myself permission, giving the process validity and importance for me. Iola [Peter's wife] immediately declared her liking for the choice even though this was made on aesthetic grounds and not the practical and emotional grounds I had used myself. But this was part of the permission process. (Peter Nelson)

Writing began to be exciting and so enjoyable that Peter looked forward to being able to 'return to my pad and let my pencil run riot again'. Here is a section from his most recent writing:

> Writing seems to be an avenue for expression and filing. Modern-day lives are so complex that our minds work incessantly. Certainly mine did professionally and even now after almost a year I have to be careful not to overload on the intake. I am certainly more relaxed than I was and the tiredness does not stonewall me at the early stages that it was. The physical and cerebral intake still has to be monitored though. Writing is a way of expressing feelings out-loud at the same time as putting them in a secure filing cabinet. Once in there they are less of a burden to the brain, the brain's desk surface is cleared for other activities. (Peter Nelson)

Peter took great justifiable pleasure and pride in the writing, finding it to be a way of expressing himself as well as of exploring his own emotions, thoughts, feelings and memories. The writing has been, furthermore, a communicating bond between him and his GP. Peter is, at the time of writing, in a very different position – new job, starting up a private business. He will have little time, and much less therapeutic need, to write. Whether he continues to write because he has caught the bug will remain to be seen.

All this work is clearly initiated in a 1:1 situation. The patient then writes on their own. But this kind of writing can be done in a group – a group of those wishing to quit smoking, asthma sufferers, new mums in the surgery, and so on.

I ran a heartwarming couple of sessions with the New Mums Group in GP Moira Brimacombe's surgery. One of the writers went on to have her piece published in *Practical Parenting* (Katie Dudley 1997). Here is part of the leaflet I gave the group:

Writing as the parent of a very new person

So much happens when you first have a baby:
so much to think about, feel, listen to, say, learn, and do.
You will want to remember so much of this,
yet it can so easily all happen too quickly.
You will need to think about much of it, in order to get it straight in your head.

Writing is a way of remembering things,
a way of sorting out difficulties or muddles,
a way of getting things off your chest and onto the paper.
You can choose with whom you share it,
or even tear it up unread!

This writing is for you,
for the baby in the future,
for others who've been involved,

Here are some ideas for you to write about at home:

What I've been told about my own birth or little childhood
A memory that's come to mind over the last month
A person who's been important to me
A gift (need not be an object)
Something someone said
A hope for the future
A memorable place
A near-disaster
A surprise
A struggle
A dream
A fear
A joy

The wider picture in primary care

The General Manager of Dudley Family Health Services has commented: 'As an ex-army man I view art in primary health care as being a bit like the invention of radar – intangible and impossible to understand at first but now we can't do without it!' (Bromley 1990, p.19).

Professor Downie and the chief medical officer Sir Kenneth Calman support this: 'The arts are the vehicles through which human beings articulate the meanings of their lives' (1996, pp.1499–1500).

Malcolm Rigler (1997) of Withymoor Village Surgery had the first writer-in-residence in a GP surgery 'encouraging visitors to write about their medical experiences as a way of helping themselves and others with the same problem … We believe communicating information in this way is of the utmost importance to health' (p.10). David Hart (1990), who is West Midlands Arts Literature Officer and who supports Malcolm Rigler, said:

> Arts in Primary Health Care could lead to a new role for the GP, who will be less of a prescribing surgery-based doctor and more of a local perceiver of social change, an observer of patterns of illness and health very broadly defined and, consequently, a teacher and stimulator of imaginative solutions. It could also lead to a blurring of the boundaries (in formal education and between professionals in various fields) between what we now think of as physical health, cultural vitality, spiritual balance, quality of life and communal well-being. (p.1)

Medical Monitor published an account by a GP about two of her patients who have written themselves out of their bad psychological situations (anonymous author 1995). The author says of one of the patients: 'I have gradually watched her change until she has once again been able to return to work.'

Chris Ellis (1989), a GP in South Africa, has reported in the *British Medical Journal* how he uses what he calls 'epistotherapy' – patients writing either unsendable letters (see Chapter Four) or sending them to him or others. The gains he details are similar to those of my GPs:

> Writing letters is … an occupier of the mind and hands and is an on the spot emotional outlet in which the patient has the opportunity to describe his or her feelings without having to race against the surgery clock. It is a continual contact with the care-giver in times of rejection, depression and despair. The letters can be dropped into the surgery and put with my mail or brought in at the next visit. They are kept in a locked drawer of my desk … Finally you can use epistotherapy on yourself.

GPs and other healthcare staff also write themselves, as members of groups which I run. They write poems or stories about their work and then discuss whatever vital issues arise from the accounts. A GPs work is generally isolated – either in the consulting room or the patient's home – this method melts the walls between peers – rather like professional therapy. Here is Bob Purdy (1996), one of the group members, writing about it:

> It is easy for GPs to work in almost total professional isolation, even in a friendly partnership, and it can be hard to admit mistakes, vulnerability, sadness and even occasionally joy. If you can commit some of these thoughts to paper, then not only can it be personally therapeutic, but by sharing them with others you may bring insights that can strike a chord and be of benefit to others.

The practitioner, as well as the patient, needs to write (see Chapter Ten); their job is getting tougher and tougher. Distressed, anxious and depressed people do turn to their primary care practitioners in the absence of strong traditional family, neighbourhood and religious support networks, yet it is often very hard for the GP to think of appropriate interventions. Here is an answer which helps both them and their patients.

Writing in the hospital

> I never knew birds sang in winter until I had cancer
>
> (A patient, quoted by Pat Pilkington 1997)

Writing therapy offered by nurses

This was a module on the BA in Health Care Practice at Sheffield Hallam University. Aesthetics, the arts and a holistic view of the patient (e.g. Smyth 1996) have been called for in nursing, just as they have in medicine. The students were all nurses: hospital, general practice, Macmillan, midwives, and so on. We discussed a different way of writing each of the twelve weeks – for example, reminiscence, dreams, making lists of anxieties, unsendable letters, and so on. The nurses wrote in these ways themselves for their course portfolio, and also used writing with appropriate patients.

Gyll Marples (see also Chapters Ten and Eight) was a night nurse on an oncology ward. She felt that the approach was particularly appropriate at night: there was time and she found it helped the patients to settle. She used writing on a one-to-one basis and isolated a range of prerequisites in the relationship between nurse and patient before therapeutic writing should be introduced. She felt that group work would require a different relationship as the patients would have elected to go to a creative writing group. 'By listening and reflecting back to the patient, nurses are able to share and release anxieties , fears and emotions.' This sharing, which includes creative writing, can only develop if the patient and nurse can build up trust and work together in partnership. Actively listening to the patient creates the groundwork for a relationship which should be built on 'trust, honesty, respect, and genuineness' and empathy. Insight into the situation of the patient can only be achieved with empathy, she maintains. Empathy is nurturing, recognising and allowing patients the validity of their own feelings.

Gyll only introduced writing to the patients once she felt that she had built up a good relationship with them and if she felt that the patient was not 'anxious and nervous' at the time, as writing can be felt to be threatening. She used list making as a non-threatening introduction to writing, such as 'things which make me anxious/prevent me from sleeping' (also see Chapter Ten). She also used diary writing (pain diary, bereavement diary, coma diary – written by relatives to tell the patient afterwards exactly what happened). Letters were also useful: a patient of another of the nurses on the course was so poorly that he found visits from his wife exhausting, although vital to his happiness. He made use of the long waits between her visits slowly writing letters to her which she could read when she came. Unsendable letters were used too, such as a very lengthy, angry, questioning letter to the cancer. A patient of Gyll:

> was an articulate 40-year-old who had recently been diagnosed as having a malignant melanoma. It was at this point she was just trying to come to terms with the disease. After showing her Gillie's article from the *Guardian* she became extremely enthusiastic. Armed with a pen and a sheaf of paper wrote reams and reams. I couldn't wait to see this writing, but to my complete dismay, she tore every page up into shreds, slowly, carefully, methodically. I was mortified all the writing gone to waste. But when speaking to her I realised she had managed to tear a lot of her negative emotions away and was then fuelled to begin in her fight back to a positive life.
>
> Reflecting on this issue made me realise exactly what a positive response I had had. In a way I had given this lady permission to write all

her thoughts down on paper in a private, non-threatening manner. (Gyll Marples)

There was, however, one near-disaster in this work: 'Nora was interested in the idea of listing her problems and sorting them through on paper. Then she cried and cried when she realised nurse expected her to write. She couldn't because of her disease.' As a good nurse, Gyll was able to cope with it by suggesting that she told stories about happy events in her past. This was a disturbing incident which taught quite a lesson. Gyll also used reminiscence writing successfully with patients about illnesses – a process which brought them together fruitfully: 'through this experience Vic and Stan have kept in touch through letter, both housebound patients who have found companionship and comradeship through writing … The reminiscence encouraged self-esteem, worth, respect, interest, added communication and above all memories which cannot be removed.'

Anna Stanford, another of the group, runs an asthma support group in the community, called 'Gaspers'. She encouraged the members to write but felt that she was only successful once she had experienced writing herself: 'It has been invaluable actually to experience creative writing.' Some of the exercises were a 'shock' to Anna, some 'threatening' and some 'comfortable'. She feels that she is now able to offer it with 'caution and preparation'. 'I have seen patients who have struggled for months or years trying to come to terms with their changed life styles, take a giant step forward just by writing about how they feel about their problems.'

Anna encouraged not only her patients but also colleagues to write. One took advantage of this method after considerable personal family illness and her team are considering it for multi-disciplinary teamwork.

One of Anna's patients, Jean Barton, 'found it difficult to express her feelings and fears, but her poetry has been her salvation. It has helped her come to terms with her condition and adjust her lifestyle'. Here is one of her poems:

Positive action

I may go out today
if it doesn't rain
the damp makes me wheezy
so I tend not to bother

I nearly went out yesterday
but it was too hot

the heat makes me cough
so I changed my mind

I might go out tomorrow
if it's not too windy
the wind makes me breathless
so I'll probably stay in again

Or I could try the medication
on a regular basis
get back in control
go out … and get a life.

(Jean Barton)

The writer-in-residence in the hospital

Nurses suggesting writing to patients has been the focus so far. There have also been many writing residencies in British hospitals, for example Fiona Sampson, Isle of Wight Hospital Arts (Sampson 1995; Senior and Croall 1993) and Rosie Cullen at Pastures Hospital (Cullen 1991).

These projects have been run by writers going in to inspire and support the patients and the staff to communicate and express themselves through writing. Fiona Sampson said that at the Isle of Wight she was steering between writing being a 'diversion' and a 'therapy' (like art therapy).

Many writer-facilitators (such as Joan Poulson below) perceive the value of creative writing to be intrinsic. Anyone who writes knows that writing is good for you, but this doesn't necessarily need to be specified by the facilitator. Writing, sharing that writing with others, receiving positive criticism and help, perhaps performing it to other patients and having it 'published' in a photocopied or printed anthology, engenders self-respect. It is absorbing – an intense involvement outside the writer and their symptoms or problems. It helps bring material up to the surface of the mind and to fit that hitherto troubling material into everyday understandings. Autobiographical writing has its own benefits (see the section Writing in the Old People's Home). Writing creates something positive out of suffering.

The very act of creativity itself is life-enhancing: a piece is created from out of the writer her/himself. The organisation for writers who have survived the NHS Mental Health system, 'Survivors Poetry', considers that to concentrate directly on the therapeutic would be detrimental to the writing and its beneficial effects (Chapter Fourteen). They feel this very focusing on the writing as a piece of art, rather than on an individual who needs therapy, creates a positive and outward response.

Here is Joan Poulson's account. She is a poet, with extensive experience working with patients in hospital, who has edited several anthologies of patients' writing (1994a and b, 1996):

> Much of my experience with writing groups has been with patients and staff in psychiatric and geriatric hospitals or in day care centres for people coping with less extreme forms of psychiatric illness. The unexpected is inevitable. During one session in a day care centre where I had facilitated a group for almost a year, Barry suddenly cried out, dropped his head onto the table and sobbed, calling out that he was 'psychotic'. Then he said he would like to write something, took pen and paper and wrote almost frantically for around thirty minutes before asking, politely and quietly, if he might leave the group. Barry was always enthusiastic and never missed a session. This was the first time he had ever left behind anything he had written. It was an autobiography, beginning when he was taken into care at the age of four and cataloguing foster homes, residential homes, abuse, bullying, illness.
>
> I find stimulating the senses to be one of the most successful ways of encouraging people to write. This is particularly so with people in long-term residential care. My workshops often start with music, live whenever possible, otherwise on audio cassette. I also use recordings of birdsong and other natural sounds. Flowers, plants, fragrant herbs in pots, jars of spices, fabrics in a variety of texture, stones, pieces of bark, tree branches, picture postcards, all provide starting-points. I might ask everyone in the group to choose a postcard, write from any perspective about what they see or imagine to be taking place. I would stipulate a time for this, say ten minutes. Then I might introduce a variety of spices in jars and packets, ask the group to make a choice and to write without taking pen from paper: anything that comes to mind but allowing less time, probably five minutes.
>
> I often use postcards in a similar way and with music or in combination with paint or richly textured fabrics, encouraging people to concentrate on the senses and not to think about words at that point.
>
> Working with long-stay patients in a psychiatric hospital I took colourful lengths of fabric, magazine illustrations and paint to one group session. Few of the patients would use paint, not wanting to 'soil' their hands, but we talked about colour in the landscape, gardens, clothes,

rainbows and made cut-up collages from the magazines. Two of the patients also wanted to write:

Rainbow

Red of tomatoes
Yellow daffodils
Orange of the dawn
Blue of the sea
Green of the grass
Indigo of love
Violet of the valentine.

Turquoise is my Auntie Lillian
Black is the dimmer nights
White is the lovely wedding dresses
Purple is the sweetness of the cooking
Beige is the lovely summer shoes
Brown is the chestnuts in autumn
Cream is the nice milky coffees.

(Margaret Howell)

In another workshop in the same hospital, working with adults who had been there for considerably shorter periods – six months to a year, I passed round a variety of boxes: wooden, silk-covered, lacquered, made of felt; and in all kinds of shapes. We looked at illustrations of large decorative cupboards, magicians boxes, posters depicting a wide variety of doors. I read Miroslav Holub's poem 'The Door' to the group and we talked around the subject of openings, possibilities, magic doors/ cupboards etc.

Castle of Light

In the Tower of the East Wing
of the Castle of Light
The Magic Cupboard contains
the crystal ball
of the Land of Unicorns.

The cupboard door faces
an old coloured glass window
of a multi-petalled flower.
When the sun reaches

the centre of the flower,
a bright beacon of light
shines through –
to the cupboard.

If the cupboard door was pen
the sunbeam would light up
the crystal ball and show
the gateway to the Land of Unicorns.

But who holds the key
to the Magic Cupboard?

Only the Keeper to the Tower
who will guard it
with the help of the Fairy of Light.

Any who enter the Tower
without permission are blinded
by the Fairy's only spell.
How do I know this?
Because I am the keeper.

(Anon)

Working with elderly people attending a day unit in a city hospital, mainly for physiotherapy, I used music as a stimulus. We listened to extracts from classical music and from popular music of the Twenties, Thirties and Forties, perhaps familiar to them in youth or when they first arrived in this country. I also found traditional music from a variety of cultures which I hoped might bridge present-day Manchester which had become home to everyone in the group and the countries where they were born and grew up. Our discussions began with the music but expanded over a wide range of subject, focusing eventually upon the past. All the written work from this group had to be scribed but the results were lively and direct, such as the one which begins: 'In 1926 I lived on a farm in Slovenia with my family and my three sisters and two brothers …'

(Joan Poulson)

Publication for patients

Publication and readings can be a vital element in the writing process. Patients writing poetry, stories and some autobiography are often writing for an audience, in a similar way to a professional writer. Not all of it will be great art but a great deal of it has much to offer a reader. This benefits the writer's self-esteem as well as the reader. Sharing writing with others who have suffered, their relatives and friends, or those who think 'there but for the grace of God go I' is a way of sharing experiences which would be difficult in any other way. Reading a well-expressed account by a fellow-sufferer is extremely valuable. Judith Thwaite perceived a need, when a patient, and gave considerable energy, time and talent to meeting it. She joined forces with Don Ayers and together they edit *Patchwork: An Anthology of Poetry from the Christie Hospital* (quarterly):

> It was in the waiting room of Christie Hospital that the idea of *Patchwork* was born. I was in the out-patients with pad and pen trying to escape into a world of words far away from Manchester when I looked round and instead of slumped anonymous shapes around me I saw others like me – a veneer of conformity, doing the expected outward gestures but inside raw and afraid. Just as one can cry oneself dry, I had poured out my hurt onto paper. Perhaps others could find this a cathartic experience.
>
> I went home determined to send out a message to other patients. I printed notes which I pinned throughout the hospital on my next visit and waited for some response. Within days, letters came with poems and pleas for them to be published. It was just my intention to begin a group, but here was a need to get thoughts into a more permanent form. I had no funds to satisfy this need, but when a letter followed from a patient who offered help I didn't feel the task was so hopeless. Don and I talked on the phone and we met at the hospital. There followed months of talks and discussions with the hospital management. Don and Debbie's patience and good humour were always there when it seemed we would never get anything off the ground.
>
> In 1992 Don produced the first prototype booklet which he illustrated. We had by then become affiliated as a branch of the Christie's Appeal Group called Creative Arts Against Cancer. We have kept the original design of patchwork squares on the cover as Patchwork is an acrostic for Poetry at The Christie Hospital, though our catchment is nation-wide.
>
> (Judith Thwaite)

Writing in the hospice

> Verse is for healthy
> arty-farties. The dying
> and surgeons use prose.
>
> (Peter Reading 1984, p.59)

This last is not true at all; the poet Peter Reading is well known for using outrageousness to make people think. Poetry is peculiarly appropriate to the dying due to its concise brevity and lyricism. The following is an account of therapeutic writing with the dying, which focuses on the writing of narratives as well as poetry. There are a range of fearful words for the dying, denoted by their initial letter. Reading's 'C' word (cancer) is one, as is the big 'G' (God), Writing is another. 'Oh I couldn't do that' a healthy person, and often a dying one, will say.

Yet, *in extremis*, the dying can find writing a deeply healing activity – just as they wish to hear the word 'God'; and often want to face up to facts about their cancer. Writing ceases to be a frightening activity associated with school, which only clever people or 'arty-farties' can do. It becomes a way of expressing some of their response to the turmoil of change taking place in this last precious bit of their lives. Not all this turmoil is negative – the knowledge of the closeness of death seems to sharpen an awareness of the beauties of life. Writing is a perfect way of celebrating these, as well as a way of bringing outside that which is causing pain inside:

> It all goes round and round in my head, you see. I'm not very good at talking. But the writing – it seemed to get it out there, stopped it going round and round. Now I can see it in writing, I can sort it out more. Reading it out to the group wasn't easy, but it gave me a way of saying something to them which I couldn't say otherwise. I said it in the writing. (Mavis Heaton)

Mavis was talking to the Ashgate Hospice day-unit nurse manager after a group writing session at which she had begun to write her autobiography. Not a verbally articulate person, she had written about her distress at friends abandoning her once they knew she had cancer. Her writing examined what their motives might be:

> Strong makes strong, they believe, weak makes weak. But for people like me one has to be strong to conquer our fears. I am weak myself and all I

want is to be strong, strong, strong. So who can help me. No-one but myself. (Mavis Heaton)

Sharing writing, hopelessness and fear

The little group, of whom Mavis Heaton was a member, met to write with me fairly often. On a later occasion, when Mavis was, unfortunately, not there, we only had half-an-hour for writing because of hair appointments, seeing the doctor, and so on. Dorothy Lewis was sitting in the dayroom saying that there was no purpose to life, feeling really dismal. I asked her to join us, saying that I had brought something really nice. She had been hesitant the previous week, asserting that there was nothing in her head, that she couldn't write. To my pleasure, she did rouse herself sufficiently from her misery to join us.

My 'something nice' was a couple of beautifully marked shells, a tom-tit's nest with my mother's hair woven into it, an egg, boxes and a tin. Examining these was almost enough. But, after a short while, I asked them to write, imagining what it would feel like to be inside one of the containers – they might either feel cosy and safe or frightened and trapped (see Chapter Four). Jan Broadwood, who has been in writing groups for years, immediately responded: 'Oh that's too open, I need you to be a bit more precise.' I responded: 'Put your pen on the page and see what comes out.' She did. So too did Dorothy, none of the previous week's nervous prevarication, she had chosen the egg and was thrilled with the writing but felt it wasn't finished.

The following week I arrived with little preparation but found there was nothing else laid on for them to do. I wished I had planned something but vaguely hoped Christmas would be enough. However, as soon as Dorothy saw me, she kept expressing disappointment that she had forgotten to bring her poem in. When I realised she meant the one I had typed, I assured her that I had a copy. All she wanted to do was write more.

The group were intrigued, so before she got writing again, she asked me to read it aloud. This really set them off talking because Jan suggested we all say in turn what it made us think of. This was so fruitful that I stopped them pretty quickly and gave out the paper and pens, suggesting that they write what was in their heads. Both Kath Chambers and Muriel Simpson said that theirs were empty, to which I responded that that was a very good thing. I didn't want them to write with their heads but their hearts. Here is part of Muriel's:

Everything seems like a ball of string
all tangled up, with crinkles in
as if it's been unknitted
that's just how I feel
it's neither going straight nor the other way
...
After Christmas
after all this darkness
I'll be able to go forwards
things will lift.

It'll be a newly rolled ball of string.

Muriel wrote another one in the Spring about how she had prayed for a change and a solution to her problems had arrived that day. Here is Dorothy's completed poem:

Let me out
I seem to have been enclosed forever,
the walls of this prison are closing in
and I must escape.

How long ago it seems I felt so safe
and secure, but no no longer,
when did this urge come upon me to escape.
I twist and turn my body,
my arms windmilling around my head,
my legs in constant motion,
God how much longer.

Suddenly through the walls of my cell
I see a light, very pale blue,
it seems to be so soothing,
my body absorbs this and I feel more calm.
What is happening.

The light is getting stronger
I have a feeling of freedom and comfort
bathed in this warm blue light,
what can it be?
suddenly I have a feeling of well-being,
can this last?
I look around me and my eyes come to rest

on a pale green broken shell;
Has this been my prison for so long?

Suddenly I am aware of a presence,
so I feel threatened!!
warm tender hands enfold me
I feel peace,
and this feeling is so good.
Will it last?

I look up and suddenly I am alone again, can this be so?

I look around me
the soothing blue light has faded,
being replaced by a cold grey light,
I feel my limbs trembling;
my head aches;
I am in despair,
I long for my shell,
to be in my cocoon,
was I safe in there?
my eyes close,
tomorrow is another day;
I can hope!!

Kath said afterwards she was horrified at being presented with paper and pen, even with the suggestion she dictate her thoughts. Luckily, Val, a volunteer, appeared like a genie at the right moment. Kath rightly trusted Val, who supported her as she cried, upset even further that she was crying. When I suggested that we all read our pieces, Kath said 'not mine because it's all rubbish'.

Val persuaded her to let her read it. Kath had expressed regret for the past, and feelings of jealousy for healthy people, adding, 'if you put that in it'll make me feel so selfish'. She ended with: 'I reckon you'd better stop before that page is full of tears.'

Kath cried quite a lot with the group that day, quite fearful of having expressed and shared so much, feeling she should be brave in front of others. But it gave the others the opportunity to say self-affirming things to her. They shared their feelings about what the cancer made them feel: depressed, angry, envious and weepy. Later, Kath and several of the others told the day-unit manager how glad she was for the session, how glad to have cried together and shared so much. (Kath Chambers died a very short time later.)

I was just setting off for the wards when the day-unit manager said that Dorothy had asked if I'd read her poem to all of the patients in the day-unit. This larger group also each said in turn what it made them think of, a real opening up about the difficulty of life, depression, coping, the value of tears. One patient had never before shared any such feelings.

Several weeks later, Mavis Heaton did some more writing with me. It was a harrowing episode in her autobiography and ended with the word 'amen'. When I queried this, she said that it seemed 'to end it off properly'. I think she wanted to parcel that experience up in the writing and the 'amen' was like a tight knot of the string. She talked at length about her previous piece of writing because doing it had seemed to 'bring it home to me'. She said that she now felt much more in control of her life and had been able successfully, though painfully, to cut the unsatisfactory friends out of her life.

A page full of tears

Several patients in this study found that writing a narrative of their fears, anxieties, anger, bewilderment or denial helped them to face, understand and, to an extent, come to terms with things. The staff reported that this reduction in stress helped relieve their symptoms.

Rita Parker, an in-patient, could not accept that she had cancer and was in great turmoil within herself. I saw her three times, each for about forty minutes. She dictated her writing, as her hands had been affected by the treatment, sitting looking away from me, talking and talking with no reference to my presence. Tears streamed down her face then, and, as she told me, for some time after I'd left her at the end of our first session. She said that she had not cried since her diagnosis over a year previously and had never before cried in front of others: 'it [the writing] must be coming from the inside, the tears are rolling down … it's a relief it really is … as if a millstone had been lifted from off my neck.' She blessed the writing over and over for allowing her to face the diagnosis and to express fearful thoughts like a desire for suicide. 'My son wanted to know what we did and I said "how can I tell you? I don't know. But this writing, it seems to get right inside you. Right into the centre of your being."'

Another patient was in such great distress that the staff could not ease his symptoms. He wrote for a mere fifteen minutes, almost unintelligibly. But he wrote the names of his first partner and those of their children. Having written, he was then able to talk about them, ask to see them and say goodbye and that he was sorry. When I called in the next day he lay there quiet, looked up at me and smiled. 'Happy', was all he said, 'happy, happy.' He died very shortly afterwards.

Marie Cox was a gentle breast-cancer patient who gained a comfort and peace from the writing. She died after a great deal of distress, including a neighbour berating her publicly as a 'bald, one-breasted woman' and leaving a family she desperately wanted to stay with. I visited her daughter after her death and Clare gained insight and comfort also from the writing. Amongst other things she wrote, Clare Godhino remembered her mother through her hands:

> Hands that remained powerful, beautiful, expressive,
> our way of always being close.
> Hands that I sat holding.
> Hands that held mine, when they were crossed and still.
> Hands that I miss.

Jayne Unwin was a young woman with breast cancer with whom I worked for several months, right up until a couple of days before her death. The staff who cared for her were all aware of the considerable benefit to her of this writing. She wrote a great deal, including letters to her daughters and one to her husband, on her last days. She also wrote to her husband several months before she died, telling and asking him loving things she could not somehow bring herself to say. The longest texts were a diary and a letter to the cancer. This latter included this:

> Yes Cancer you damned thing you've mucked up my life, I can't plan ahead when I do plan to do something you come along and mess it up again.
>
> I look through the mirror in the morning and I don't like what I see. Dark round the eyes and a worrying look on my face – wondering what today's going to bring.
>
> I wish I could share people's happiness and troubles like I used to. They talk but sometimes I'm not listening. It's hard being shut off from what's happening to me. Then I feel bad and angry with myself because they must see me as a right selfish person what can't let go.
>
> (Jayne Unwin)

These patients and relatives were in great need of a vehicle to enable communication both with themselves and with others. They needed to express fears caught inside them and to explore issues which they didn't know were troubling them. So when I told them they would be writing from a strong dependable healing self inside themselves, they believed me, and that was where they wrote from. They nearly all began with a great deal of anxiety and inhibition, of course – 'Me. Write???!!!'. There were those who could not trust either themselves or me, of course. With a few of the patients it was clear that they knew what I was offering them but could not take the plunge, for whatever reason.

The account given here is of myself, an outside writing therapist, working with the patients, but it could just as effectively been offered by healthcare staff – medical/nursing/occupational therapist.

The sharing (and publication) of writing can be of value to both writer and reader, as I said above. Eleanor Nesbitt has written in *Linkup* about her experiences of writing as a cancer sufferer, encouraging others to do the same:

> I felt a strong inner compulsion to record what I was going through and made sure I had plenty of paper and pens in hospital. Even in the dark, one sleepless night, I wrote blindly, capturing images and fleeting thoughts without the fear that they would have evaporated by the morning medicine round. I would rather throw them away in the cold light of day than feel I had let something precious and fleeting slip past irrevocably. Both writing and reading my diary entries have clarified my feelings and ideas. (Nesbitt 1997, pp.7–9)

Joanna Drazba's poetry collection (1997), published posthumously, has made her something of an emblematic figure in Polish hospice circles. In Australia, Elizabeth Mosely and Tarja Ahokas have published a poetry and painting account of their 'healing journey' through 'grief, fear, anxiety and the myriad other emotions' (1997).

Conclusions

When, and in what way, is writing right?

For a health professional to suggest a personal journey of exploration like writing, the relationship between themselves and the patient must be one of trust and empathy and they must be in a position to be willing to, and know how to, listen to the patient. For example, in an empathetic, listening situation writing would not be suggested to an illiterate patient or one who was unable to write because of debilitation. Similarly, the practitioner would need to be confident that the patient had sufficient psychological strength to tackle this kind of writing and/or sufficient support from friends or family –

it would be inappropriate for a psychotic patient, for example, unless the practice or hospital could offer back-up psychotherapeutic support. The stages of writing are gentle, however. Unless felt to be pushed, those who start to write will generally only take the steps right for them to take. The practitioner or writer-in-residence should suggest writing in this way as an option to be taken up entirely at the patient's discretion.

Within an occupational therapy setting, Nick Pollard (1990) states: 'Defended patients need to know what is expected, to know the surroundings, and to be able to trust the therapist'. He quotes Winnicot as saying that creativity requires 'somewhere to put what we find'. Advising anxious or depressed people to put their feelings, thoughts, ideas, images onto paper in a controlled way is often a tremendous relief – they are put somewhere, rather than endlessly going round and round in their own heads.

Patients then need to know where to put the product of their creativity. Every writer needs to know who their audience is for every act of writing. A diary is clearly for oneself at a future date; a letter is intended to be read by the recipient; reminiscence work is for the children and future generations. A knowledge of their intended reader must be clear to the patient who is embarking on writing. Within a writing group (whether therapeutic or not), the audience is clearly the group. It is important to celebrate this. An essential of every writing group I run is the 'readaround', with everyone listening and commenting constructively. The production of an in-house anthology, if the course is long enough, is vital. The patient must decide whether they wish their writing to be private, destroyed or shared with the doctor, a relative or a friend.

The practitioner should be clear why they are suggesting this writing to their patient: to support them in understanding the patient better; to help the patient express deep-seated anxieties; to help the patient clarify and organise their thoughts, feelings, ideas or compulsions; to help the patient communicate with the doctor better; or to remind the patient of happier past times, perhaps. The practitioner also has to be aware that material may be distressing or disturbing to themselves. Issues of informed consent, confidentiality and ethical dilemmas also need to be clear to both patient and practitioner.

Writing seems to be a gentle and effective way of encouraging those who are sick or near the end of life not to repress, but to tell their story. 'What the mind represses, the body expresses' (Daniel 1997).

CHAPTER TWELVE

Writing in Prison, the Old People's Home

'Reach for the Stars'

> One can afford to be hurt, one can afford to reach for the stars, if there is a built-in safeguard against crippling depression or disorganising excitement.
>
> (Molly Harrower, *The Therapy of Poetry,* p.3)

> Writing could keep me company when I was isolated
>
> (Jackie Kay, *Young Poetry Pack,* p.4)

> My grandfather and grandmother never spoke. Everyone in that little house was miserable, and although they knew they were miserable and why they were miserable, they couldn't explain why ... I realised the only way I could express my feelings was by writing them down.
>
> (Brian Patten, *Young Poetry Pack,* p.15)

Writing can not only keep you company when isolated from everyday contact with other people during everyday activities, and enable you to express your feelings when those around you cannot, it can also help you to reach for the stars, even from the restrictions of institutional life. All that has been said about therapeutic writing in the rest of this book is relevant here but institutional life makes additional demands which this chapter addresses. Annie Dalton graphically describes how a group of prisoners wrote a musical and John Killick and I tell of our work with older adults – mine in old people's homes and John's with dementia sufferers.

Writing in the prison

I am a mole,
a mole burrowing in myself,
and making mounds of words

(Yana Levieva 1991, p.40)

A new hero, by Annie Dalton

The men enter and, without a word, wrench and kick the chairs out of position. In seconds my new students are slumped at bizarre angles round the room, seemingly hurled there by centrifugal force. They furiously avoid eye contact. The room is now about as welcoming as the waiting room of an autistic dentist, despite my care to arrange the chairs in a circle, as I would before any normal class. It's my first session as writer-in-residence in Wellingborough Prison.

This is my introduction to the chaotic parallel universe of prison, where voices are either pitched too low to carry or else carry stridently from wing to wing. Prison is toxic to living things, causing its inhabitants to skew, like seedlings deprived of natural light. A simple paper cut takes months to heal, yet vicious fights erupt bewilderingly form nowhere. Some days you can taste the unexpressed energy in the air, like the build-up of ions before a storm. Words mean little (inmates have heard them all). Nerve endings are on perpetual red alert. Prison is the ultimate dysfunctional family writ large.

Two years later: it's high summer, hot and humid. My group is working on a rock musical. The project is not my idea but theirs, growing out of a songwriting workshop. Like all true creative enterprises, PRESSURE has a life of its own from the start. Mingling the speech and music of 1990s urban life with metaphysical elements of Dante's *Inferno* and *A Christmas Carol,* it tells the story of Stone, black, street-wise and dead and Robbie, an adopted white youth with zero self-esteem.

First we write the scenes, then, as prison routine permits, we record them in our cupboard studio at the end of the education corridor. Some days up to eight members of the cast can be found crouched in cramped immobility for fear of stray sounds being picked up on mikes. They not only remain civil in this sweltering hutch but insist on take after take, missing tea breaks, mealtimes, and even that most sacred slot on the prison timetable, weight-training. 'Gotta get it right', they say fiercely. And often, 'They think we're animals, but this play will blow their socks off'.

Their literacy skills are minimal, their life experience universally bleak. Except for the musicians amongst them, their experience of collaboration is confined to high-adrenaline activities: football, drugs, burglary.

The officers say I'm wasting my time. These men are antisocial scum, irresponsible losers, going nowhere fast.

These losers wait impatiently for me each morning so they can get back to work. Some days the truth of the words we first improvise, then write down, sobers us all. Other times we laugh so much that I drive home with aching stomach muscles.

Everything takes longer in prison. Even the air is stagnant. Time, having been commandeered by the institution itself, has little meaning. Tension levels are high, attention spans short and prison endlessly rich in soap-opera distractions. At first the delicate spell of our creative concentration is easily shattered by an outburst of rage in the corridor or the cheery arrival of an officer to cart someone away for a piss test.

Yet as we work, over weeks and months, it gets increasingly hard to remember we are in prison. Whoever and whatever these young men may be elsewhere, here in a magic circle of their own creation they blaze with integrity. Even the inevitable ego clash has become a grail-like absolute, not despite, but, I suspect, because of its sheer improbability.

When Paul, who created and is to play the part of Stone, wins his appeal the day before we start recording, a new hero steps promptly into his shoes. After a while, I almost expect this curious phenomenon. Long-term creative projects are usually killed off by the erratic comings and goings of prison existence. Yet for the year-and-a-half it takes to complete, the crew tenderly pass our play from one to another like a precious egg no one wants to break. When I fail to arrive one morning, the guys simply go ahead and record the scenes without me. And, damn their eyes, they're brilliant!

Did I accomplish this miracle? Yes and no. My contribution is best described as learning (the painful way) *not* to do things; learning, in other words, to become still. Still enough to subdue my initial panic, to give up my addiction to good words, my thirst for validation. Still enough to be myself, simply present, with no agenda. Only then can I see what was at first invisible to me: the hidden beauty in these men.

But the search for the right words, the gritty determination to win through, the reclamation work, the graveyard humour, the power and the glory – was all theirs. By utilising me as a kind of human lightning rod, that raw chaotic energy, the kind which flings chairs randomly about the room, changed into something else, a third force which Julia Cameron calls aptly spiritual electricity.

Like many writers, I take for granted the transforming effects of plugging myself into this power. To experience them in a group is especially inspiring. But when they materialise in that archetypal wasteland of human hopes which is the prison system, this appearance of a third force approaches the miraculous.

'It was not just the quality of the poetry, the music the drama and computerised electronic whizz-bangs which filled the small prison theatre,' wrote David Rousel-Milner, reviewing PRESSURE for the *Carribean Times*. 'There was pathos, pain, sorrow, remorse and some anger. But most of all it was the almost tangible aura of love which bound the performance together. An unexpected sensation to find within the austere high-fenced razor-wired boundary of a punishment and correctional facility...'

None of us ever kidded ourselves that our prison-cupboard musical could reverse decades of damage in the young men who wrote it. Yet it would be equally false to deny the extraordinary changes which occurred as they wrote and rewrote their profoundly redemptive drama. For not only did they seem to be rewriting themselves in the process but actually *rewiring* themselves to take account of the third force, that mysterious spiritual electricity, becoming transformers of chaos in their own right.

Barnes, who took over the lead, applied for college, using PRESSURE as part of his music portfolio. At the time of writing he is in his second year. Kevin, a furiously self-hating young man, became our most constructive critic and, to his astonishment, earned the respect of everyone. A desperately shy young lifer, a talented guitarist, agreed to take the part of Robbie, wanting to help youths as confused as he had been.

Ant spent his last evening in the prison recording the final rap of the musical he had written especially. 'I hope it's all right,' he said anxiously as he left for yet another jail, clutching the bin bags which held his possessions. 'I put my heart and soul into it, Annie.'

(Annie Dalton)

* * * *

The therapeutic value of this work was life-changing for the prisoners. The bulk, perhaps all of them, had probably never experienced anything like this. Their expression and experience was suddenly valued – Annie not only listened and supported and criticised constructively but also valued it.

Eventually, this rubbed off onto them: 'this play will blow their socks off'. For the first time, probably in their lives, these lads and men were realising that they could and should pay attention to their own feelings and thoughts. They were encouraged to enjoy and be stimulated by collaborating, by listening to each other. Had this work been followed through instead of being an island in their experience, and had it been supported by other authorities around them (the officers continued to treat them as scum), the prisoners might have been able to change their attitudes and begin to alter their way of life. Unfortunately, this is not normally what prison is for. But these men did have this brief experience and one did become a music student on leaving prison.

Writing in the prison is, and has been, happening all over the country. The reports of these residencies all contain similar elements, ranging from frustration and fear to delight and intense creation (Edge 1989; Jenkins 1991; Peaker and Vincent 1994; Williams 1996). Michaela Morgan has facilitated the inmates at Stocken near Peterborough to write children's stories (Williams 1996). Not only is this intensely therapeutic for the writers but it also helps fill a gap – there are few books to help children make sense of having a parent in prison. These illustrated and bound books are put in the visitor centre for inmates' children to read, which they do avidly.

These writer-facilitators work in a range of ways with the prisoners. Annie's was a very individual approach – writing and performing a musical. Here is another point of view from Jane Richardson, whom I met as my student at Northern College, a remarkable institution for people who missed out on education first time round (one of the eight residential colleges, Ruskin in Oxford being the best known). I held my classes in a gracious room in the Palladian wing of Wentworth Castle, with huge windows overlooking the south lawn, rhododendrons and azaleas, and my supervisions in my own room in the Gothic wing. My people said, enthusiastically, how much they had learned about creative writing. I think they also learned a great deal about themselves, each other and our culture. Here is one of the things Jane did with the experience.

Time in prison, by Jane Richardson

When I first started to write, I wrote little rhyming couplets to fit Christmas cards, etc.... I joined a small writing group, and then the opportunity to go to Northern College came up. What more could I want, a place that could inspire my writing to perfection? It didn't though. I was inspired by ideas, imagination, settings, moods, feelings and emotions, but at the end of it I had to put it together: structure it, rewrite it and edit it. When at the end of the week I was told to go away, and learn, and come back in a couple of years time, you can imagine how I felt. Three years later I had my second chance.

After I went home I got an idea. A new prison had opened up in Doncaster. I offered my services for free. I found the ones who'd never written before were the most challenging and the most rewarding. One lad in particular was at rock bottom, everything looked black, there was no way out. Then as we worked together, experiences, feelings and thoughts were put down on paper for no other than himself. After some time, we read through what he had written until it could be put into some kind of diary system and he was finally writing on a lighter note and could see a light at the end of the tunnel. He called it *Diary of an Inmate.* Others throughout the prison could see a difference. Here are two poems from the prisoners:

Officers peeping through my door
A world of my own, I care no more
Then a hand comes through my wall
I screw up tight in a tiny ball
Scared as hell, my mind runs wild
Like I did as a little child
When this happens I want my Mum
The most I get is feeling numb
I get so mad and shout out no

(Anon)

I pray to God that they will go.
We're known as mugs
When we use drugs
Stop using!!! I've tried
Couldn't do it!!! I cried
I made money from crime
For drugs every time
Only wanted to forget
All the things that upset
The things in my mind.

(Anon)

(Jane Richardson)

Autobiography or reminiscence writing with older adults

An old person never wants a tale to tell.

(Proverb)

I am, I am, I am.

(Sylvia Plath, *The Bell Jar,* p.256)

Only in snow do I see/the trees I drew as a child.

(Hilda Cotterill 1992)

Writing not telling

'I'm going to write a whole book. I hope you are ready to read so much. It's quite a story.' 'Oh no, duck, I can't remember anything. You wouldn't want to hear about all that, anyway.'

Two responses to the same offer of an opportunity to be involved in writing reminiscence work in old people's homes. Reading the final products at the end of the project, one would be hard put to guess which writer had said which. The stories were varied and vital – full of humour and tragedy.

Perhaps, if the Ancient Mariner (Coleridge 1878) had been able to go to a reminiscence writing workshop, he wouldn't have had to stop so many people in the street over so many years telling the same story over and over again. Reminiscence work is often undertaken (Bender 1994). But nearly all the work reported in the literature is oral to written: taped and transcribed. The importance of the sparking of memories, encouraging people to express them and then giving them back their words, printed or typed, cannot be doubted. The writing of one's own reminiscence, and having written up and published, has a power even greater than the telling (see Chapter Seven, Autobiography, for further information and discussion).

> She thought to herself, 'This is now.'
>
> She was glad that the cosy house, and Pa and Ma and the firelight, and the music, were now. They could not be forgotten, she thought, because now is now. It can never be a long time ago. (Ingalls Wilder 1963, p.138)

These are the final words of the first volume of Ingalls Wilder's autobiography about her childhood, pioneering in America's Wild West in the 1880s. They could not be part of an oral reminiscence. They are essentially written: inherent within them is that private sense, that reflectiveness, which comes with writing.

Hilda Cotterill, who is in her late eighties, has said that writing poetry has been a saviour to her. She started writing a few years after her husband died – this greatly facilitated her coming to terms with his loss. Much of her writing has been autobiographical, depicting her present situation as well as past ones.

She told me that writing has been of such value to her because she has been able to express deep emotions and feelings and create something worthwhile. The mulling over a poem in her head before she writes it down helps keep depression and introspection at bay. Her writing has offered her a purpose in life as well as new friends (in the local poetry world) and some welcome fame.

The power of autobiography

This may be one of the best ways of cultivating feelings of self-esteem and control over life. It enables the retrospective viewing of a life. This can help to uncover, and recognise, strengths and weaknesses by viewing the stages of life. It can facilitate a coming to terms with present relationships and conflicts. It can help connect the present self with the child or young person – a therapeutically unifying process. As Mere (1994) said: 'Reminiscence is a dynamic process in which there is a seamless quality where past, present, and future ebb and flow, backwards and forwards' (p.133).

Physical problems

Helping frail old people to write is a skill all of its own. In one of the homes I went into the staff were adamant that none of their residents would be able to write – this would have to be an oral project. They accordingly seated us in a comfy sitting room for the first session. Thereafter, we took a corner of the dining room, around serviceable tables. Ernest wanted to write a book but told me I'd have to scribe for him. On my laughingly encouraging him, he wrote several pages, astonishing (and delighting) himself. I was sorry this was such a mini-project, he clearly would have liked many more sessions.

One lady's writing was a mere series of squiggles (to my eyes), so I had to transcribe it at the end of each session while she read it to me slowly. But this was still written reminiscence. She was rereading what she had written, not orally telling me. Some people needed help in beginning to wield the pen after so many years/months of manual inactivity and they tired quickly. Some were initially anxious about lack of spelling ability and so on, and needed encouragement. Some wrote for a short time and then relapsed into blankness, they needed 'waking up' and having their last few words read to them to remind them where they'd got to.

One person out of six or eight needed all their reminiscences scribing for them. We coped with this – myself and the care assistant – keeping an eye on the whole group and dodging about to offer whatever support was necessary.

There must be people for whom this kind of work would not be appropriate, or only appropriate under very carefully set up circumstances. Each individual is special and must be treated as such. We trusted the staff to know who would benefit and the old people themselves to choose to do it.

We laughed a lot. And we cried over some terrible events shared with us. I was left with the odd knowledge that people either felt they had had a terrible life or a fortunate one. One or other of these stances was reiterated time and again. Whether those whose experience was of a life of ups and downs, or perhaps just uneventful, didn't come to our groups, or were remarkably silent, I don't know.

The old people were delighted and stimulated to hear their previous week's writing read back to them at the start of each session. The staff's understanding and knowledge about the residents was deepened – they seemed to have little time and opportunity in their day-to-day contact to listen. Through the stories written during these few hours, the old people were able to present themselves as ordinary (or extraordinary) citizens, rather than just inhabitants of the tiny enclosed world of the home. A few of the resident's stories were ones the staff knew well from their day-in, day-out care but many gave fresh insights. Faced with these frail old people, one wouldn't guess the frolics they'd got up to, nor the suffering they'd endured.

There were some subjects which they were very keen to write about, such as the War, weddings and 'how we used to do things in the old days'.

Two stories

One of Annie's memories

I had gone for a walk in Hillsborough Park in Sheffield and me and my friend flirted and got off with these two boys. We just continued walking round and around the fish-pond, looking at the fish and that. When accidentally my knickers fell down. The boy looked embarrassed and looked away. That was the end of my first romance. I was about sixteen.

My knickers were around the waist in a band with buttons on. The buttons must have given way. They stopped at just above the knees. They fell around my ankles and I stooped, and tried to pull them up. But I couldn't, then I had a job getting them off around the toes and heels of my shoes. The boy walked away and needless to say that was the last I saw of him. I put them under my arm and carried them.

The beginning of Ernest's autobiography

When I was 5 years old the headlamp of a Bentley hit me in my jaw and knocked me 24 yards up against a wall. I was unconscious for 21 days and semi-conscious for 21 days. I lost my memory for 8 years …

How we worked

Some of the work was one-to-one but we mostly worked in a group, where they could share their writing with each other. Here is a digest of the way I worked and the issues I felt to be vital (in addition to those discussed elsewhere in this book):

- I only worked with people who wanted to be involved and they were encouraged to feel that everything they wrote was the right thing
- the residents/patients/clients must be comfortable, warm, have a drink and have been toileted
- I worked at their pace, which, of course, proved to be sometimes pretty slow
- the care staff who were involved wrote alongside each group, writing their own stories. Several members of staff found their own writing and each other's valuable and we loved their accounts. This gave the residents confidence as well – everyone has a life to tell, we were all in the same position.

What we did

'Think of a time when …?' is a useful start. It might be when they learned something important, such as tying their shoelaces or that Father Christmas was really only mum, or when something exciting happened or when a major change happened in their lives.

I usually suggested they think of only one occasion and describe it in detail as much as they could, including the time of year, whether they were warm or cold/comfortable, any smells associated with the memory (baking bread is popular with old people), any particular tastes, colours, textures, who else was there, what did they say, and so on.

Talking gently to them in this way as they sat and thought, seemed to encourage them to round out the memory.

There are an infinite number of ideas for inspiring this kind of writing – old photographs/postcards, precious mementoes, memories of food. Suggestions from any of the other chapters in this book can be used. Objects to be handled or music or smells are very good. (Age Exchange has published a creative ideas handbook for reminiscence (Osborn 1993).)

Now they could begin to write, but fears about handwriting, spelling and so on needed to be allayed. The only thing that matters is the process of committing a memory to paper.

Their writing was read back to them as they went along, particularly when they appeared stuck. There were all sorts of leading and supporting questions we asked to encourage them to remember more widely and write more.

Then everything was typed and read back to them the following week. This ensured we had read it right (the handwriting wasn't always easy) and gave great pleasure. Though, sometimes, when the memory had been painful, the rereading caused distress. It is part of the power of writing that words can flow onto the page in an almost unconscious way. Realising what those words mean on rereading can be a shock.

The last stage was making the writings into a little book, with a picture of Mabel's wedding dress on the cover. They have something to keep and be proud of.

The reminiscence process

Senex bis puer (an old man is twice a boy) is a Latin saying which gives the feel of the way old people live their childhoods twice – once when they are little and again in reminiscence later (the other interpretation of the saying is a great deal less complimentary). As they get older, the past seems to appear with greater and greater clarity and the concerns of the present to recede. In the 1960s and 1970s elderly people were discouraged from dwelling in the past in this way. It was considered one of the signs and disadvantages of senility, a mere brooding on the past.

The value of this natural-seeming process is now well studied and respected by researchers. It is encouraged as a therapeutic process and a healthy pastime in residential homes, as well as a way of fostering better memory. It exercises the mind, helping to keep mental facilities supple and functioning. A vital part of life has thus had to be institutionalised and offered by paid people to the elderly. The elderly have been dislocated from everyday life, they no longer live with their families. They are like a severed limb which feels as if it is still there, it itches or hurts, so specialists go in and care for them, offering to facilitate their remembering in order to improve the quality of their lives.

The very being in a home – cut off from normal life and associations – possibly encourages some residents to feel their life is of no further value, irrelevant, uninteresting. They need help to be able to re-value their life. Memory is coloured by present emotion. Those who feel a sense of present well-being are more likely to have a sense of satisfaction about their past life.

There are many oral history projects being carried out which value these reminiscences for their own sake. Accounts of how things used to be done – from washing with a dolly tub and posher to carrying the coal from the face by donkey cart – have been taken down and published by small presses (e.g. Gatehouse, Manchester). Otherwise, this knowledge would die with these old people.

In oral cultures old people would have been the repository of wisdom, experience and history. The sages, healers, historians would have had to instruct the younger generation before they died. And they would have been respected for it. The grannies and aunts would have told tales of long ago to soothe, amuse and inform the children.

I loved my great-aunt's stories – like kicking sparks against the cobbles in borrowed clogs, hoping my great-grandmother wouldn't catch her – nice girls did not wear clogs. My grandmother used to tell the tale of how my great-grandfather (Mad Jack Bolton) was killed by his own bull in his own stack yard. My own children repeatedly asked me to tell them about my boarding-school days. We were being connected up with our heritage, to lives and ways of living totally different to our own. We were also being offered a continuity with our forebears – this is who I am, where I come from.

Facilitating the reminiscence process

Older people often tend to reminisce naturally. Encouraging it in this way deepens its therapeutic value. From the relatively cut-off position of old age, reviewing life in this way can offer a greater sense of consistency and coherence of life, control over it and a greater understanding of their relationships to others. It can become a celebration of the older adults' own ordinary way of living and a recognition of their own achievements and experiences.

Some older people have painful memories. If the process is handled sensitively, a recognition of, and healing confrontation with, past pain and distress can take place. They can also be supported towards finding positive memories, in order to create a more comfortable life view to live with. This can be very beneficial to those who are stuck in a spiral of grief, in which there is nothing positive. They can be supported to find good episodes with the deceased, gradually build on these and move onwards and outwards within a more positive grieving.

This kind of activity can help these people in their present situation as well. It can help them create connections, which they might not hitherto have made, between present circumstances and past episodes. It can foster a greater degree of intimacy and friendship between the residents – this can be based on a greater understanding of them and their circumstances.

Reminiscing in this way can also help those who feel they need to boost their ego within the environment of the home by aggrandising their past. They will gain from hearing the memories of others, but also by discovering the joy of ordinary memories of their own.

I have already mentioned the way in which listening to these memories can enable carers to have a greater sense of understanding and insight into their patients. It can help them search for islands of lucidity with those suffering from dementia (see below).

Pause for thought

These older people *do* have something vital to say. Some texts (e.g. Coleman 1986) speak of 'allowing' elderly people to have a voice and opportunity of genuine expression in order to achieve a 'sense' of control over their lives. To encourage them to 'reminisce' merely in order to keep them happier and more alert is not respectful. It is up to us to listen and take these people seriously.

Slipping into a patronising tone would be very easy with these institutionalised older adults, whether that tone comes from an attitude towards class, race or gender. These people's experience is very different from many of ours (whether 'down t' pit', or 'skivvying') and a sensitive awareness is needed. The stimuli must be open, not reliant on being Christian, working class, white. John Killick (1994) has expressed hesitation in using standard (published) material for encouraging reminiscence (oral or written). He feels that there is no substitute for the relationship between writer and elderly person. I endorse this finding.

The writing of autobiography

There are several values that are specific to the writing of autobiography with older adults, over and above the therapeutic benefits discussed elsewhere in this book.

Older adults can think of themselves as offering material to our society's bank of social history, increasing self-confidence and self-respect. Small everyday events and habitual ways of doing things by their nature go unremarked – one always devalues one's everyday mundane existence. But, of course, when lifestyles change such information can be lost for good.

By writing autobiographical material, these older adults are creating an artistic product. The pride and self-confidence this engenders must not be undervalued. I have worked for many years with unemployed people in the Barnsley area, an area of high unemployment due to coalmine closures. The effect on these people of the writing of stories, poems, autobiographical material, plays is immense. It was the same for the old people.

Other projects

The Age Exchange Reminiscence Project (Arigho 1997) runs many projects in institutions. The Reminiscence Project of Manchester has run placements in Salford and Manchester (e.g. Poulson 1994a and b, 1996). Faith Gibson (1994) has written a *Guide to Good Practice* for Age Concern. A geriatric programme in New York most successfully instituted poetry groups on the initiative of one of their nurses (Sluder 1990). The staff found that the writing deepened their understanding of the patients a very great deal – many patients could express in writing what they had never been able to verbalise.

John Killick has reported at length his work with the elderly and dementia sufferers (1994, 1996a and b), and published a collection of their poems (1997). Working one-to-one has offered him time to discuss with the subjects the shaping and/or extension of writing. He feels that this reflection time is as vital as the reminiscence time.

Please Give me Back my Personality, John Killick's (1994) booklet from the Dementia Services Development Centre, includes a set of guidelines for the writer undertaking this work. 'You must have respect and curiosity and love in the presence of your subject ... You must be using all your powers of empathetic attention.' Proper attention must be given at all times to the elderly person – this might well include the appropriate offering of 'hugs and kisses'. On the other hand, this will also include an understanding that a rebuff (sometimes vituperative from a dementia sufferer) must not be taken personally.

'A lot of time working with an individual is spent waiting, and then the insights often come in a rush.' This work, and the attitudes of the worker, cannot be planned. The writer has to have a mixture of confidence and spontaneity in their ability to act instinctively. Yet when it comes to redrafting the old people's texts, Killick says that it is not the facilitator's job to alter the text in the interest of normal use of language, but only to edit where a thread is clear.

John Killick makes a strong case for individual work with people in which the writer is saying: 'May I accompany you on a journey into your own life?' In groupwork the writer is merely saying: 'Paint me a picture in words of what it was like.' Here is an account from John Killick:

Letting it all out

A lady said to me the other day 'I'm blethering from beneath the surface. I'm tired, but I don't want to go to sleep because I'm thriving'. The phrase 'blethering from beneath the surface' suggests an awareness that the talk stems from the unconscious mind, and that matters of significance are thrown up. She is *thriving* because the conversation is stimulating her.

A man said 'that chap who's doing what you are doing could be onto quite a big thing'. The significance of the work seems to be appreciated by some at least of the people I work with.

For a proportion of those with whom I work speech is no longer possible, or it is very difficult to unscramble. I am still able to communicate with them, though, by means of eye-contact, tone of voice, body language and touch:

> Alice, a Scottish lady is bent over in a chair, rocking and mumbling. I crouch down to make eye-contact and ask 'Do you like singing?' She nods, and I begin. Soon she is joining in, but is reduced to tears by the lament 'Will y no come back again?' because her 'Charlie' will never return. An embrace comforts her, and we sing a more cheerful song together until she falls asleep in my arms.

Sometimes what people tell me constitutes a vivid expression of a state of mind.

When this has been interpreted and shared with staff it can lead to immediate action to relieve tension and mood.

Much of the language used by people with dementia is figurative. It is as if the disease has attacked the reasoning faculty but left the more creative approach to language intact, and the disinhibiting effect of the disease removes the barrier to expression in imaginative ways. So a lady suffering from depression can say:

> It's like you're on a roundabout,
> but it's inside o' you.

and a man can express his confusion in the following terms:

> Have you any openings?
> Have you got a guide?
> Could you come along
> and turn a key in a lock for me?

Some of the transcripts become poems with very little in the way of editing:

> ... Say I was who I am.
> and you're doing what you're doing,
> d'ye think my wife would come?
>
> Write me your name and address,
> and don't let me lose it,
> so you keep it for me.
>
> Opened the door, let it all out.
> That's about all for now.
> Put 'etc. etc. etc.' for the rest.

One message of the work is that people retain their individuality to a late stage. They seem to understand far more than they are able to confirm to us in their conversations. And at all stages of the disease there appear to be windows of clarity. One lady whom it had been suggested to me was too confused for me to speak with, came up and asked 'is there a moment between birth and death when one becomes more important than the other?'

Another lady said: 'I'm talking, talking, talking all the time. I didn't know if you would understand with you living on the other side.' We share a common humanity, and must learn to listen and respond so that we can be with them in their condition. Writers have the privilege of being able to give a lead in this process. We are not 'living on the other side'.

(John Killick)

CHAPTER THIRTEEN

Approaches to Therapeutic Writing

'But Who Are *You*?'

> In the beginning was the word.
>
> (St John 1:1)

> Give sorrow words: the grief, that does not speak,
> Whispers the o'er-fraught heart, and bids it break.
>
> (*Macbeth* III iv 24)

> Art gives a voice to suffering.
>
> (Stephen K Levine)

Who are you? What is your suffering? Does it want to be heard? Why? How can this be done? Who can best facilitate this to help me with the question: who am I? Different approaches to the use of writing in attempting to respond to these questions is examined in this chapter.

Words and voices

The three statements which precede this chapter would seem to contradict each other. If there is the word before anything else, why do we need writing (and psychotherapy, etc) to express sorrow and suffering? We need them because the heart becomes 'o'er-fraught' when words of pain and suffering have gone round and round in the head silently – unexpressed and uncommunicated. The value of therapy lies in its facilitation of communication and development of respect for feelings. In the quote from *Macbeth* at the beginning of this chapter, Malcolm is chiding Macduff for not sharing the pain he is clearly feeling at hearing of the murder of his wife and children, for not giving it the space it clearly warranted. Levine continues from his above quote: 'To dance suffering, to paint it or put it into poetic form is to confront it directly and give oneself up to it.' Not only are the feelings properly acknowledged and expressed, in this process, but also respected. (The use of image in dance or painting can be as much a communication and channel of expression as speaking or writing can).

"But who are *you*?'

said the Caterpillar. "I – I hardly know sir, just at present – at least I know who I was when I got up this morning." ' (Carroll 1865, p.35). Alice is struggling, just as we all struggle, with the biggest philosophical question of all time. And this is the unanswerable question at the heart of psychotherapy and the arts therapies. The Caterpillar had the solution when Alice turned the question back on him: ' "I think you ought to tell me who you are, first." "Why?" said the Caterpillar.'

Why indeed. Why *not* settle for not knowing who I am essentially and spend my energies instead on finding out about all the potential people I might be? The previous chapters suggest many ways of doing this. I will now turn to looking at other practitioners' understandings of the self and other approaches to offering and supporting therapeutic writing, as well as different understandings of its value. This is followed by four examples of writing within therapy or counselling.

Mirror or model

What is the nature of the sorrow referred to by Shakespeare and Levine; and who am 'I' who is suffering or who could (should) 'I' be? It would be too easy to imagine that sorrow or suffering is held in a finite pit in ourselves which can be emptied of its painful contents through expression and communication with a therapist, page or canvas – resulting in a fit, well or whole person. This way of understanding assumes a perfect self who is in there waiting to be relieved of the burden of carrying this painful lump within them. Levine carries on to say: 'As we enter unreservedly into ourselves, we encounter healing energies and experience the hope of integration. Though this ultimate wholeness is never given to us, it remains a vision that animates our work on ourselves' (1992, p.23). Levine's model is of a potentially whole (unsuffering) person. He admits this is unattainable, but, even so, it is his vision. This vision is a notion of a perfect me which is there somewhere – if only I could find it, I would be happy and at peace. This assumption underlies much of medicine and psychology and it is not helpful.

The theory and practice of therapeutic writing outlined in this book is based on a model in which different aspects of ourselves can be experimented with and explored, where stories can be written and then rewritten with different endings or in a different voice. There is no whole and integrated me, which is the ultimate aim, the vision, of this therapeutic work. The writing described here is a process of exploring; an expression of different aspects of myself and an encouragement of these disparate voices within me to communicate with each other, and with other people. This can lead to greater understanding and greater respect for the diverse aspects of myself, and an increased ability to listen attentively and fruitfully to them.

It is as though the writing is a multicoloured packet of plasticine which I can model variously. It is not a mirror. The art therapist, R Simon has said: 'Art as therapy is a mirror that the patient makes to find his own self reflected.' (1992, p.9) If, as I suggest, there is no *one* own self to be reflected, the reflection will be different every time I look. It is, moreover, a multifaceted image – three-dimensional – moving and breathing more like those model clay characters we see on the television (e.g. *Wallace and Gromit*) than the cold hard stare of a looking- glass reflection.

There is no more a single reservoir of artistic creativity within us than there is a single pit of pain.

> In the act of writing, especially of writing verse, one is always convinced that what appears on the page is only a distorted fragment of what, somewhere or other inside you, wanted to appear, and would have appeared too, if only we knew how to listen to it more subtly and widely and deeply, and record it more boldly. The progress of any writer is marked by those moments when he manages to outwit his own inner police system which tells him what is permissible, what is possible, what is 'him'. Writers have invented all kinds of 'games' to get past their own censorship ... One thing such times have in common is a willingness to relax expectation, and to experiment, to let flow – a willingness to put on masks and to play. (Hughes 1982, p.7)

Writing can be a letting go of expectations and assumptions and a playing with possibilities, as Ted Hughes says. But instead of envisaging myself as a definite *me* who puts on masks, I would more suggest that we are trying out, listening to varied internal voices – *each voice as valid as the other.*

The notion of there possibly being different aspects of ourselves has long been a fear in our culture, expressed vividly by Robert Louis Stevenson in *Dr Jekyll and Mr Hyde* (1886), in which Mr Hyde – a dangerous sub-personality, hidden within the urbane Dr Jekyll – has to be exterminated. Pat Barker has explored this fear of our potentially split nature in her *Regeneration* trilogy where the sufferers from shell shock and fugue repeatedly examine their hands for Mr Hyde's hairiness. We are fascinatedly fearful (see also Lesley Glaister's powerful fiction about a split personality: *Private Parts of Women* (1996)). Herman Hesse's *Steppenwolf* is yet another example from literature.

Our fear is capitalised on in these fictions. Yet the notion of there being different people in us can be most fruitfully harnessed in therapeutic work (we are not here talking about psychiatric states of dissociated personality but about the workings of the mind of you or me). Freud suggested that each of us is divided into three essential elements: ego, id and superego. Since Freud and Jung there have been many theories about the different elements of ourselves and many different psychotherapies making active use of these theories, such as psychodrama, gestalt, transactional analysis. John Rowan (1990) and James Hillman (1975, 1981) argue strongly for there being no essential self and suggest many methods for allowing the different elements within ourselves to be heard, and to hear each other, therapeutically. Most of the suggestions in this book (such as letter writing to parts of oneself) are adapted from such theories and practices.

We are afraid of the self who emerges in dreams. It is not surprising that we incarcerate those we consider to be mad, since the insane speak with voices beyond our narrow frightened definition of the normal and allowable. If, instead, we can bear to listen to the words which come from this suffering, this sorrow, listen to our dream voices and those of the insane, we stand to lose a crippling fear and open out our understandings, empathy and wisdom.

Writing can give a voice to suffering. Pennebaker, in the United States of America, used a scientific paradigm to create random controlled trial evidence for the value of writing on health.

Research into the power of post-trauma writing

The natural way of dealing with an upheaval is to talk about it extensively over a long period. This time is often too long and too repetitive for audiences who tire of the subject or find it stressful. Pennebaker and Short undertook an unpublished study in 1990 which shows that talking about a trauma reduces the teller's anxiety level but increases that of the hearers. They found that those who provide social support to another person in distress suffer significantly higher physical and mental illness rates than they would otherwise. Only too often, friends expect a bereaved wife/husband to be feeling better after a few weeks. Those of us who have been bereaved, or bereavement counsellors, know it can take years, especially if the relationship had not been a satisfactory one. So those who have suffered unusually (death of a child, incest) and those who suffer because they are unwell (chronic depression, etc) will tend to have to repress the normal coping mechanism of talking through their situation endlessly.

Expressing thoughts and feelings about a massive upheaval enables people to learn more about the event and their own reactions to it, and the way in which it is represented in the memory. Once it has been put into words, it should be easier to organise and assimilate. If this doesn't happen, longstanding personality processes are affected, a trauma is cognitively prolonged and, because the person cannot talk to friends and relatives about the distressing subject, they can become socially isolated. Pennebaker quotes Wegner (1988), who demonstrated that intrusive thoughts of a white bear intensified when asked not to think of one. 'Intrusive thoughts get much of their propulsive force from unexpressed emotion ...' The problem is not the memories themselves but 'the unassimilated emotions that drive these memories to the surface of consciousness' (Pennebaker 1993, p.101).

Pennebaker (1988, 1993) found that students who were asked to write about their deepest thoughts and feelings about the most traumatic event in their lives for a short period on four consecutive days showed consistently significant drops in physician visits for illness in the two to six months after the study, in comparison with control subjects who wrote about trivial matters. They were asked to write with candour, without regard for spelling, grammar or punctuation.

A significant increase in the experimental subjects' immune function, their ability to withstand infection, was noted, compared to the controls', from before to after the writing period. The subjects received no feedback from the researchers; it was purely the impact of writing that made the effect.

The more organised the subjects' writings were, the more they increased in organisation over the four days of writing, the more it succeeded as a narrative – organised, emotionally compelling, vivid and fluid – the more their immune function improved. This is corroborated by the findings of other researchers.

Over 75 per cent of the subjects described the long-term benefits in ways such as: 'it made me think things out ...'; 'it helped me look at myself from the outside/sort out my thoughts ...' Only about 10 per cent used venting or cathartic words to describe their writing, and those who did showed less improvement.

Pennebaker concludes that narrative expression, whether written or spoken, has a naturally organising (controlling and structuring) effect. But 'writing permits subjects to engage their traumas to a degree and at a rate at which they feel comfortable' (1993, p.110). Writing in this controlled and structured way also enables the traumatic memories to be associated with non-traumatic ones. This helps to re-integrate them into the normal network of the sufferers' memories and beliefs.

Pennebaker's conclusions on the beneficial effects of writing support those of this book. But he is working from a different assumption about the self – a different model. He assumes that people have a normal network of memories and beliefs and that writing helps them to sort out the abnormal ones which won't fit in in a controlled and structured way. In other words, writing helps these traumatic memories to become normal. I would suggest that this model of there being a controlled and structured normality, and all sorts of elements outside it causing problems, is far from useful. People are composed of a stewpot of beliefs, understandings, memories, terrors and hopes. Different elements bubble up at different times, wanting and needing to be attended to. Dealing with these in an appropriate way then and there will lead to a more balanced and happy individual. But there are no *right* or *wrong* elements.

Pennebaker's data also suggest that a chaotic cathartic splurge of writing is not enough. People need to carry on writing (possibly redrafting and rewriting) until they understand what their writing means for their own personal development. A piece of writing created with an emotional charge about an event in the past is very often therapeutic and creative. There seems to be a right time to write about deeply-felt events in order to create effective writing – not straight away when it would be jumbled, nor too late when the emotional need for expression might have gone cold. Wordsworth called this 'emotion recollected in tranquillity'. Writing, done at the right stage, which makes sense and accurately conjures up a past situation, will offer its writer the most release and relief because it will have expressed and communicated their feelings effectively.

Pennebaker concludes that although circumstances allow few people to share as much about a harrowing event as they need to for psychological health, disclosing on paper at a later date can do much to undo this original harm. Pennebaker's research concerns the effectiveness of writing for the disclosure and emotional reintegration of subjects' worst memories of trauma.

Writing (and reading) can also be therapeutically supportive in a gentler manner. There is, potentially, a spectrum of different ways of using writing for therapeutic support. *The Therapeutic Potential of Creative Writing* offers, on the whole, an in-depth therapeutic approach and Pennebaker's findings back up one aspect of this. I would like to give a glimpse of some of this wide spectrum. Here follows a description of a lighter set of methods, possibly appropriate to an even larger number of people, which are being looked into in Britain.

Research into the soothing and healing power of poetry

Poetry (both reading and writing) can have a calming and soothing effect on the sick and depressed, according to the research of Robin Philipp, Consultant Occupational and Public Health Physician and Director of The Centre for Health in Employment and the Environment. Robin describes how poetry makes you feel better and why it should be more integrated into mainstream healthcare:

> There is accruing evidence that looking inwards or 'inscaping' and the process of linking and giving coherence to different thoughts, feelings and emotions, and articulating them as poetry can be beneficial to health. It can have a calming effect for many people, especially if the words are written with cadence and rhythm. Such expression can even evoke a resonance with aspects of and factors in the external environment. This personal creativity, sometimes spontaneously flowing whilst in a relaxed, half-awake, half-asleep state when the mind is in a state of 'stillness' and untroubled by external stimuli, allows the gentle surfacing to consciousness of inner tensions and delights and the outward expression of innovative, imaginative, evocative, ingenious, inspired and inventive thoughts.
>
> In January 1994, in a letter published in the *British Medical Journal* (BMJ), we asked if reading, writing or listening to poetry benefits health, and if we should encourage our patients or ourselves, to express thoughts as poetry? (Philipp *et al.* 1994). By January 1996 when we completed the first qualitative study of responses to our letter in the BMJ, it had evoked 60 news media reports and letters from 84 health professionals and 218 members of the public in 14 different countries.

The responses were all positive and supportive. The health professionals included psychiatrists, general practitioners, psychologists, psychotherapists, counsellors, nurses, and occupational, speech and drama therapists. They reported they had successfully used poetry with patients suffering from anxiety, depression, bereavement, terminal illnesses, post-traumatic stress and eating disorders. Amongst 196 members of the UK public, three-quarters said that reading reduced stress and two thirds that writing it had the same effect and provided an outlet for their emotions. Ten per cent reported that reading poems improved their mood. These benefits also enabled 13 of the UK respondents to stop the antidepressive or tranquilliser medication they had been taking (Philipp and Robertson 1996). The personal testimony was powerful (Philipp 1995, 1996). It included the following comments:

- Writing poetry helps me to get something off my chest.
- I feel the need to write when I feel something very intensely.
- Poetry is infinitely preferable to a pill, has no adverse side effects and revitalises and enhances the human psyche.
- Reading poems is inspiring, therapeutic and calming.
- Provided one enjoys writing, the penning of poetry has a cathartic effect. Reading a poem with a relaxing rhythm can be almost hypnotic.
- The most tranquillising effect comes from poetry with rhythm, and when in need of calm, the natural 'rocking' sound of the words takes me back to being a child and I find the effect very soothing.
- Creative writing can be used to get the world into perspective and encourage understanding that allows us to see the reasoning behind other peoples, as well as our own actions.
- Hymns speak to one of the crying needs of our day – the need for space in one's life for times of quiet amidst excessive noise and over-activity.

We have identified similar findings in two other unpublished studies amongst 80 members of the National Association of Writers in Education. They also identified the healthcare settings where poetry workshops are being successfully held. These settings include general practice surgeries, hospices, adult and paediatric in-patient general and psychiatric hospital wards, psychiatric day hospitals, community psychiatric clinics, psychogeriatric units and long-stay residential care units for persons with learning disorders, mental health problems, chronic physical handicap and problems of ageing.

The news media have spontaneously reported their interest in this work. Amongst the 80 news media reports brought to our attention, some of the newspaper headlines have been as evocative as the public testimony:

- GPs to be versed in therapy
- Try the rhythm method
- A poem a day keeps dejection at bay
- Let iambics take the measure of your stress
- Rhyme that can restore reason
- Exam blues? An ode could ease your load
- From bad to verse.

Poetry and other forms of creative writing can, we believe, be used to:

- unburden negative thoughts, feelings and emotions
- broaden the way we look at our present-day patterns of living and help us identify ways we can enrich our own lives
- express our delight, wonder and enjoyment of life and living
- improve our personal well-being
- identify ways we can help others and share thoughts, ideas and experiences.

We have prepared a framework to help evaluate the effectiveness of the arts in healthcare. Further research is being planned, with the purpose of determining if more health practitioners should include poetry in their therapeutic tool-kit (see also Philipp 1997 and Bolton and Ahmedzai 1997).

(Robin Philipp)

This chapter has so far looked at how there are different ways of understanding the nature and status of those parts of ourselves where therapeutic writing comes from, what kind of thing this writing is and proof that can it work in certain ways. There are also different ways of understanding the relationship of the writer with a support person (therapist, facilitator, reader, teacher, supervisor) and the role of writing within the developing understandings of the writer. Here follows a brief look at some other ways of working.

Some more examples of practice and theory

Therapists in the USA have been at the forefront of examining the potential of therapeutic writing (often called scriptotherapy), so far. The (American) National Association for Poetry Therapy, which offers post-graduate training in developmental (or clinical) interactive bibliotherapy, only has fewer than 370 members (17 in other countries), however. Much of their emphasis is on reading or listening to poetry. On the process of therapeutic writing, they state: 'Finding one's own voice is a self-affirming process often followed by cathartic release, greater self-awareness and new insight.'

Luciano L'Abate's approach, however, in common with many other American writers on this subject, involves:

> intervening by relying on self-paced, self administered homework assignments varying in their degree of structure and content … Although self-administered by patients, completed assignments are scrutinised by the therapist who then provides corrective feedback. These assignments are used as a springboard for further discussion and exploration in therapy. Generalisations, distortions, deletions and other errors in thinking are pointed out by the therapist and worked through. (1991, p.90)

This is didactic and completely lacks respect for the client and any writing they may create – a totally different approach to that suggested in this book. It must create very different writing, and self-understandings, from the kind of writings suggested in this book, and from the examples offered below in this chapter. One of the main advantages of the therapeutic writing outlined in this book is that it can offer the patient or client much more autonomy and sense of control over their own symptoms and illness. L'Abate would seem to be using it to tie the client even more securely to the therapist's apron strings. He even reports that there are 'workbooks' published in the USA to direct clients in therapeutic writing.

Considerable success is reported using this 'programmed writing', however. L'Abate even goes so far as to claim: 'Writing aims to offer a method that, in the hands of sensitive, experienced, and knowledgeable professionals, should help them improve their own effectiveness and efficiency. It is not unlike using a calculator or a computer rather than our ten fingers to solve mathematical problems' (1991, pp.82–98) He adds that one of the advantages of using writing within therapy is: 'How hard, how well, how frequently patients work on these assignments is another more direct way to assess whether they are motivated or not.' Writing becomes a real test in the hands of this therapist.

There are a considerable number of ways of using writing documented (mostly in the USA). A few of them are outlined below. They are all effective ideas, if used with an open attitude to the writer (client) and the relationship between writer and supporter.

1. Summaries of therapeutic session written by therapist, or client or both, and read and commented on by both in order to share their understandings of the event (Yalom 1970). Yalom has found these offer great insight. In fact, some summaries even exploded his own assumptions about what had happened during sessions he had run!

2. Scenario writing – This is fictional written accounts of anticipated future events in order to help the client to cope with fears and apprehensions (Haddock 1989). This method is based on the theory that 'it is the *expectation*, not the objective conditions of uncontrollable events, that is the crucial determinant of helplessness and depression'.

3. Writing letters to, and dialoguing with, other parts of the self – such as the child, the assertive managing self, the over-protective self, etc. – as a way towards understanding dissociative and dysfunctional behaviour (Torem 1993). Torem reports using this when hypnosis is not appropriate. The approach he has used is, however, once more very didactic – patients are 'instructed' to write 'homework', 'tasks', and 'assignments'. The same way of working could be introduced without this autocratic approach.

4. Within 'couples therapy', to help each client examine their own feelings and enable them to hear each other (Jordan and L'Abate 1995).

5. The writing and redrafting of poetry (Lester and Terry 1992). Poetry communicates through images, often metaphors, as do the symptoms of mental and emotional disturbance. Lester and Terry cite the example of Anne Sexton, who 'revised her poems extensively. In the process of revision, the poet must concentrate no

longer on content but rather on form. This allows for both the action that therapists deem to be therapeutic and the distancing of the self from one's problems'. (See also the work of Atlas, Smith and Sessoms (1992), who used therapeutic poetry writing with hospitalised adolescents, and Chapters Seven (poetry) and Fourteen.)

6. As a method for clearing the mind and giving perspective to troubling thoughts and feelings that stand in the way of important tasks, such as in diary writing (Riordan 1996).
7. For diagnosis – for suicidal themes in young people's poetry, for example (Sharlin and Shenhar 1986) – and for assessing disorders, personality functioning and behaviour (Silverman 1986).
8. The writing of fiction. A rape victim was enabled to remember and face her trauma by writing an account as if it had happened to a fictional character (Graves 1984). She was able to master the trauma by altering the fictional circumstances and create a new account. This extension of the fictional writing is similar to scenario writing, above, and to my own reflective writing (see Chapter Eight).
9. Sent letters (as well as unsendable ones). This is from Britain and is of a three-year postal psychotherapeutic relationship which relied on the sending of verse. Interestingly the therapist noted that the patient's poetry improved in quality as the treatment advanced (Morrice 1983).

I could carry on. There has been a great deal of invention in the use of writing within therapy and the approach has been very varied. If suggested and supported by the therapist with respect for the client's writing and autonomy, the above ideas could be useful within therapy, or for the writer to try on their own. There are also some extremely valuable books from both the USA and Britain containing ideas and suggestions which are not expressly therapeutic, though two of them have self-discovery in their titles. I recommend Schneider and Killick (1997), Lane (1993), Baldwin (1991) and Sellers (1991).

I now offer examples as models of using writing within therapy/counselling. These descriptions are all written by the therapists themselves, with quotes from their clients' writing.

A hand to hold the hand which holds the pen

A poem, story or drama offers relatively secure boundaries to the writer, who can explore and express their inner self, just as a visual artist is contained by the picture frame. If the writer is further supported and guided by a therapist or counsellor, the insights have the potential to be very great.

Many therapists and counsellors use writing as an adjunct to their work with clients, without it ever reaching the literature. It is such an obvious thing to do, with such a range of benefits. Writing aids a sense of responsibility in clients because they can do it on their own and for themselves, it extends the therapeutic hour and it can enhance understandings since clients are often willing to write things in the security of their own homes which they would find impossible to say to the therapist. It prevents issues or images from uselessly twisting round and round in the client's head by putting them firmly down on the paper; the very deliberateness of writing helps the writer to take seriously whatever appears on the paper. Writing is unequivocal and is less likely to be misunderstood than talk when it is given to the therapist to read (see Chapter Eleven – GP: 'you can't mis-hear what is written') and offers a lasting record to be worked on. In creating an object out of intangible thoughts and ideas, to which the writer can relate, writing provides a testimony of the process. Here follow some examples of good practice.

Writing in therapy

Gloria was unconventional: from an East End (London) background, she had settled very happily in her home on the edge of the Forest where she brought up her family. A very warm personality, she looked after and loved not only her grandchildren, but the birds and squirrels who would come to her.

She had left home in her teens to escape the unwelcome attentions of her stepfather. After a very difficult life, she had, at 30 years old begun to make her peace with her mother. Unfortunately mother died rather young and very suddenly. Gloria found this very painful; so much unfinished business; so many *if onlys.*

I suggested she wrote a letter to her mother, telling her all the things she regretted not saying; afterwards she could keep it, or burn it so the smoke would go upwards like a prayer. The response was in keeping. 'Me write?! I can just about manage a shopping list!'

At the next visit I found a very different Gloria: much happier. Yes, she had written the letter, could not stop once she started: three pages. Then she took it to the cemetery, set fire to it and sat and watched the smoke go up to heaven. She felt at peace as she buried the ash in the grave.

An elderly woman attending her husband's grave came to see what was happening, having watched the flames, and Gloria explained. 'What a good idea,' exclaimed the old woman; 'I am going to send a letter to *my* husband.'

Gloria felt Mother had heard, and that she was blessed.

(Doreen Padfield)

Marguerite Dixon's writing in therapy

Marguerite is a therapist who habitually harnesses the power of writing within her work. Here is an example from her:

> Penny was a private person, not wishing to share all her deepest thoughts with another, yet she was unhappy, confused, stuck and mildly depressed. Through empathetic listening I helped Penny identify themes she could explore and develop in writing. A description of different ways of doing this: free-flowing writing, completing sentences, lists, comparisons, dialogues, and letter and story writing, enabled Penny to choose what seemed most helpful to her at the time of writing. In therapy, Penny disclosed what she wished of her own writing, and I helped clarify and affirm insights. Here is some of her writing:
>
> *It seems good to be writing all this stuff because now I've started talking to Marguerite there are lots of ideas in my head. Well, they are all muddled up right now, and if they don't sort themselves out I'll burst!...*
>
> *I'm lost – I don't know who I'm supposed to be any more. Any more – because I* was *a worker and a mum and a housewife. But I just* did *all those things and, not thought about who I was at the time.*
>
> *I'm beginning to feel that WHO I AM is hidden inside me somewhere and has been there all the time. I think that writing about ME will help me work it all out as well as talking. It's good I can write anytime I like – when ideas come into my head and I don't have to wait for counselling sessions. And I can keep what I want private too. That's all good – I don't feel quite so stuck now there is at least something I can DO!...*
>
> Penny has got in touch with her inner child needs and begins to work out how to satisfy them now in a series of writings. I had introduced the concept form Transactional Analysis of Parent/Adult/Child which Penny found helpful in her written explorations. She went on to do

dialogues with her inner child and even a story, written as a young child. Here is more, written towards the end of therapy:

The best thing has been able to follow up ideas just when they came in between sessions. I've got better at knowing when the odd thought coming in my head needed me to put it down on paper so all kinds of other thoughts could follow and I could get to understand myself better.

Writing things down has sometimes turned into a sort of dialogue between my unsure and my sure self – the best of that was that it just grew and I surprised myself by what got written! I suppose that means I've partly become my own therapist.

Another example of writing in therapy

This therapist, unfortunately, has to remain anonymous:

> Sarah's inner rage stemmed from unfinished business relating to Sarah's having repeatedly been sexually abused by her uncle when a child. Sarah was not comfortable with writing initially. Although verbally articulate in general, she had not found writing easy at school. With encouragement Sarah found after initial attempts that she could write freely albeit in a sometimes disjointed and untidy fashion. She used different styles of writing, different sizes of letters and capitals randomly as these best reflected her feelings.
>
> After a few sessions of therapy Sarah found it easy to disclose what had happened to her by writing it as a third person story about 'little Sarah aged 7'. Doing this gave her confidence to disclose at a distance from her feelings which she was afraid would over-power her:
>
> *Sarah didn't like Uncle Alan much he had funny eyes but she couldn't say so. After the biscuits Uncle Alan sat her on his lap and put his hand down her pants and tuched her. Sarah didn't like it. She tried to get off but he held her. He put her hand down his trousers to tuch his hard thing. She hated it but he held her tite and made her. he got all red and egcited. In the end he let Sarah go and told her to keep it secret or her Mum would get cross. Sarah went home and did not tell her Mum cus she didn't like it when her mum got angry and shouted at her. Uncle Alan did it lots of times and Sarah never told on him.*
>
> Sarah had been reassured that handwriting, correct spelling and so on did not matter. She wrote in a rather childish hand with childish spelling mistakes which she did not repeat in later writing.
>
> Therapy after this writing centred on enabling Sarah to own the experience as her own and to get in touch with unresolved feelings. She

was able in writing, to rewrite the story, writing in the first person and disclose the terror, fear and disgust of her experiences.

Sarah wrote letters to 'Uncle Alan' telling him what she thought about him. This helped her release further anger, although she had thought that because he was now dead it would not help. She also wrote angry letters to her mother who she felt should have known she was upset. Therapy helped her understand her mother's situation at the time and she forgave her in a letter which, as an adult she decided was best not sent.

It helped to write it down – it was hard to write, but it got some things out of me that I couldn't just have said out loud. They were to awful to say to my therapist, but after writing, I could *say them to her.*

If I get angry again I can write things down just how I want to – *just for me – anyhow I like. I've decided it's not going to mess up my life any more.*

(Anon)

The self as source

A therapeutic writing method from Cheryl Moskowitz

Cheryl, a psychodynamic counsellor, describes how she came to develop her therapeutic creative technique which involves the client creating and developing different characters from aspects of herself (see also Moskowitz 1998). It originated with a woman who was in remission after lengthy treatment in isolation for leukaemia:

> The illness had caused a feeling of total disintegration, similar to that which is experienced after any major crisis in life either physical or emotional. She felt herself to be split in many ways, fearful and hopeful, living and dying, loving and hating, angry and forgiving. She talked about herself in relation to how she was before the illness and now, how changed she felt in its aftermath. I began to work on an exercise with her which we called *the ill self and the well self.* She explored each of these sides of herself as if they were different people. Together we brainstormed words, ideas, phrases that fitted each and later searched for visual images and verbal metaphors to flesh them out.
>
> The next stage was to give each of these split parts that had now become separate people in their own right, an identity and a name. She christened the ill self Eileen, and the well self Sally. We endowed the two characters with biographical details: age, profession, physical char-

acteristics and personality, place to live, car to drive, personal likes and dislikes.

The third stage was to create a way, through story, for Eileen and Sally to meet one another. The objective of the story was for the two women to exchange something of mutual value. The story could be anywhere and the exchanges could be anything: material or in the form of ideas or quality of self. The discovery for her as well as myself was that the creation of characters from split parts of the self provides a richness of emotion and spirit, which is beyond initial imagining. The further discovery was that these characters, once created and given dimension, do not remain static in their approach or reaction to circumstances around them. They are changed by events and, in fact, become people with the same real contradictions and splits from which they were initially created.

Inside me I have a man who is a juggler and acrobat, an ageing New Age hippy woman, and a boy, and a girl. I suppose there may be more. I'd like to try Cheryl's suggestion of them meeting in a fiction. Jane Rogers' (1984) novel, *Her Living Image*, is about a woman whose husband has an affair with her alter ego, a book which adds even more understanding to Cheryl's approach.

Who are you?

This is a question with which Gillian Massereene-James has clearly been faced. She says that 'my poems are turning point poems … linked with movement – changing one life for another, holding the thread while that happens'. She uses writing as part of her 'struggle to know what I have to do next'. Her first poem below expresses 'anger – healthy anger – wanting to change my relationship with the world. The second poem is about being very content with the freedom of being "just me", brand new':

1

Get in touch with yourself
they said

They didn't know
I hadn't got a self
my blueprints rejected
before they were drawn
But I worked hard

took all advice
and got in touch
with somebody else
Helped them out of a hole
and ruined my health
Somewhere
in the world's waste paper
lies an almost thought
which could be me

I'd like it back now
please

2

There is no record
that I have ever been
My friends have never
heard of me
my family have never seen
anything
I've looked in
the hardest places
found nothing
that could have been me

Does that mean I'm no-one?
Does that mean I'm free?

(Gillian Massereene-James)

CHAPTER FOURTEEN

Conclusions

Thought Made Flesh

We write before knowing what to say and how to say it, and in order to find out, if possible.

(J.-F. Lyotard, *Explaining the Postmodern to Children*, p.119)

Trying to learn to use words, and every attempt
Is a wholly new start, and a different kind of failure
... And so each venture
Is a new beginning, a raid on the inarticulate

(T.S. Eliot, *East Coker*)

That process of raid, or persuasion, or ambush, or dogged hunting, or surrender, is the kind of thinking we have to learn and if we do not somehow learn it, then our minds lie in us like the fish in the pond of a man who cannot fish.

(Ted Hughes, *Poetry in the Making*, p.57)

Writing has a power quite different from talking or thinking. Its power is similar to the other arts but dissimilar in that it uses words, our everyday communicating medium. This chapter looks at this difference, explores the relationship between writing and mental illness or depression and examines whether therapeutic writing is or can be art.

Some of the ways in which writing is different from thinking and talking have been studied in the rest of this book. One of these is that the act of writing creates an object to which the writer can relate tangibly, visually and aurally. The writing is seen, it can be heard, it can be touched on the page – framed, filed with care, screwed up in a ball, or burnt. And this tangibility lasts over time, to be re-experienced in different frames of mind, different stages of life.

The act of creating this object is a physical one, which itself can provide powerful release and creative energy. Shaun McNiff (1992) an art therapist, tells people: 'Just paint ... Start painting as though you are dancing with your whole body, and not just using your fingers and your wrist' (p.33). He adds: 'The beginning painter often tries to represent images visualised in the mind in advance, making failure inevitable'. One must paint or write with the body rather than the mind, with no assumptions or expectations as to what is going to appear (see Helene Cixous below). In order to paint or write therapeutically (or effectively), we must let go of that controlling mind and allow the expression to be from our whole selves (from the fish, the pond *and* the watcher on the bank) and this means we have to entertain failure. Paradoxically, we are, therefore, far more likely to succeed, since our whole selves know a great deal more than just our minds.

This process can be more enjoyable and certainly far less aggressive than Ted Hughes' 'process of raid, or persuasion, or ambush, or dogged hunting, or surrender' or Eliot's 'raid' might suggest.

But why is this kind of writing different from talking or thinking; why is writing not just talking or thinking which happens to have been put on the page? What makes it different?

It seems that writing in a free-intuitive way (Chapter Three) can take you into an altered state of consciousness close to a dream state, perhaps almost into a hypnogogic or trance-like state. Sometimes it even seems to do more than this and takes the writer into an altered state of being, different from the everyday self – a state we might otherwise consider as being not sane. Here is the poet Carole Satyamurti speaking of her own experience:

> Writing a poem seems to involve a simultaneous opening up and a reaching inwards – like an intense form of day-dreaming – a state a bit like madness. And there's a fear that if I am interrupted, I'll fall apart and not recover my 'normal' self; or that what I'm groping after, that elusive form I'm trying to make more substantial, will disappear. (1989, p.14)

Anna Freud, a psychoanalyst, talks about the very first attempts made by the beginning painter and the nervousness experienced once the realisation strikes that this process does make contact with vital, hitherto inarticulate, material. The process she describes is much the same as for writing:

> The amateur painter, who first puts pencil or brush to paper, seems to be in much the same mood as the patient during his initial period on the

> analytic couch. Both ventures, the analytic, as well as the creative one, seem to demand similar external and internal conditions. There is the same need for 'circumstances in which it is safe to be absent minded' (ie for conscious logic and reason to be absent from one's mind). There is the same unwillingness to transgress beyond the reassuring limits of the secondary process and 'to accept chaos as a temporary stage'. There is the same fear of the 'plunge into no-differentiation' and the disbelief in the 'spontaneous ordering forces' which emerge, once the plunge is taken. There is, above all, the same terror of the unknown. (1971, p.xvii)

Exhilaration and the excitement of discovery, rather than terror of the unknown, are more often experienced, once the process is started. Shaun McNiff (1992) suggests the art therapist is a shaman. Many cultures have shamen as healers: they take on a trance state (induced by drumming, dancing, fly agaric mushrooms or other hallucinogenic plant) and 'fly' to other 'worlds' to bring healing or to fetch back a wandering, alienated soul. In therapeutic writing the writer themselves can be their own shamen, entering an altered state of consciousness in which to make contact with their own wandering soul. They are then able to create images which will help them to understand how to retain contact with their soul, and become more integrated.

Some theories of why writing is different

Researchers have attempted to understand the way in which the artistic process can take writers into different and deeper territories than talking. Juliet Mitchell (1989) offers the theory that artists subject themselves repeatedly to 'as-it-were' trauma (an affective living-through of trauma that has not been personally experienced) to give them 'anxiety-pain' which offers energy and material for creativity. 'So, in its most simple form, anxiety obviously motivates people to be creative.' Yes, but this doesn't mean people invent trauma in the pursuit of their art.

A much simpler explanation could be offered: that artists who subject themselves to imaginative experiencing of trauma are, in fact, attempting to gain contact with forgotten or temporarily unavailable material for the kind of therapeutic purposes outlined in this book (as well as to create powerful writing). Fictional writing can offer a safer-seeming entry into painful and forgotten experiences than direct autobiographical writing. I have written a fiction about a woman who killed seven men, poetry about the death of a child, about Sleeping Beauty even. I know these fictions had therapeutic value for me, but to someone who did not know me I may appear to have subjected myself to 'as-it-were' trauma.

Wenz and McWhirter (1990) also suggest fictional writing enables the writer to explore a wider range of material:

> The function of writing is a way to express ideas, attitudes, and feelings in an indirect manner as though they are abstract or belonging to someone else. This indirect exchange seems to pave the way for more direct statements. This affect grows (it is suggested) from the inner-self which is tapped through intuitive, creative writing. (p.39)

Atlas, Smith and Sessoms (1992) have used a similar understanding when using poetry psychotherapeutically with hospitalised adolescents (see Chapter Seven). According to them, the client, when creating art, regresses into trauma which has been personally experienced:

> Ernest Kris, an artist and practising psychoanalyst, described a process of 'regression in the service of the ego' underlying artistic accomplishment. Assuming a moderate level of psychological intactness, a creative person may briefly (for minutes or hours) 'suspend' critical apprehension of reality while letting her or his awareness plumb depths of experience and memory that are typically unconscious. In returning to full consciousness, the creative person integrates elements of unconscious awareness with conscious experience to fashion an artistic product offering new meaning, conveying images of a different reality. (p.282)

I would not make such a clear distinction between unconscious and conscious. My model is more of a bubbling soup with different elements at the bottom of the pot at different times.

Why do writers need or want to explore in this way, fishing around in the stew? Are writers madder than those who do not write? Does the writing keep them saner than they would be otherwise? In offering therapeutic writing we are suggesting the therapeutic route found naturally by writers.

Are writers mad?

Felix Post (1996) has conducted research into the lives of one hundred American and British writers. This followed up his original study of 291 world-famous men (Post 1994). He narrowed his field to writers for the second study because he found writers had more psychopathological problems than any other famous people. Out of the sample of 100 writers, he discovered that only nine of them displayed an absence of classifiable mental illness. The playwrights are the worst and the poets the most stable.

Even given the problems of the narrow scientific paradigm within which he is working, this does not make it clear enough whether Post is suggesting that writers are unusually unbalanced people who turn to writing for therapeutic support. This theory would be seem to be supported by Sigmund Freud (1925), who implied that artists found works of art served them better than symptoms would have done – artists might display even more psychopathologies if they had no artistic expression. It would also be consistent with the view of Survivors Poetry (see below) and with this book. *The Therapeutic Potential of Creative Writing* describes a form of therapeutic writing which offers insight and understandings at a rate, and in a way, which can be worked on without causing further untherapeutic disturbance (for a writer not suffering from a classifiable mental illness). 'You cannot write the wrong thing' is a basic tenet – painful and difficult to face, yes, but overwhelming or destabilising, no.

Mind, the Mental Health Charity, celebrated its fiftieth anniversary by publishing an anthology of 'matters of the mind' written by well-known authors: *Mind Readings* (Dunn, Morrison and Roberts 1996). These pages contain more evidence of brilliant writing from the mentally distressed.

Writing through mental illness

Schizophrenia

Linda Hart hears the voice of her father telling her to kill herself, that her stomach is full of maggots. She was sectioned under the mental health act and spent more than nine months in psychiatric hospital, where she tried to commit suicide. She says:

> My only solace was my writing, which I started to stop myself from going totally insane. Expressing my fears and emotions in a diary was more effective than drugs and custody. It helped me to come to terms with my illness. I let my family read it. My mother cried for a week, and my sons were devastated. For years, they'd thought I was suffering from stress or, at worst, depression. Now that they know the truth we are closer than ever. (1996, p.53)

Linda kept up her diary writing while she was in hospital and it was published when she came out (Hart 1995).

Here is some of her writing, from just before she was taken into hospital. This writing is so powerful that it is almost frightening just to read it. There are so few words here, yet they give such a graphic picture of feelings and experiences way beyond the experience of most of us (thankfully). But Linda wrote because she wanted to, with only gentle encouragement:

> Far away knitted sheep graze in woven fields stitched on to a landscape to keep them still. A pause between rough birth and the butcher's knife.
>
> A village in the cleavage of the hills huddles tight against the hard, milkless earth. The village is veined with streets cut through hedges tough as muscle
>
> The flies are telling secrets, writing names in the air. Neighbours, reading fly-script, gossip…
>
> …The sheep unravel and bleed. The village suckles stone. Hedges stretch out across the streets and the flies are writing my name.

Depression

'I could not write about being depressed while actually depressed. I can only write about it and its effect *in retrospect*, when well,' says poet Roy Blackman. Even writing cannot pierce the 'blank, black mattress pressing down to smother'. Writing comes from a contact with our innermost being, but this is not accessible in depression. Alice Miller saw 'depression as denial of the self. [It] consists of a denial of one's own emotional reactions' (1995, p.67).

Roy Blackman reflects on the non-depressive state: 'When one comes out of a period of depression, the relief is so wonderful, the world, the everyday, ordinary, humdrum world, is so vivid and warm and re-assuring that you see it with a *poetic* vision and notice, with delight, so many *little* things that it is so easy to overlook.' So the writing is a celebration of being out of the depression. Perhaps the joy in the non-depressive world Roy is describing is similar to the wonder I have heard patients with life-threatening or terminal illnesses express (see the quote at the beginning of Chapter Eleven). Beauties, joys and delights are noticed and celebrated when they are likely soon to be taken away or have just been given back after a period of deprivation.

Silence

Not all personal horrors can be approached through writing or any other therapy. A creative writing student of mine, Harry, had been one of the first to enter Belsen when it was liberated, as a squaddie. In a tutorial he started telling me the less horrific of these memories (which will always remain with me). He tried to write them, at my suggestion, but told me that he simply could not do so. He could find no way of turning them into a story – the protagonist was a character he wanted to forget.

Possibly, attempting to face those memories was an ordeal for which he was not strong enough, just as King Lear tried to prevent himself reflecting on his daughters' ingratitude, saying 'that way madness lies'. (See also the experience of holocaust survivors and their children reported in Chapter Five.) For the rest of the course he wrote fictional fantasy stories and told a great number of jokes with the lads. We never mentioned the war again and I supported his writings as if nothing else had ever been suggested.

Survivors Poetry

This is an organisation initiated and run by and for survivors of the mental health system, offering poetry workshops, readings, performances, publishing, outreach and training. They train their own paid workshop leaders, who often joined originally as group members. Survivors Poetry concentrates on the art form, rather than the therapeutic need of each writer, and on the artistic quality of the work (see Chapter Seven). The work they do together is not labelled 'therapeutic'. Yet the impact of this forward and positive way of thinking is deeply therapeutic, they have found – survivors begin to see themselves as artists, or potential artists rather than patients or clients. The creative writing workshops offer constructive criticism, advice, support and fresh ideas on the poetry; performance workshops increase confidence and skills; and publication (often small-scale) offers recognition and response. All this increases self-esteem, confidence and self-value.

Joe Bidder, one of the founder members, says: 'Poetry saves lives. Many lives have been transformed: people have moved out of the despondency of being mental health users, and have become writers, magazine editors, and so on.' He continued by pointing out how many writers suffer from mental distress, so 'a possible payback for their suffering may be a hope that their mental distress may be part of our literary heritage.' An anthology, *Beyond Bedlam: Poems Written out of Mental Distress* (Smith and Sweeney 1997) marks the 750th anniversary of the original 'Bedlam' Hospital. Many survivors and users are represented here. If you want to know what madness feels like, and how poetry can help, read this book.

Foreknowledge through poetry

The line between madness and sanity is notoriously indistinct. Many cultures have revered sages, soothsayers, shamen as bringing wisdom and foreknowledge; in others the same people would be considered to be mad. Writing can also have a prophetic or diagnostic effect, like dreams, because it is drawing on those deeper, wiser levels of ourselves which know more than we do. Here is the experience of three poets.

Catherine Byron: Poetry as divination

I have made the disconcerting discovery that some of my poems have been writing my future, and that physical as well as psychic dis-ease has been my unconscious subject. Ten years ago now, I was writing a prose book about following Seamus Heaney's trail to St Patrick's Purgatory. His 'Station Island' sequence drew me there, on what I imagined would be a literary pilgrimage. It turned out, in the doing and even more the writing up, to be a disturbing and distressing revisitation of my own Catholic girlhood in Ulster. During the writing of *Out of Step* (1992), I wrote very little poetry, just one long, intense narrative inspired by the mock funeral that VIP pilgrims had undergone, in the pilgrimage's late medieval heyday, before being ceremonially sealed into St Patrick's subterranean cave for ten days and nights, with a bare survival ration of bread and water. Fasting is still a big deal on the three-day modern pilgrimage to Station Island, which is unfailingly popular, especially with Ulster Catholics. I put my coffin poem away for several years. I forgot about it, but not about my time at the Purgatory, Ireland's very own entrance to the Underworld.

Eating and not eating had never presented me – as they have many of my close friends – with psychological problems, but about five years after writing in prose about the fasting on Station Island, and Heaney's stark linking of it with the 1981 IRA hunger strikes, I began to have severe physical problems with food. Eventually I was surviving on prescription nutrition drinks and a fierce drug regime. I felt very low, physically and in spirit. I wasn't writing anything at all, poetry or prose. Then a commission came out of the blue, to write a long poem for performance on London's South Bank. The theme of the evening was – uncannily? – 'Ghosts'! It was only when I was right up against the deadline, and desperate, that I remembered that coffin narrative, and dug it up. Quickly, other poems grew out of and around it, and they were all about renunciations of the flesh, whether eating it, or pleasuring it. Then the final poem sang in unbidden: an invocation to the Lord Hades:

> Come, Hades, lord of the inner channels
> prince of peristalsis, pot-holer extraordinaire.
> You alone know there is nothing at my core –
> an extended nought, a hole from mouth to anus.
> I have fasted for three days, and drunk no water
> this last day – light-headed, leaving home –
> I am pure pink for your pleasure. Thread me through.
> This is the purest form of penetration.
> This is the going up into the gaps.
> This is the airy way of the hunger artist.
> I beseech ye, o my bowels,
> that I may not be mistaken.

As it sped onto the paper I was thinking that it concerned one of the many medical investigations I had been conscious for, an endoscopy, and that Hades was my surgeon. Then I gave it the ambiguous title *Consumption*, posted it to the South Bank Centre, went and read it on the appointed night, and forgot it – again.

A friend whose husband had died at forty-two, of late-diagnosed anorexia, told me months later what *Consumption* was really saying: that I was giving up, giving in. Saying a warm hello to death. I think she was right.

But by the time she told me this, in distress and some anger with me, I knew that the poem recorded a state of mind that I had already left behind. It felt as though my unconscious writing of it had, again unconsciously, exorcised the very death-wish it expressed. I still needed her to point it out to me, though. For I only recognised my own returning will to go on, to live, when she helped me to read aright my own serenade to Death. I was already on the path up and out from Hades' underworld, and, unlike Rilke's Eurydice, had chosen not to stay, not this time.

Within months I allowed my surgeon in, and he was not the dead ringer for Hades that I'd feared – and nearly fallen for. He was, of course, invasive, and I was unconscious in the literal rather than the metaphorical sense, but his skill has enabled my body to work again, to go on – as my soul had already told me that he could.

(Catherine Byron)

Robert Hamberger: It puts us in touch with ourselves

Adrienne Rich (1980) stated: 'poems are like dreams: in them you put what you don't know you know'. In the eighteen months or so before my marriage ended, when with my conscious mind and in my daily life I was working hard to repair and renew our relationship, I was writing poems whose metaphors included a woman in a fairy-tale walking out on a wolf; a trapped starling beating its head against a window to get free; anger biting 'anything with a whiff of the human'; a short sequence focusing on fear in seven languages; rising like 'Adam from the valley in her side; a male frog gripping a dead female frog in the act of mating. All signs or premonition that the poetry-writing part of me was clearly driven to express, but messages whose meaning my daily life was not yet prepared to decipher.

I would also like to suggest there can be 'fortune-telling' aspect to some poetry writing, where you write lines envisaging a life or event you haven't yet lived. This relates to Rich's statement in the same essay that: `if the imagination is to transcend and transform experience it has to question, to challenge, to conceive of alternatives, perhaps to the very life you are living at that moment.' Around 1982 I wrote a poem called *Warpaint Angel* (1997) about my mother's husband, the man I had seen as my father, who died in 1981. It ends:

> I dream of meetings:
> the grand reconciliation,
> holding you, weeping
> as a father would a child.

In 1989 I met my natural father after thirty years. When we talked about my birth and childhood my father cried and I held him as he wept. The scene I described in 1982 without any conscious hope of realising it, was enacted seven years later. When I showed my father the *Warpaint Angel* poem he called the ending 'witchy'. My dictionary definition of a witch is 'a woman believed to have supernatural powers'. Perhaps tuning into the powers of our imaginations, and unleashing them in writing even if we're not fully conscious of where that writing is leading, puts us in touch with powers beyond the accepted laws of nature. It puts us in touch with ourselves.

(Robert Hamberger)

Liz Cashdan: Ironies

Ironies

She used to watch him at the ironing board

proud of his prowess in the tug of war
between his new-learned skill
and the ebb and flow of shirt.

She'd hear the steamer hiss
across recalcitrant waves of silk.
Bravely he'd guide the silver prow
determined on its head-strong course.

Now as they argue over every rucked-up
detail of their lives
she sees him falter and begin to doubt –
realises he's ironed the creases in
not out.

(1995, p.40)

* * * *

I heard Liz deliver this poem with emotive force at a reading, though she wrote it long before she and her husband had any real inkling that they were going to separate and not see each other again. An additional irony.

But is it art?

True ease in writing comes from art, not chance
As those move easiest who have learned to dance

(Alexander Pope)

A literary product is not the prime aim of therapeutic writing. The discoveries, or the satisfaction of expressing thoughts and images hitherto kept down inside the mind, are the primary aim – an intensely creative process, of value in its own right. But, however vital and important the writing is to the writer, however exciting or angst-ridden its production, this does not indicate that it will communicate any such emotion to a reader without careful, considered reworking. Indeed, the writer's bleeding heart has to be taken off the page for the writing to work as a piece of literature for the reader (see autobiography section).

A work of art is the result of a powerful charge of inspiration and a very large input of crafting skill, patience, observation, contemplation and the taking of experienced advice. The crafting of the initial writing to form a finished product is often long and laborious, unfortunately. A work of art is a construction, not an outpouring of emotion, although invariably it is based on powerful experiences of some sort.

> O the mind, mind has mountains; cliffs of fall
> Frightful, sheer, no-man-fashioned. Hold them cheap
> May who ne'er hung there.
>
> (Gerard Manley Hopkins 1953, p.61)

No one could doubt Gerard Manley Hopkins' experience of acute depression. But this sonnet is an artefact based on this experience. It is a creation designed to take the reader into the experience of depression. Writers very often write therapeutically and work on this material to create publishable works. Poems, as well as people, grow and mature; they go through stages of maturation. To begin with they are often a very personal expression, a communication with the self. Through the stages of redrafting they become less personal and become part of the writer's relationship with others. In an annual poetry competition I have judged, the entries consisted of emotional splurge or sweet rhyming metrical ditties (doggerel). The couple of *poems* (which had clearly been crafted) which were the winners stood out with an almost painful clarity.

The experience of using the tools of art can be immensely therapeutic. The writing suggestions in this book, to encourage people to express themselves, are those used by many writers to gain their notes towards a first draft. I recommend redrafting not so much for its value in refining the writing as for clarifying and distilling the experience for deeper therapeutic benefit (see Chapter Seven).

Creative writing which communicates to a reader, and is publishable, cannot be taught. But it can be fostered. The student, patient or client may come to have the blend of essential ingredients (primarily patience, doggedness and time) for making a writer-artist.

> A writer develops the muscles of his mind. This training … demands suffering, weakness, setbacks, exhaustion, mourning, insomnia, exercises

> which are the reverse of those which develop the body. (Cocteau 1930, p.139)

> Composing is hard work, an unyielding effort, a struggle with material to make it bend to the forms and colours you want to. (Kokkonen 1997)

There is no benefit to patients or clients to think they will be creating a publishable form of art as soon as they pick up a pen. Yet advice on publishing the unsifted contents of a troubled mind is very often sought from me. People should be encouraged to express themselves, work on their writing to whatever level seems appropriate and share this writing through in-house publications, readings and display. Achieving national publication of poetry, in particular, is extremely difficult. But if the work (and it *is* work) of crafting and publishing works of art is right, the writer will have the impetus to persevere (Levertov 1982).

For writing to have a therapeutic impact, it must generally be felt to be only for the self or a known and trusted audience. The writer will then feel sufficiently secure and confident to explore and express their deepest feelings and emotions. Plans for publication at first draft or note stage are rarely useful for any writer other than the experienced. It leads to a self-conscious stilted tone and unnatural subject matter. It is not useful for the therapeutic or beginning writer to confuse what they are doing with the activity of the published (and perhaps famous author), who, in fact, is pursuing a skilled craft of which the patient or beginner knows nothing.

The way of writing outlined in this book, however, is likely to produce fresh, clear, powerful images which will be worthy of being crafted. Many published writers use approaches similar to the ones suggested here to gain their first draft material. The heart of a successful piece of writing must come unbidden and retain its integrity throughout all the redrafting stages. Listen to this from Keats (1918):

> If poetry comes not as naturally as the leaves of a tree it had better not come at all.

and from Helene Cixous (1989):

> Writing is a primary act. It comes from within. I feel it welling up inside me, growing out of me, transforming itself into language. The still dumb flow of writing passes through my woman's body, searching for words...
>
> I write because I have to. I need to write, like I need to eat, like I need to sleep, like I need to make love. It's like a second heart. I feel that, by writing I continually renew myself and replenish vital forces. I need the

> incessant movement from body to symbol, from symbol to body; for me the two things are intrinsically linked. (p.198)

Chris Woods here recounts an experience which proves that effective writing *can* sometimes take us by surprise and just happen:

> Withington Library, Manchester. Early evening, one summer before they closed libraries in the evening. Five of us in a back room with the din of the traffic. Closed windows. Open them and the traffic noise runs you over.
>
> He was a new face and voice. A public poetry workshop. Anyone could bring anything they considered poetry and copies for each of us. Anything could happen.
>
> Five of us. Four hard-core, and a newcomer. Comfortable chat before-hand, then down to business. My turn to lead the group. I got him to deal his copies and we read.
>
> A visceral response first. Tingly. Satisfying. Timeless. Rather out of time. A suspension of time. Then excitement. Nothing conscious formulating. Then a realisation of what I was reading.
>
> The writing was fresh as first time. Images surprised and challenged. An energetic flow of language. I was gobsmacked.
>
> The poem came third in the National Poetry Competition. It should have won.
>
> (Chris Woods)

Final words

Traditional cultures know and knew the value of storytelling and listening to ballads. We cannot return to sitting round the fire telling them, singing them and listening ritually and socially. We have to use the medium we are used to – writing. Artists have traditionally played the role post-renaissance society has assigned to them: creative dreamers on the margins. This is changing dynamically and needs to change still further. Writers are not different, they just happen to be brave people who are willing to voyage into uncharted waters; they are just people who are willing to trim and trim their sails until they are sailing as close to the wind as they can get, in order to understand, clarify, explain, communicate. Anyone can get into their own clipper, trimaran or dinghy and set out onto their own stretch of water, whether it is a gravel-pit or the Antarctic, and taste artistic waters. It is exhilarating but not at all easy. It is also one of the most self-illuminating things anyone can do.

And who knows, you may bring back material from those waters which others will want to read and hear.

Cocteau kept a journal through his opium cure. It was partly this which helped him through the pain, humiliation, depression and fear. And the document not only helped him, it is an extra-ordinarily artistic and educative text to read. He said the experience:

> would have dissolved leaving no other trace behind except a deep depression, if a fountain pen had not given it a direction, relief and shape... The only possible style [for this kind of writing] is the thought made flesh. (1930, p.139)

APPENDIX

Useful Contact Addresses

Organisations

Age Concern
Astral House, 1268 London Road, London, SW16 4ER
Tel: 0181 679 8000, Fax: 0181 679 6069

Arts Council of England
14 Great Peter Street, London, SW1P 3NQ
Tel: 0171 333 0100, Fax: 0171 973 6590
Literature Officer: Alison Combes

Arts for Health
The Manchester Metropolitan University, All Saints, Oxford Road, Manchester, M15 6BY
Tel: 0161 236 8916, Fax: 0161 247 6390
Practical help, information, advice for all involved in the arts as a complementary part of healthcare

The Arvon Foundation
(Creative Writing Courses)
Totleigh Barton, Sheepwash, Beaworthy, Devon, EX21 5NS
Tel: 01409 231338, Fax: 01409 231144

Creative Writing and Personal Development
(Postgraduate Diploma)
University of Sussex, Celia Hunt – Convener
Further details and application forms from: Yvonne Barnes, Continuing Education, University of Sussex, Falmer, Brighton, BN1 9RG
Tel: 01273 678537

Healing Arts
Isle of Wight, St Mary's Parkhurst Road, Newport, Isle of Wight, PO30 5TG
Tel: 01983 524081, Fax: 01983 525 157
Comprehensive range of arts in healthcare projects, in particular Creative Writing

Health and The Arts (MA)
Director: Terry Smyth, Head of Health and Social Studies
Colchester Institute, Sheepen Road, Colchester, Essex, CO3 3LL
Tel: 01277 264504

Healthcare Arts
233 Springfield, Dundee, DD1 4JE
Tel: 01382 203099

Hospital Arts
St Mary's Hospital, Hathersage Road, Manchester, M13 0JH
Tel: 0161 256 4389
Working with groups to improve the environment in caring establishments

Lapidus
Membership secretary: Christina Dunhill, BCM Lapidus, London, WC1N 3XX
The Association for the Literary Arts in Personal Development – conferences, workshops, newsletter, database

Medical Humanities (MA)
Director: Martyn Evans, Head of the Centre for Philosophy and Health Care
Admissions tutor: HR Upton, University of Wales Swansea, SA2 8PP
Tel: 01792 295611, Fax: 01792 295769
A part-time and full-time course

The National Association of Writers in Education
PO Box 1, Sheriff Hutton, York, YO6 7YU
Tel/Fax: 01653 618429
Conferences, courses, journal – for novelists, poets, playwrights etc. in residencies in education – primary, secondary, tertiary, higher

Patchwork, Poetry from the Christie Hospital
(Quarterly Poetry Anthology)
Judith Thwatie, Don Ayers (Editors)
Christie Hospital NHS Trust, Wilmslow Road, Manchester, M20 9BX

The Poetry Society
22 Betterton Street, London, WC2H 9BU
Tel: 0171 420 9880, Fax: 0171 240 4818
Membership organisation to help poets and poetry thrive; Poetry Review, Poetry News, National Poetry Competition

Survivors Poetry
Diorama Arts Centre, 34 Osnaburgh Street, London, NW1 3ND
Tel: 0171 916 6637, Fax: 0171 916 0830
Poetry Workshops and Performances by and for Survivors of the Mental Health System

The Unit for the Arts and Offenders
CRSP, Social Sciences Department,
Loughborough University, Loughborough, LE11 3TU
Tel: 01509 223374
Supports the development of creative arts opportunities for people in prison, etc; news bulletin

Practitioners and researchers

Writing and Dementia
John Killick
Dementia Services Development Centre, Department of Applied Social Science, University of Stirling, FK9 4LA

Lorna Dexter
Dreamworker and Therapist
Quarry Garden, Farnah Green, Belper, DE56 2UP

Davidoff Imago
Leslie Davidoff – Dream Consultant and Writer
6 Beverley Gardens, York, YO3 7TH
Tel.: 01904 424198, email davimago@aol.com

Brenda Mallon
Counsellor and Dream Consultant
7 Didsbury Park, Didsbury, Manchester, M20 5LH
Tel: 0161 448 8780

Cheryl Moskowitz
Writer and Psychodynamic Counsellor – The Self as Source
Contact via Jessica Kingsley Publishers

Simona Parker
Creative Journal: Life Integration Workshops
11 Brackley Road, London, W4 2HW

Poetry Therapy Research
Dr Robin Philipp, Centre for Health in Employment and the Environment, Department of Occupational Health and Safety, Bristol Royal Infirmary, Bristol, BS2 8HW
Tel: 0117 928 2352, Fax: 0117 928 3840

Therapeutic writing

Stories at Work: Writing as a Reflective Practitioner
Gillie Bolton
Institute of General Practice and Primary Care, Sheffield University, Community Sciences Centre, Northern General Hospital, S5 7AU
Tel: 0114 271 5830, Fax: 0114 242 2136, email gbolton@sheffield.ac.uk

Caroline Wilson
Writing Therapist
Stoops Cellars, Broadhemston, Nr Totnes, Devon, TQ9 6AQ
Tel: 01803 813135

Writing for Self-Discovery Courses
John Killick and Myra Schneider
5 Slater Bank, Hebden Bridge, W Yorks, HX7 7DY
Tel: 01422 842093

Bibliography

Adams, P.T. *et al.* (1997) *The Guided Hand.* Liverpool: Sunny Moon Publications.

Alexander, L. (ed) (1990) *Now I Can Tell.* London: Papermac.

Allende, I. (1995) *Paula.* London: HarperCollins.

Anonymous author (1995) 'Writing to ease the pain of abuse.' *Medical Monitor,* 15 November, 60.

Arigho, B. (1997) 'Reminiscence work with older people in Health Care Settings.' In C. Kaye and T. Blee, *The Arts in Health Care: A Palette of Possibilities.* London: Jessica Kingsley.

Ashbridge, E. (1713–1755) Journal. In the Quaker Library, Woodbrooke College.

Atlas, J.A., Smith, P. and Sessoms, L. (1992) 'Art and poetry in brief therapy of hospitalised adolescents.' *The Arts in Psychotherapy,* 19, 279–283.

Baldwin, C (1991) *Life's Companion: Journal Writing as a Spiritual Quest.* New York: Bantam.

Bankhead, T. (1996) quoted in 'Keepers of the diaries', Anita Chowdhuri, *The Guardian,* January 4.

Barrie, J.M. (1967) *Peter Pan.* Middlesex: Penguin.

Bauby, D. (1997) *The Diving Bell and the Butterfly.* Translated by J. Leggat. New York: Knopf.

Bender, M. In J. Bornat (ed) (1994) *Reminiscence Reviewed: Perspectives, Evaluations, Achievements.* Buckingham: Open University.

Beowulf. (1973) Translated by M. Alexander Middlesex: Penguin.

Berger, J. (1995) *To the Wedding.* London: Bloomsbury.

Bettelheim, B. (1976) *The Uses of Enchantment: The Meaning and Importance of Fairy Tales.* London: Thames & Hudson.

Birren, J. and Deutchman, D. (1991) *Guiding Autobiography Groups for Older Adults.* Baltimore: Johns Hopkins University Press.

Blackman, R. (1996) *As Lords Expected.* Ware: Rockingham.

Blodgett, H. (1988) *Centuries of Female Days: Englishwomen's Private Diaries.* New Jersey: Rutgers.

Bolton, G. (1992) 'Just a bobble hat: The story of a writing as therapy training workshop.' *Changes, International Journal of Psychology and Psychotherapy 11,* 1, 37–43.

Bolton, G. (1992) 'Skills on call.' *Times Educational Supplement.* 13 March.

Bolton, G. (1994) *Writing the Spirit, Material for Spiritual Exploration. London: Quaker Resources for Learning.*

Bolton, G. (1995) 'Taking the thinking out of it: Writing, a therapeutic space.' *The Journal of the British Association for Counselling*, 6, 3, 15–218.

Bolton, G. (1995a) *Writing from the Source, Research for Spiritual Writing.* London: Quaker Resources for Learning.

Bolton, G. (1995b) *Writing Yourself, Keeping a Spiritual Portfolio.* London: Quaker Resources for Learning.

Bolton, G. (1996) 'The process of writing gets me in touch.' *Artery, The Journal of Arts for Health 14,* 15–16.

Bolton, G. (1997) 'Buttoned.' *Writing in Education*, 11, 10–14.

Bolton, G. and Ahmedzai, S. (1997) 'Project will assess effects of patients writing about their terminal illness on self-perceived quality of life.' *British Medical Journal*, 314, 7092, 1486.

Bolton, G. and Styles, M. (1995) 'There are stories and stories.' In Julia Swindells (ed) *The Uses of Autobiography.* London: Taylor and Francis.

Bornat, J. (ed) (1994) *Reminiscence Reviewed: Perspectives, Evaluations, Achievements.* Buckingham: Open University.

Brimacombe, M. (1996) 'The emotional release of writing.' *GP*, December.

Brody, H. (1987) *Stories of Sickness.* Yale: Yale University Press.

Bromley, J. (1990) 'Healthy art in the heart of the Black Country: The family health spokesman.' In M. Miles (ed) *Arts in Primary Health Care.* Dundee: British Health Care Arts.

Brown, J. (1993) *Thinking Egg.* Todmorden, Lancs: Littlewood Arc.

Byron, C. (1992) *Out of Step.* Bristol: Loxwood Stoneleigh.

Byron, C. (1995) 'Writers on teaching.' In S. Thomas (ed) *Creative Writing.* Nottingham: Nottingham University.

Caduceus (1996) 'How do the arts heal?' 31, 38–9.

Calman, C. and Downie, R. (1996) 'Why arts courses for medical curricula?' *The Lancet 347,* 1499–1500.

Calvi, J. (1988) 'Six Healing Sayings'. *Friends Journal*, May, 6–9.

Campbell, D. (1995) 'A book with long sentences.' *The Guardian,* 2 September.

Carroll, L. (1865) *Alice's Adventures in Wonderland.* London: Dent.

Carroll, L. (1871) *Alice Through the Looking Glass.* London: Dent.

Cashdan, E. (1995) *Laughing All the Way.* Nottingham: Five Leaves.

Cixous, H. (1989) 'The "double world" of writing.' In Sellers (ed) *Delighting the Heart.* London: Women's Press.

Cixous, H. (1989) Writing as a second heart. In S. Sellers (ed) *Delighting the Heart.* London: The Women's Press.

Clare, J. (1997) *John Clare.* London: Dent.

Cleveland Peck, P. (1995) 'Doubts, psychosis? Get a diary.' *Independent Weekend*, 30 December.

Cocteau, J. (1930) *Opium: the Diary of a Cure.* London: Peter Owen.

Coleman, P. (1986) *Ageing and Reminiscence Processes.* Chichester: John Wiley.

Coleridge, S.T. (1878) *The Ancient Mariner.* New York: Harper & Brothers.

Coleridge, S.T. (1975) *Biographia Literaria.* London: Dent.

Coleridge, S.T. (1993) 'Kubla Khan.' In J. Wain (ed) *The Oxford Library of English Poetry.* London: BCA.

Cotterill, H. (1992) *Changing the Décor.* Sheffield: South Yorkshire Writers.

Cullen, R. (1991) 'Report'. *Openmind,* 16 August.

Daniel, R. (1997) Spirituality and Health Conference, Durham, Sept/Oct.

Day Lewis, C. (1974) The Poetic Image.

Doherty, B. (1993) *Walking on Air.* London: HarperCollins.

Doty, M. (1996) *My Alexandria.* London: Jonathan Cape.

Downie, R.S. and Charlton, B. (1992) *The Making of a Doctor, Medical Education in Theory and Practice.* Oxford: Oxford University Press.

Drazba, J. (1997) *Behind the Screen of the Eyelids.* Media Rodzina of Poznan.

Dudley, K. (1997) 'Our son had meningitis.' *Practical Parenting,* July, 85–88.

Dunn, D. (1985) *Elegies.* London: Faber.

Dunn, S., Morrison, B. and Roberts, M. (eds) (1996) *Mind Readings.* London: Minerva.

Edge, B. (1989) 'Inside story.' *Writers in Education, the Journal of the Association of Writers in Education,* 5, 5–6.

Eliot, T.S. (1936) *Collected Poems.* London: Faber.

Eliot, T.S. (1951) *Selected Essays.* London: Faber.

Ellis, C. (1998) 'Epistotherapy'. *British Medical Journal,* 299, 1230.

Fine, D. (1995) 'Writing is a healthy activity'. *Artery,* 11, 6.

Frampton, D.R. (1986) 'Restoring creativity to the dying patient.' *British Medical Journal,* 293, 6562, 1593–1595.

Frank, A. (1947) *The Diary of Anne Frank.* London: Macmillans Children's Books.

Freud, A. (1950) Foreword and Introduction. In M. Milner *On Not Being Able to Paint.* London: Heinemann.

Freud, S. (1959a) 'An autobiographical study.' *Standard Edition of the Complete Works of Sigmund Freud,* Vol. XX 64-65. London: Hogarth.

Freud, S. (1959b) *The Standard Edition of the Complete Works of Sigmund Freud,* Vol.V. London: Hogarth Press.

Fuchel, J. (1985) 'Writing poetry can enhance the psychotherapeutic process: observations and examples.' *The Arts in Psychotherapy,* 12, 89–93.

Gendlin, E.T. (1986) *Let Your Body Interpret Your Dreams.* Illinois: Chiron.

Gersie, A. and King, A. (1990) *Storymaking in Education and Therapy.* London: Jessica Kingsley.

Gibran, K. (1926) *The Prophet.* London: Heinemann.

Gibson, F. (1994) *Reminiscence and Recall: A Guide to Good Practice.* London: Age Concern.

Glaister, L. (1996) *Private Parts of Women.* London: Bloomsbury.

Goldberg, N. (1986) *Writing Down the Bones.* Boston, Mass: Shambhala.

Graham, E.H., Hinds, E., Hobby, E. and Willcocks (eds) (1989) *Her Own life: Autobiographical Writings of Seventeenth Century English Women.* London: Routledge.

Graves, P.L. (1984) 'Life Event and Art'. *International Review of Psychoanalysis,* 11, 355–365.

Grubrick-Simitis, I. 'From concretism to metaphor: thoughts on some theoretical and technical aspects of the psychoanalytic work with children of Holocaust survivors.' *Psyche,* 38, 1–28.

Haddock, B.D. (1989) 'Scenario writing: A therapeutic application.' *Journal of Mental Health Counselling,* 11, 3, 234–243.

Hall, E. (1990) 'Strategies for using journal writing in counselling gifted students'. *Gifted Children Today,* 13, 4, 2–6.

Hamberger, R. (1997) *Warpaint Angel.* Leicester: Blackwater.

Harrison, B.T. and Bolton, G. (1990) 'Realising through writing.' *The Creative Self in the New Era.' Journal of Institute of Education, Hull University,* 42, 96–108

Harrower, M. (1972) *The Therapy of Poetry.* Illinois: Charles C Thomas.

Hart, D. (1990) 'Healthy art in the heart of the Black Country: The arts spokesman.' In M. Miles (ed) *Arts in Primary Health Care.* Dundee: British Health Care Arts.

Hart, D. (1998) 'The expressive community: Our place as writers.' *Writing in Education 14,* 12–15.

Hart, L. (1995) *Phone at Nine Just to Say You're Alive.* London: Douglas Elliot Press.

Hart, L. (1996) 'I'm learning to live with schizophrenia.' *Woman's Realm,* 1 October, 52–3.

Hartley, L.P. (1953) *The Go-Between.* London: Hamish Hamilton.

Heller, T. (1997) 'A GP writes.' In B. McDonnell (ed) *Serious Fun: The Arts in Primary Health Care.* Yorkshire and Humberside Arts.

Henzell, J. (1995) 'Research and the particular: Epistemology in art and psychotherapy.' In A. Gilroy and C. Lee (eds) *Art and Music: Therapy and Research.* London: Routledge.

Herzog, J. (1982) World beyond Metaphor. In Bergman and Jucovy pp103-119.

Hillman, J. (1975) *Revisioning Psychology.* New York: Harper Collophon.

Hillman, J. (1981) 'Psychology: Monotheistic or polytheistic.' In D.L. Miller (ed) *The New Polytheism.* Dallas: Spring.

Hippocrates (1983) *Hippocratic Writings.* Middlesex: Penguin.

Hjelmstadt, L.T. (1993) *Fine Black Lines: Reflections on Facing Cancer, Fear, and Loneliness.* Denver: Mulberry Hill Press.

Hopkins, G.M. (1953) *Poems and Prose.* Middlesex: Penguin.

Hudson Jones, A. (1997) 'Literature and medicine: Narratives of mental illness.' *The Lancet,* 350, 359–61.

Hughes, T. (1967) *Poetry in the Making.* London: Faber & Faber.

Hughes, T. (1982) Foreword. In S. Brownjohn *What Rhymes with Secret?* London: Hodder & Stoughton.

Ingalls Wilder, L. (1963) *Little House in the Big Woods.* Middlesex: Penguin.

Ivison, I. (1997) *Fiona's Story: A Tragedy of Our Times.* London: Virago.

Jacobs, D. and Mack, J.E. (1986) 'Case report of psychiatric intervention by mail: a way of responding to a suicidal crisis.' *American Journal of Psychiatry,* 143, 1, 92–93.

Jenkins, J. (1991) 'Write inside.' *Writers in Education, the Journal of the Association of Writers in Education,* 9, 7–8.

Jordan, K.B. and L'Abate, L. (1995) 'Programmed writing and therapy with symbiotically enmeshed patients.' *American Journal of Psychotherapy,* 49, 2, 225–236.

Jung, C.G. (1963) *Memories, Dreams, Reflections.* London: Collins.

Karr, M. (1995) *The Liars Club.* London: Picador.

Kay, J. (1995) *Young Poetry Pack.* London: Poetry Society.

Keane, F. (1996) *Letter to Daniel.* Middlesex: Penguin.

Keats, J. (1818) Letter to John Taylor, 17 Feb.

Keats, J. (1906) *John Keats Poems (Lamia Part 1)* London: Dent.

Killick, J. (1997) *You are Words: Dementia Poems.* London: Journal of Dementia Care.

Killick, J. (1996a) 'Communicating as if your life depended on it: Life history work with people with dementia.' In T. Heller *et al.,* (eds) *Mental Health Matters.* London: Macmillan.

Killick, J. (1996b) 'A far fetch (conversations with Alice).' *Changes, International Journal of Psychology and Psychotherapy,* 14, 4, 289–294.

Killick, J. (1994) *Please Give Me Back My Personality.* University of Stirling: Dementia Services.

Kokkonen, J. (1997) Crucible Studio Theatre 'Music in the Round', Sheffield. Concert programme. Unpublished.

Kopp, S. (1972) *If you Meet the Buddha on the Road Kill him.* London: Sheldon Press.

L'Abate, L. (1991) 'The use of writing in psychotherapy.' *American Journal of Psychotherapy,* 45, 1, 87–98.

Lane, B. (1993) *Writing as a Road to Self-Discovery.* Ohio: Writers Digest Books.

Lao Tsu (1973) *Tao Te Ching.* Edited by Gia-fu Feng and J. English. London: Wildwood House.

Latham, J. (1996) *The Unbearable Weight of Mercury.* Calstock, Cornwall: Peterloo.

Lester, E. and Terry, R. (1992) 'The Use of Poetry Therapy: Lessons from the life of Anne Sexton.' *The Arts in Psychotherapy 19,* 47–52.

Levertov, D. (1982) 'Paper for literature and medicine symposium.' In J. Trautmann (ed) *Healing Arts in Dialogue.* Southern Illinois University Press. pp.147–156.

Levieva, Y. (1991) (trans Grinberg, B. and Flint, R.) *Graphite.* Varna: Andina.

Levine, S.K. (1992) *The Language of Psychology and the Speech of the Soul.* Toronto: Palmerston Press.

Luidens, P.M. (1997) 'Paper thinking: the process of writing.' In A.L. Costa and R.M. Liebman (eds) *Envisioning Process as Content: Toward a Renaissance Curriculum.* London: Sage.

Lyons, P. (1997) 'Creative Writing and healing.' *Lapidus News,* 4, 4–5.

Lyotard, J.F. (1992) *Explaining the Postmodern to Children.* London: Turnaround.

Mallon, B. (1987) *Women Dreaming.* London: HarperCollins.

Mallon, B. (1989) *Children Dreaming.* Middlesex: Penguin.

Mantel, H. (1996) *An Experiment in Love.* Middlesex: Penguin.

McLellan, M.F. (1997) 'Literature and Medicine'. *The Lancet,* 349, 1618–20.

McLoughlin, D. (1985) 'Creative writing in hospice.' *Hospice Bulletin.* October, 8–9.

McLoughlin, D. (1987) 'Teaching writing in a hospice day centre.' *Writing in Education, The Journal of the National Association of Writers in Education,* 11, 7–9.

McNiff, S. (1992) *Art as Medicine: Creating a Therapy of the Imagination.* Boston: Shambhala.

Mere, L. 'Arthos Wales: Writing in hospitals.' In J. Bornat (ed) (1994) *Reminiscence Reviewed: Perspectives, Evaluations, Achievements.* Buckingham: Open University.

Miles, S. (1996) 'Writing as a way of self-knowing: creative writing.' *Caduceus,* 31: 29–32.

Miller, A. (1995) *The Drama of Being a Child.* London: Virago.

Milligan, S. (1968) *Silly Verse for Kids.* Harmondsworth: Penguin.

Milner, M. (1971) *On Not Being Able to Paint.* London: Heinemann Educational Books.

Milner, M. (1986a) *An Experiment in Leisure.* London: Virago.

Milner, M. (1986b) *A Life of One's Own.* London: Virago.

Milner, M. (1987) *Eternity's Sunrise: A Way of Keeping a Diary.* London: Virago.

Mitchell, J. (1989) 'Anxiety and creativity.' Lecture at Sheffield University reported in *Asylum 3,* 3, 31–35.

Morrice, J.K.W. (1983) 'Poetry as therapy.' *British Journal of Medical Psychology,* 56, 367–370.

Morris, I. (ed) (1967) *The Pillow Book of Sei Shonagan.* London: Penguin.

Mosely, E. and Ahokas, T. (1997) *Palette and Pen, A Healing Journey.* Brisbane: Spokespress.

Moskowitz, C. (1998) 'The self as source: creative writing generated from personal reflection.' In C. Hunt and F. Sampson (eds) *The Self on the Page.* London: Jessica Kingsley.

Nesbitt, E. (1997) 'Writing cancer out of your life.' *Linkup,* 46, 7–9.

Novotny-Hunter, J. (1995) 'Writing for children'. *The Journal of East Midlands Arts Literature Dept.,* Autumn, 10–11.

Nussbaum, M. (1994) *The Therapy of Desire: Theory and Practice in Hellenistic Ethics.* New Jersey: Princeton University Press.

Oates, J.C. (1988) 'Selections from a journal, Jan 1985–Jan 1988.' *Antaeus 16,* Autumn, 332.

Osborn, C. (1993) *The Reminiscence Handbook: Ideas for Creative Activities with Older People.* London: Age Exchange.

Parker, S. (1993) 'Writing yourself towards wholeness: The creative journal.' *International Journal of Complementary Medicine,* November, 27–28.

Parks, P. (1990) *Rescuing the Inner Child.* London: Souvenir Press.

Patten, B. (1995) *Young Poetry Pack.* London: Poetry Society.

Peaker, A. and Vincent, J. (1994) *Writers in Residence in Prison.* London: Arts Council of England.

Pennebaker, J.W. (1993) 'Overcoming inhibition: rethinking the roles of personality, cognition, and social behaviour.' In C. Harald and J.W. Pennebaker (eds) *Emotion, Inhibition and Health.* Seattle: Hogrefe & Huber.

Philipp, R. (1994) 'General practice, the science and the art.' *GP Weekly,* Wellington, New Zealand, 20 February.

Philipp, R. (1995) 'Metred health care.' *Poetry Review 85,* 1, 58–59.

Philipp, R. (1996) 'The links between poetry and healing.' *The Therapist,* 3, 4, 15.

Philipp, R. (1997) 'Evaluating the effectiveness of the arts in health care.' In C. Kaye and T. Blee (eds) *The Arts in Health Care: A Palette of Possibilities.* London: Jessica Kingsley.

Philipp, R., Coppell, K. and Freeman (1996) 'Poetry and the art of medicine.' *British Medical Journal 308,* 63.

Philipp, R. and Robertson, I. (1996) 'Poetry helps healing.' *The Lancet,* 347, 332–333.

Pilkington, P. (1997) Summing up of Spirituality and Health Conference, Durham Sept/Oct.

Plath, S. (1963) *The Bell Jar.* London: Faber & Faber.

Pollard, N. (1990) 'Uses of Creative Writing as a Therapeutic Medium in Occupational Therapy.' Dissertation: Diploma of the College of Occupational Therapists. Unpublished.

Pope, A. (1966) *Poetical Works.* Oxford: Oxford University Press.

Pope An Essay on Criticism p.362.

Post, F. (1994) 'Creativity and psychopathology, a study of 291 world famous men'. *British Journal of Psychiatry* 165, 22–34.

Post, F. (1996) 'Verbal Creativity, Depression and Alcoholism, An investigation of one hundred American and British writers.' *British Journal of Psychiatry,* 168, 54, 545–555.

Potter L.L. (1990) 'Write therapy.' *Daily Mail, 17 October.*

Poulson, J. (ed) (1996) *Ladywell Lives: Stories from Ladywell Hospital.* Salford: The Reminiscence Project.

Poulson, J. (ed) (1994a) *Window on Winwick: an anthology of stories, poems and reminiscences from Winwick Hospital.* Salford: The Reminiscence Project.

Poulson, J. (ed) (1994b) *Those Were the Dream Days: Memories from Platt Day Hospital.* Salford: The Reminiscence Project.

Pritchard, P. (1997) *Deep Play.* London: Baton Wicks.

Progoff, I. (1987) *At a Journal Workshop.* New York: Dialogue House.

Purdy, R. (1996) 'Writing refreshes my practice.' *Medical Monitor,* 6 March.

Rainer, T. (1978) *The New Diary: How to Use a Journal for Self-Guidance and Expanded Creativity.* London: Angus & Robertson.

Reading, P. (1984) *C.* London: Secker & Warburg.

Reynolds, A. (1996) *Insanity.* London: Fourth Estate.

Rich, A. (1995) *What is Found There: Notebooks on Poetry and Politics.* London: Virago.

Rich, A. (1980) 'When we are dead awaken: writing as re-vision. In *Lies, Secrets and Silence: Selected Prose 1966–1978.* London: Virago.

Rigler, M. (1996) *excerpt Liddle and Scott Greek-English lexicon.* Withymoor Village Surgery, material. unpublished.

Rigler, M. (1997) *Withymoor Village Surgery – A Health Hive.* Dudley Priority Health Trust.

Riordan, R.J. (1996) 'Scriptotherapy: therapeutic writing as a counseling adjunct'. *Journal of Counseling and Development.* 74, 263–269.

Rogers, J. (1984) *Her Living Image.* London: Faber & Faber.

Rowan, J. (1990) *Subpersonalities: The People Inside Us.* London: Routledge.

Sansom, P. (1994) *Writing Poems.* Newcastle upon Tyne: Bloodaxe.

Sampson, F. (1995) 'Perspectives on a writing project.' *Artery,* 11, 6.

Satyamurti, C. (1989) 'Lady scribbler.' In S. Sellers (ed) *Delighting the Heart.* London: The Women's Press.

Schneider, M. and Killick, J. (1997) *Writing for Self-Discovery.* Dorset: Element Books.

Sellers, S. (ed) (1991) *Taking Reality by Surprise.* London: The Women's Press.

Senior, P. and Croall, R. (1993) *Helping to Heal, the Arts in Health Care.* London: Calouste Gulbenkian.

Seth-Smith, F. (1997) 'Four views of the image.' In K. and J. Schaverien *Art, Psychotherapy and Psychosis.* London: Routledge.

Sharlin, S.A. and Shenhar, A. (1986) 'The fusion of pressing situation and releasing writing on adolescent suicide poetry.' *Suicide and Life Threatening Behaviour,* 16, 3, 343–355.

Silberman, H.L. (1986) 'Poetry Therapy'. *Arts in Psychotherapy,* 13, 343–345.

Simon, R. (1992) *The Symbolism of Style: Art as Therapy.* London: Routledge.

Simons, J. (1990) *Diaries and Journals of Literary Women from Fanny Burney to Virginia Woolf.* London: Macmillan.

Sluder, S. (1990) 'The write way: using poetry for self-disclosure.' *Journal of Psycho-Social Nursing.,* 28, 7, 26–28.

Smith, B.H. and Taylor, R.J. (1996) 'Medicine – a healing or a dying art?' *British Journal of General Practice,* 46, 405, 249–251.

Smith, K. and Sweeney, M. (1997) *Beyond Bedlam: Poems Written out of Mental Distress.* London: Anvil.

Smith, S. (1983) *A Selection.* London: Faber & Faber.

Smyth, T. (1996) 'Reinstating th person in the professional: reflections on empathy and aesthetic experience'. *Journal of Advanced Nursing,* 24, 932–937.

Stevenson, R.L. (1886) *The Strange Case of Dr Jekyll and Mr Hyde.* Middlesex: Penguin.

Stoker, B. (1897) *Dracula.* London: Penguin Classics.

Thomas, R.S. (1973) *Selected Poems.* Newcastle-upon-Tyne: Bloodaxe.

Thomson, M. (1989) *On Art and Therapy.* London: Virago.

Tomlinson, T. (1997) *Dancing Through the Shadows.* London: Julia McRae.

Tooth, D. (1990) 'Creative expression and chronic pain'. *The Lancet,* 1336, 1240–1241.

Torem, M.S. (1993) 'Therapeutic Writing as a Form of Ego-State Therapy'. *American Journal of Clinical Hypnosis,* 35, 4, 267–276.

Waller, D. and Dalley, T. (1992) 'The theoretical perspective.' In *Art Therapy.* Buckingham: Open University Press.

Warren Wilson, G. *Hanging Windchimes in a Vacuum.* Dorset: Tears in the Fence.

Wegner, D.M. (1988) 'Stress and mental control.' In S. Fisher and J. Reason (eds) *Handbook of Life Stress, Cognition, and Health.* Chichester: Wiley.

Wenz, K. and McWhirter, J.J. (1990) 'Enhancing the group experience; creative writing exercises.' *The Journal for Specialists in Group Work,* 15, 1, 37–42.

Wilde, O. (1995) *The Oscar Wilde Quotation Book (The Importance of Being Ernest).* London: Robert Hale.

Williams, E. (1996) 'Tales told within Walls'. *Times Educational Supplement,* March 8.

Wilson, C. (1997) 'Writing therapy'. *Holistic Nurses Association UK Newsletter,* 4, 1, 5–6.

Woolf, V. (1979) *The Diary of Virginia Woolf (Jan 1919).* Middlesex: Penguin.

Woolf, V. (1997) *The Waves.* London: Hogarth Press.

Woolf, V. (1993) *The Crowded Dance of Modern Life.* London: Penguin.

Wordsworth, D. (1987) *Dorothy Wordsworth's Illustrated Lakeland Journals.* London: Collins.

Wordsworth, W. (1976) Preface. *Lyrical Ballads.,* edited by Derek Roper. Plymouth: Macdonald and Evans.

Wordsworth, W. (1977) 'Lines composed a few miles above Tintern Abbey.' *Poems,* Vol.I. Harmondsworth: Penguin.

Wordsworth, W. (1985) *The Prelude,* edited by Jonathan Wordsworth. Cambridge: Cambridge University Press.

Yalom, I.D. (1970) *The Theory and Practice of Group Psychotherapy.* New York: Basic Books.

Yeoman, M. (1995) *Recalled to Life: Christopher's Story.* London: Alderney Books.

Young, E. (1975) *Selected Poems.* Cheadle, Cheshire: Carcanet.

Subject Index

Author Index